A TEXT BOOK OF

# DIGITAL SYSTEM AND MICROPROCESSOR

FOR
**Semester – III**

Second Year Degree Course in Information Technology

As Per New Revised Syllabus of
Shivaji University, Kolhapur, June 2014

**Dr. ST PATIL**
M. Tech. (CSE) PhD. (Computer)
Professor, Computer Engineering Deptt.
Vishwakarma Institute of Technology (VIT),
Pune - 411 037

**SS KULKARNI**
M. E. (E & TC)
Associate Professor, I.T. Deptt.
Sinhgad Academy of Engineering
Kondhawa, Pune

**DIGITAL SYSTEM AND MICROPROCESSOR (S.E. IT – SEM. III SU)**    ISBN 978-93-5164-246-6

**First Edition** : September 2014

© : Authors

The text of this publication, or any part thereof, should not be reproduced or transmitted in any form or stored in any computer storage system or device for distribution including photocopy, recording, taping or information retrieval system or reproduced on any disc, tape, perforated media or other information storage device etc., without the written permission of Authors with whom the rights are reserved. Breach of this condition is liable for legal action.

Every effort has been made to avoid errors or omissions in this publication. In spite of this, errors may have crept in. Any mistake, error or discrepancy so noted and shall be brought to our notice shall be taken care of in the next edition. It is notified that neither the publisher nor the authors or seller shall be responsible for any damage or loss of action to any one, of any kind, in any manner, therefrom.

**Published By :**
**NIRALI PRAKASHAN**
Abhyudaya Pragati, 1312, Shivaji Nagar,
Off J.M. Road, PUNE – 411005
Tel - (020) 25512336/37/39, Fax - (020) 25511379
Email : niralipune@pragationline.com

**Printed at**
**Repro Knowledgecast Limited**
**India**

## DISTRIBUTION CENTRES
### PUNE

*Nirali Prakashan*
119, Budhwar Peth, Jogeshwari Mandir Lane
Pune 411002, Maharashtra
Tel : (020) 2445 2044, 66022708, Fax : (020) 2445 1538
Email : bookorder@pragationline.com

*Nirali Prakashan*
S. No. 28/25, Dhyari,
Near Pari Company, Pune 411041
Tel : (022) 24690204 Fax : (020) 24690316
Email : dhyari@pragationline.com
bookorder@pragationline.com

### MUMBAI
*Nirali Prakashan*
385, S.V.P. Road, Rasdhara Co-op. Hsg. Society Ltd.,
Girgaum, Mumbai 400004, Maharashtra
Tel : (022) 2385 6339 / 2386 9976, Fax : (022) 2386 9976
Email : niralimumbai@pragationline.com

## DISTRIBUTION BRANCHES

**NAGPUR**
*Pratibha Book Distributors*
Above Maratha Mandir, Shop No. 3, First Floor,
Rani Jhanshi Square, Sitabuldi, Nagpur 440012,
Maharashtra, Tel : (0712) 254 7129

**BENGALURU**
*Pragati Book House*
House No. 1, Sanjeevappa Lane, Avenue Road Cross,
Opp. Rice Church, Bengaluru – 560002.
Tel : (080) 64513344, 64513355,
Mob : 9880582331, 9845021552
Email:bharatsavla@yahoo.com

**JALGAON**
*Nirali Prakashan*
34, V. V. Golani Market, Navi Peth, Jalgaon 425001,
Maharashtra, Tel : (0257) 222 0395
Mob : 94234 91860

**KOLHAPUR**
*Nirali Prakashan*
New Mahadvar Road,
Kedar Plaza, 1st Floor Opp. IDBI Bank
Kolhapur 416 012, Maharashtra. Mob : 9855046155

### CHENNAI
*Pragati Books*
9/1, Montieth Road, Behind Taas Mahal, Egmore,
Chennai 600008 Tamil Nadu, Tel : (044) 6518 3535,
Mob : 94440 01782 / 98450 21552 / 98805 82331, Email : bharatsavla@yahoo.com

## RETAIL OUTLETS
### PUNE

*Pragati Book Centre*
157, Budhwar Peth, Opp. Ratan Talkies,
Pune 411002, Maharashtra
Tel : (020) 2445 8887 / 6602 2707, Fax : (020) 2445 8887
*Pragati Book Centre*
Amber Chamber, 28/A, Budhwar Peth,
Appa Balwant Chowk, Pune : 411002, Maharashtra,
Tel : (020) 20240335 / 66281669
Email : pbcpune@pragationline.com

*Pragati Book Centre*
676/B, Budhwar Peth, Opp. Jogeshwari Mandir,
Pune 411002, Maharashtra
Tel : (020) 6601 7784 / 6602 0855
*PBC Book Sellers & Stationers*
152, Budhwar Peth, Pune 411002, Maharashtra
Tel : (020) 2445 2254 / 6609 2463

### MUMBAI
*Pragati Book Corner*
Indira Niwas, 111 - A, Bhavani Shankar Road, Dadar (W), Mumbai 400028, Maharashtra
Tel : (022) 2422 3526 / 6662 5254, Email : pbcmumbai@pragationline.com

# PREFACE

It gives us immense pleasure to present this book on **'Digital System And Microprocessor'** to the Students of Second Year Degree Course in Information Technology it is strictly written as per New Revised Syllabus of Shivaji University, Kolhapur (2014).

The text includes information about basic concepts of 8085 Microprocessor. It Various building blocks of the 8085 Microprocessor Architecture are explained in detail. Programming treatment of various concepts are given wherever necessary. Number of solved programs and exercises are given to strengthens the concepts. The working of Microprocessor system is explained with extensive instructions and programming to get an insight into the subject.

Our sincere hope is that the material presented in the book will be useful in understanding the subject as well as for attempting examination questions.

We take this opportunity to express our thanks to **Shri. Dineshbhai Furia** and **Shri. Jignesh Furia** and **Shri. M.P. Munde** for publishing this book in time.

We also take this opportunity to express our thank all the staff members of Nirali Prakashan namely Mrs. Shilpa Kale, Miss. Mandakini Jadhvar, Mrs. Pratibha Bele, and Mrs. Sarika Wagh for their tremendous dedication and hard work in bringing out this book in an excellent form.

We also thankful to **Mr. Virdhaval Shinde**, Branch Manager, Kolhapur Offcie and **Mr. Ashok Nanaware**, Branch Manager, Sangli District for their valuable help and efforts for promotion of our book.

Our special thanks to our family members, students and all those who directly or indirectly supported us in this project.

Any suggestions and feedback shall be appreciated and acknowledged.

September 2014    Authors
Pune

# SYLLABUS

### Unit I : Fundamental Concepts                                    (4 Hours)

Analog and digital systems, representation of signed numbers, 2's complement arithmetic, BCD addition & subtraction, octal & Hexadecimal addition and subtraction, Derived gates.

### Unit II : Boolean Algebra & Combinational Logic Design           (7 Marks)

Reduction of Boolean expressions, Boolean function representation, expansion of Boolean expression (standard SOP & POS), simplification of boolean expressions using K-map (upto 5 variable), prime implicants, Adders & Subtractors design using gates, Multiplexer, implementation of expression using MUX, Demultiplexer, decoder(74138), BCD to 7 segment decoder.

### Unit III : Sequential Logic Design                               (7 Hours)

Classification, Flip-Flops(S-R, J-K,T,D)using gates, Race around condition Master –Slave J-K Flip Flop, Counters (Asynchronous & Synchronous), Design examples, Shift registers, State transition diagram, excitation table.

### Unit IV : 8085 Microprocessor Architecture & Memory Interfacing  (6 Hours)

The 8085 MPU, Microprocessor communication and bus timing, De-multiplexing address and Data bus, Generating control signals, The 8085 Architecture, op-code fetch machine cycle, memory read and write machine cycle. Memory interfacing-memory structure, memory interfacing & address decoding.

### Unit V : 8085 Programming Techniques                             (10 Hours)

8085 instruction groups, addressing modes Writing and execution assembly languageprogram, counters & delays, Stack, Instruction related to stack execution of CALL and RET, The 8085 interrupt, RST instructions, vectored interrupts, RIM and SIM instructions.

### Unit VI : Interfacing I/O Devices                                (6 Hours)

Basic interfacing concepts, peripherals I/O instructions - IN, OUT, I/O execution, memory mapped I/O, I/O mapped I/O. The 8255 programmable peripheral interface, operating modes (I/O, BSR).

# CONTENTS

## DIGITAL SYSTEM

1. Fundamental Concepts — 1.1-1.22

2. Boolean Algebra & Combinational Logic Design — 2.1-2.54

3. Sequential Logic Design — 3.1-3.72

## MICROPROCESSOR

4. 8085 Microprocessor Architecture & Memory Interfacing — 4.1-4.26

5. 8085 Programming Techniques — 5.1-5.48

6. Interfacing I/O Devices — 6.1-6.24

# Unit - I

# FUNDAMENTAL CONCEPTS

## 1.1 INTRODUCTION

- An analog signal is a continuous signal varying with time. Any electronic system which processes an analog signal is referred to as an analog system in which the output can be controlled continuously by input.
- Digital signal is discrete with respect to time and has only two distinct voltage levels denoted by logic '1' (high) and logic '0' (low). Digital systems process digital signals and store information in the binary form. Modern computers and electronic systems operate on digital data. So the analog signals are first converted into digital form and then processed using digital techniques.

**Advantage of using Digital Technique**

- The devices used in digital circuits operate in one of two states, known as ON and OFF, results into very simple operation.
- Digital circuits are easy to understand.
- A large number of ICs are available for performing various operations. These are highly reliable, accurate small in size and the speed of operation is high. A large number of programmable ICs are also available.
- The fluctuations in characteristics of the components, ageing of components, temperature and noise etc. is very small in digital circuits.
- Digital circuits have memory capability which makes these circuits highly suitable for computers, calculators, watches, telephones etc.
- The display of data and other information is very convenient, accurate using digital technique.

## 1.1.1 Types of Number Systems

The different types of number systems are :

- Binary Number System
- Decimal Number System
- Octal Number System
- Hexadecimal Number System

## 1.1.2 Binary Number System

- The binary number system is used in digital electronics. It has the following characteristics.

   Two digits : 0, 1

   Base : 2

   Weights : Powers of Base 2 ($2^0$, $2^1$, $2^2$, $2^3$...) or (1, 2, 4, 8).

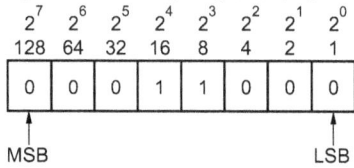

**Fig. 1.1 : Binary number system**

- In the binary system, 1's and 0's are arranged into columns.
- Each column is weighted. The first column on the right has a binary weight of $2^{10}$. This equivalent to decimal 1 and is referred to as the Least Significant Bit (LSB).
- The number in the far left hand column is called Most Significant Bit (MSB).

## 1.1.3 Decimal Number System

- In decimal number system, we can express any decimal number in units, ten hundreds, thousands and so on.

e.g. 6597.8 this number can be represented as

$$6000 + 500 + 90 + 7 + 0.8 = 6597.8 = 6597.8_{10}$$

radix and base of decimal number system is 10.

| In power of 10 | $10^3$ | $10^2$ | $10^1$ | $10^0$ | • | $10^{-1}$ |
|---|---|---|---|---|---|---|
| | 6 | 5 | 9 | 7 | • | 8 |
| | $6 \times 10^3$ | $5 \times 10^2$ | $9 \times 10^1$ | $7 \times 10^0$ | • | $8 \times 10^{-1}$ |

**Fig. 1.2**

## 1.1.4 Octal Number System

- The octal number system consists of eight digits of decimal number system : 0, 1, 2, 3, 4, 5, 6 and 7. So its base is 8.

e.g. The octal number 8531.74 can be represented in power of 8 as shown in Fig. 1.3.

| $8^3$ | $8^2$ | $8^1$ | $8^0$ | | $8^{-1}$ | $8^{-2}$ |
|---|---|---|---|---|---|---|
| 8 | 5 | 3 | 1 | • | 7 | 4 |
| $8 \times 8^3$ | $5 \times 8^2$ | $3 \times 8^1$ | $1 \times 8^0$ | • | $7 \times 8^{-1}$ | $4 \times 8^{-2}$ |

**Fig. 1.3**

## 1.1.5 Hexadecimal Number System

- The hexadecimal number system having a base of 16 having 16 characters.
0, 1, 2, 3, 4, 5, 6, 7, 8, 9, A, B, C, D, E, F.
- It is easy to convert hexadecimal number to binary and vice versa.

e.g. 3FD. 48 can be represented in power of 16 as shown in Fig. 1.4 below.

| $16^2$ | $16^1$ | $16^0$ | . | $16^{-1}$ | $16^{-2}$ |
|---|---|---|---|---|---|
| 3 | F | D | . | 4 | 8 |
| $3 \times 16^2$ | $F \times 16^1$ | $D \times 16^0$ | . | $4 \times 16^{-1}$ | $8 \times 16^{-2}$ |

Fig. 1.4

## 1.2 SIGNED BINARY NUMBER REPRESENTATION

- Signed Magnitude
- One's Complement
- Two's Complement

### 1.2.1 Signed Magnitude

- The simplest way to indicate negation is signed magnitude. In signed magnitude, the left-most bit is not actually part of the number, but is just the equivalent of a + / − sign.
- "0" indicates that the number is positive, "1" indicates negative. In 8 bits, 00001100 would be 12 (break this down into (1*2 ^3) + (1 * 2 ^2)). To indicate - 12, we would simply put a "1" rather than a "0" as the first bit : 10001100.
- The +ve or –ve signs are also represented in the binary form i.e. by using 0 or 1 so a 0 is used to represent the (+ve) sign and 1 is used to represent (–ve) sign.
- The most significant Bit (MSB) of binary number is used to represent the sign and the remaining bits are used for representing the magnitude.

e.g. 8 bit signed binary number show in Fig. 1.5

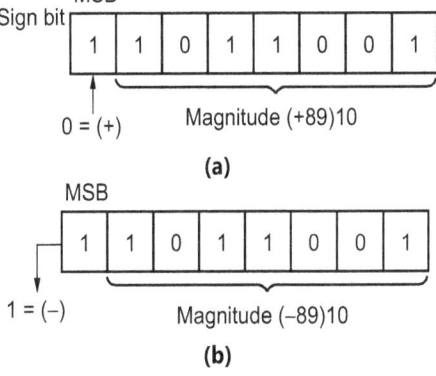

Fig. 1.5 : 8-bit signed binary numbers

This type of numbers is called number or signed magnitude number.

- For an 8 bit sign magnitude number the largest negative number is (−127) to largest positive, number is (127) i.e. from 0 to 255.

**Advantages :**

- We can easily find out the magnitude by deleting the sign bit.
- The simplicity of sign magnitude.

**Disadvantage :**

- Signed number require complicated circuits.

## 1.2.2 One's Complement

- In one's complement, positive numbers are represented as usual in regular binary. However, negative numbers are represented differently. To negate a number, replace all zeros with ones, and ones with zeros-flip the bits. Thus, 12 would be 00001100, and −12 would be 11110011.
- As in signed magnitude, the leftmost bit indicates the sign (1 is negative, 0 is positive). To compute the value of a negative number, flip the bits and translate as before.

## 1.2.3 Two's Complement

- Begin with the number in one's complement. Add 1 if the number is negative. Twelve would be represented as 00001100, and − 12 as 11110100. to verify this, let's subtract 1 from 11110100, to get 11110011. If we flip the bits, we get 00001100, or 12 in decimal.

**Example 1.1 :** Represent the decimal numbers 25 and − 25 in the 8 bit signed magnitude 1's complement and 2's complement forms.

**Solution :**

**Step 1 :** Representation of 25 signed magnitude

$$25 = 0 \quad 0011001$$
$$\downarrow \quad\quad\quad \downarrow$$
$$\text{sign} \quad \text{Magnitude}$$

**Step 2 :** Representation of −25 in signed magnitude form.

$$25 = 1 \quad 0011001$$
$$\downarrow \quad\quad\quad \downarrow$$
$$\text{sign} \quad \text{Magnitude}$$

**Step 3 :** Representation of – 25 in 1's complement form

$$25 = 00011001 \text{ ...sign magnitude}$$
$$\downarrow$$
$$\text{invert all bits}$$
$$-25 = 11100110 \text{ ...1's complement form}$$

**Step 4 :** Representation of – 25 in 2's complement form

$$25 = 00011001 \text{ ...sign magnitude}$$
$$\text{invert all bits + add 1}$$
$$-25 = 11100111 \text{ ...2's complement form}$$

## 1.3 BINARY ARITHMETIC

### 1.3.1 Binary Addition

- The binary addition is the most basic operation of binary arithmetic. The two bit binary digit addition is shown in following table.

**Table 1.1 : Truth table for half adder**

| Sr. No. | Operations | Sum | Carry |
|---------|-----------|-----|-------|
| 0 | 0 + 0 | 0 | 0 |
| 1 | 0 + 1 | 1 | 0 |
| 2 | 1 + 0 | 1 | 0 |
| 3 | 1 + 1 | 0 | 1 |

- The 3 bit (i.e. two significant bit and a previous carry) is called a full addition is shown in following table.

**Table 1.2 : Truth table for full adder**

| Inputs | | | Outputs | |
|---|---|---|---|---|
| A | B | $C_{in}$ | Sum | Cout |
| 0 | 0 | 0 | 0 | 0 |
| 0 | 0 | 1 | 1 | 0 |
| 0 | 1 | 0 | 1 | 0 |
| 0 | 1 | 1 | 0 | 1 |
| 1 | 0 | 0 | 1 | 0 |
| 1 | 0 | 1 | 0 | 1 |
| 1 | 1 | 0 | 0 | 1 |
| 1 | 1 | 1 | 1 | 1 |

**Binary addition method steps :**

**Step 1 :** Add bits column wise from LSB with carry if any

**Step 2 :** If carry is generated write at the top of next column.

**Step 3 :** Write the sum at the bottom of the same column.

**Example 1.2 :** $(8)_{10}$ and $(12)_{10}$

**Step 1 :** First convert both number into binary.

$$(8)_{10} = (1000)_2$$
$$(12)_{10} = (1100)_2$$

**Step 2 :** Add bits column wise from the LSB with carry if any.

```
       1        ...carry
    + 1000      ...number 1
      1100      ...number 2
      -----
     10100
```
$= (10100)_2$

## 1.3.2 Binary Subtraction

- The subtraction for 2 bit procedure is given below in table 1.3.

**Table 1.3**

| Sr. No. | Operations | Sub | Borrow |
|---------|------------|-----|--------|
| 1 | 0-0 | 0 | 0 |
| 2 | 0-1 | 1 | 1 |
| 3 | 1-0 | 1 | 0 |
| 4 | 1-1 | 0 | 0 |

**Subtraction method steps :**
1. Subtract bits column wise starting from LSB with borrow if any.
2. Write borrow at the next column top.
3. Write difference bottom of the same column.

**Example 1.3 :** Perform binary subtraction $(11101100)_2 - (00110010)_2$
**Solution :**

```
              10
         0 0 10 0 10
         1 1 1 0 1 1 0 0    ...number 1
       - 0 0 1 1 0 0 1 0    ...number 2
         -----------------
         1 0 1 1 1 0 1 0    Result
```

### 1.3.2.1 Binary subtraction using 1's complement method

**Steps :**
1. First take 1's complement of second number.
2. Add first number and 1's complement of second number.
3. If the carry is generated then result is + ve and true form. Then add carry to the result to get final answer.
4. If the carry is not generated then result is –ve and in 1's complement form.

**Example 1.4 :** Perform binary subtraction using 1's complement method.

$$(28)_{10} - (15)_{10}$$

**Step 1 :** First convert both numbers into binary.

$$(28)_{10} = (011100)_2$$
$$(15)_{10} = (001111)_2$$

**Step 2 :** Take 1's complement of second number i.e. $(15)_{10}$

$$(001111) = (15)_{10}$$
$$\downarrow \text{1's complement}$$
$$110000$$

**Step 3 :** Add first number and 1's complement of second number.

```
  011100
+ 110000
--------
 1001100
       ↓
     carry
```

**Step 4 :** Carry is generated so result is positive add carry to the result to get final result.

```
  001100
+      1
--------
  001101   final answer
```

$$001101 = (13)_{10}$$

### 1.3.2.2 Binary subtraction using 2's complement method

**Steps :**
1. First take 2's complement of second number.
2. Add first number to the 2's complement of second number.
3. If carry is generated then result number is positive and true form. Remove carry or ignore carry.
4. If carry is not generated then the result number is –ve and in the 2's complement form.

**Example 1.5 :** Perform following substructure using 2's complement method

(a) $(4)_{10} - (9)_{10}$.

**Step 1 :** First write both number in the binary form.

$$(4)_{10} = 0100$$
$$(9)_{10} = 1001$$

**Step 2 :** Obtain 2's complement of $(9)_{10}$

$$(9)_{10} = 1001$$
$$\downarrow \text{2's complement}$$
$$0111$$

**Step 3 :** Add $(4)_{10}$ to 2's complement of $(9)_{10}$

$$(4)_{10} = 0100$$
$$+$$
$$\text{2's complement of } (9)_{10} = 0111$$
$$\underline{\phantom{XXXXXXXXXXXXXXXXXXXXXXXX}}$$
$$\phantom{XXX}0 \quad\quad 1011$$
$$\phantom{XXX}\downarrow \quad\quad \downarrow$$
$$\text{final carry} \quad \text{answer}$$

zero shows the result is negative and in its 2's complement form.

**Step 4 :** Convert the answer into true form

$$\text{Answer} \quad 1011$$
$$\text{Subtract} - \quad \underline{\phantom{X}1\phantom{X}}$$
$$\phantom{XXXX} 1010$$
$$\phantom{XXXX} \underbrace{\phantom{XXXX}}$$
$$\downarrow \text{ invert all bits}$$
$$0101 \quad\quad \text{(answer in true form)}$$

Thus the answer is – $(0101)_2$ i.e. $(-5)_{10}$.

(b) $(10011)_2 - (1101)_2$

**Step 1 :** Take 2's complement of second number.

$$01101$$
$$\downarrow \text{ invert all bits}$$
$$10010$$
$$\underline{+ 1}$$
$$10011$$

**Step 2 :** Add $(10011)_2$ to 2's complement of $(01101)_2$.

$$\phantom{XXX}10011 \quad\quad \text{...number 1}$$
$$+ \phantom{X}\underline{10011} \quad\quad \text{...number 2 2's complement}$$
$$\phantom{XXX}\underline{100110}$$
$$\phantom{XX}|\text{ result answer}$$
$$\phantom{XX}\text{carry}$$

**Step 3 :** Carry is 1 so number is positive discard carry.

$$\text{final answer} = 00110$$

## 1.3.3 Binary Multiplication

- Binary multiplication process for binary numbers is similar to decimal number. The two bit binary multiplication shown below

Table 1.4 : Rules for binary multiplication

| Sr. No. | A | B | Ans. |
|---|---|---|---|
| 1 | 0 | 0 | 0 |
| 2 | 0 | 1 | 0 |
| 3 | 1 | 0 | 0 |
| 4 | 1 | 1 | 1 |

**Example 1.6 :** $(1011)_2 \times (101)_2$

```
      1011    ...multiplicand
    × 101     ...multiplier
    ─────
      1011
   + 00000
   + 101100
   ───────
     110111   ...final answer
```

## 1.3.4 Binary Division

The division process of binary number is same as the decimal number table 1.6 show the rules for binary 2 bit division.

Table 1.5 : Rules for binary division

| Sr. No | Numbers | | Division |
|---|---|---|---|
| | A | B | |
| 1 | 0 | 1 | 0 |
| 2 | 1 | 1 | 1 |

**Example 1.7 :** $11011011_2$ by $110_2$

```
        11011011 by 110₂
          100100
      ┌─────────
   110) 11011011
        110
        ───
        0001100
           110
           ───
           00011
```

Quotient = $(100100)_2$, Reminder = $(11)_2$

## 1.4 OCTAL ARITHMETIC

### 1.4.1 Octal Addition

- The sum of octal digit is same as decimal sum. If the decimal sum is greater than 8 or equal to 8, subtract 8, from the addition result to obtain the octal digit. A carry of 1 is produced when the decimal sum is in above condition.

**Example 1.8 :** Add $(634)_8$ and $(152)_8$

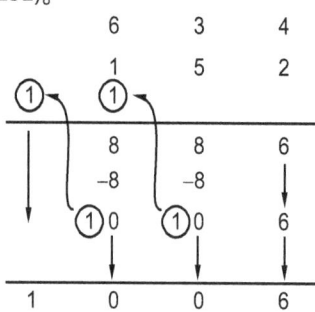

final answer = $(1006)_8$

### 1.4.2 Octal Subtraction using 8's Complement

**Steps :**

1. First take 8's complement of second number. To take 8's complement, first take 7's complement of number then add 1 to 7's complement answer.
2. Add first number and second 8's complement number
3. If carry is produced in the addition it is ignored otherwise find 8's complement of sum as a result with negative sign.

**Example 1.9 :** Perform subtraction using 8's complement method.

$(516)_8 - (413)_8$

**Step 1 :** Subtract second number each digit of a number from 7 to get the 7's complement of the number and add 1 to answer to get 8's complement.

```
        777
      - 413
      -----
        364   7's complement
        + 1
      -----
        365   8s complement
```

**Step 2 :** Add first number to the 8's complement of second number.

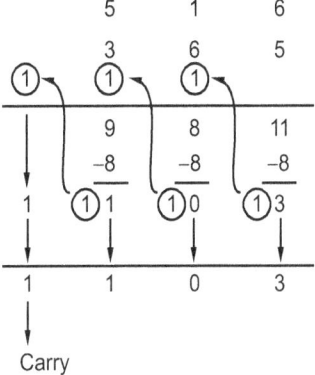

**Step 3 :** Carry is generated ignore carry.

final answer = $(103)_8$

**Example 1.10 :** $(316)_8 - (451)_8$

**Step 1 :** First take 8's complement of second number. i.e. $(451)_8$

```
   777
 - 451
 -----
   326   7's complement
 + 1
 -----
   327   8s complement
```

**Step 2 :** Add first number to 8's complement of second number.

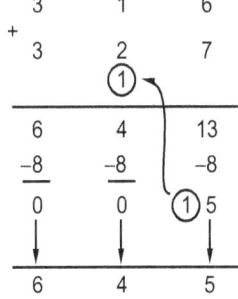

**Step 3 :** No carry generated hence take 8's complement of answer (645)

```
   777
 - 645
 -----
   132   7's complement
 + 1     add 1
 -----
   133   8s complement of (645)_8
```

$(316)_8 - (451)_8 = (-133)_8$

## 1.5 HEXADECIMAL ARITHMETIC

### 1.5.1 Hexadecimal Addition

**Rules:**
- The sum of two hexadecimal digits is the same as their equivalent decimal sum, provided decimal equivalent is less that 16.
- If the sum is greater 16 or equal to 16, subtract 16 from the result and a carry of 1 is produced when the decimal sum is corrected to obtain final answer.

**Example 1.11 :** $(658)_{16} + (975)_{16} = ?$
Add given two numbers.

$$
\begin{array}{r}
(6)_{10}\ (5)_{10}\ (8)_{10} \\
+\ (9)_{10}\ (7)_{10}\ (5)_{10} \\
\hline
(15)_{10}\ (12)_{10}\ (13)_{10} \\
\downarrow\quad\ \downarrow\quad\ \downarrow \\
(F)_{16}\ (C)_{16}\ (D)_{16}
\end{array}
$$

$\therefore \quad (658)_{16} + (975)_{16} = (FCD)_{16}$

### 1.5.2 Hexadecimal Subtraction using 16's Complement

- The 16's complement of a hexadecimal number is found by adding a 1 to the least significant bit of the 15's complement of hexadecimal number.

**Example 1.12 :** $(587)_{Hex} - (4EB)_{Hex}$.

**Step 1 :** First take 16's complement of second number.

$$
\begin{array}{r}
15\ 15\ 15 \\
-\ 4\ \ E\ \ B \\
\hline
B\ \ 1\ \ 4 \quad \text{15's complement} \\
+\ 1 \\
\hline
B\ \ 1\ \ 5 \quad \text{16's complement}
\end{array}
$$

**Step 2 :** Add first number to the 16's complement of second number

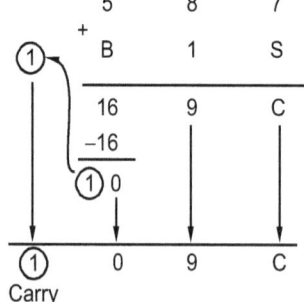

**Step 3 :** Discard carry

$\therefore \quad (587)_{Hex} - (4EB)_{Hex} = (09C)_{16}$

## 1.6 BCD CODE

- Each digit of decimal number is represented by four bits. For example digit '5' is represented as '0101'. The BCD code is also called as 8-4-2-1 code where 8,4,2 and 1 represent weights of binary symbol in the respective positions. The examples of BCD codes are given below ;

| Decimal | 4 | 2 | 8 | 6 | 3 |
|---------|------|------|------|------|------|
| BCD | 0100 | 0010 | 1000 | 0110 | 0011 |

- BCD code for 0 to 9 digits are given as;

| Decimal digit | BCD code |
|---------------|----------|
| 0 | 0 0 0 0 |
| 1 | 0 0 0 1 |
| 2 | 0 0 1 0 |
| 3 | 0 0 1 1 |
| 4 | 0 1 0 0 |
| 5 | 0 1 0 1 |
| 6 | 0 1 1 0 |
| 7 | 0 1 1 1 |
| 8 | 1 0 0 0 |
| 9 | 1 0 0 1 |

The remaining 4 digit binary representations i.e. 1010, 1011, 1100, 1101, 1110 and 1111 are invalid BCD codes.

**BCD Arithmetic :** The arithmetic of BCD code is complex. It can be used to perform addition and subtraction.

**Rules :**

1. If four bits sum is equal to or less than 9, no correction is needed. The sum is in proper BCD form.
2. If the four bit sum is greater than of 9 or if a carry is generated from the four bit sum, the sum is invalid.
3. To correct the invalid sum add 6 $(0110)_2$ to the four bit sum. If carry results from this addition, add it to the next higher order BCD digit.

## 1.6.1 BCD Addition

- In BCD addition, each digit of decimal number is first represented using it's four - bit BCD equivalent numbers.
- The addition of two BCD numbers is carried out using simple binary addition. After the binary addition the result may be invalid or valid BCD.
- If the result is invalid BCD then the it is converted into the valid BCD by adding $(0110)_2$ or $(06)_{10}$. If carry is generated after the addition of $(0110)_2$ then it is added to next bit.

**Example 1.13 :** $(569)_{10} + (687)_{10}$

**Step 1 :**

$$(569)_{10} = 0101 \quad 0110 \quad 1001$$
$$+ (687)_{10} = 0110 \quad 1000 \quad 0111$$
$$\overline{\phantom{XXXXXXX} 0111 \quad 1111 \quad 0000}$$

invalid   invalid   valid BCD
BCD number   BCD   with carry 1

**Step 2 :** Add $(6)_{10}$ to each one

```
  1011 1111 0000
+ 0110 0110 0110
  ───────────────
  10010 0101 0110
↓
  1    2    5    6   ...final answer
```

$(569)_{10} + (687)_{10} = (1256)_{10}$

## 1.6.2 BCD Subtraction

- Subtraction is nothing but addition of a signed number i.e. A − B = A + (−B). The negative BCD number can be expressed by taking the 9's or 10's complement of the BCD number which is to be subtracted.

### 1.6.2.1 BCD subtraction using 9's complement

- The 9's complement is obtained by subtracting the given number from 9. Thus 9's Complement of 3 is 6 (9 − 3 = 6).

**Steps to perform BCD subtraciton using 9's complement.**

- Find the 9's complement of subtractor.
- Perform the BCD addition of the first number and 9's complement of second number.
- If carry is generated, then result is positive. Add the carry into the result to get the correct result.
- If carry is not generated then result is negative and it is in 9's complement form.

**Example 1.14 :** Subtract 4 from 8 in BCD (8 − 4 − 2 − 1) using 9's complement of subtraction.
**Solution :**         8 − 4 = 8 + 5         where 5 is 9's complement of 4

**Step 1 :**

```
        1000     ← BCD code of 8
      + 0101     ← BCD code of 5
        ────
        1101     ← Invalid BCD answer
        0110     ← add (0110)₂
          11     ← Carry
       ─────
       10011
```

Because carry is generated, the answer is positive

**Step 2 :** Add carry into answer

```
        0011
      +    1
      ──────
           1
        0100     ← valid BCD answer
```

### 1.6.2.2 BCD subtraction using 10's complement

The 10's complement of a number is obtained by adding '1' into 9's complement.

**Step to perform BCD subtraction using 10's complement.**
- Find the 10's complement of the subtraction.
- Perform the BCD addition.
- If carry is not generated then the result is negative and it is in 10's complement form.
- If carry is generated then the result is positive. Discard the carry.

**Example 1.15 :** Perform 8 − 3 using 10's complement.
**Solution :**     8 − 3 = 8 + 7     where 7 is 10's complement of 3 i.e. [(9 − 3) + 1 = 7]

```
        1000     ← BCD code of 8
      + 0111     ← BCD code of 7
        ────
        1111     ← Invalid BCD code
        0110     ← add (0110)₂
          11     ← Carry
       ─────
       10101
```

The carry is generated. ∴ The result is positive. Discarded the carry
∴ The answer is (5).

**Example 1.16 :** Represent $(7)_{10}$ using all the weighted 4-bit BCD codes

1. 3321 code

$$(7)_{10} = 3\ 3\ 2\ 1$$
$$\downarrow\downarrow\downarrow\downarrow$$
$$1\ 1\ 0\ 1$$
$$= (1101)_{3221\ BCD}$$

2. 4221 code

$$(7)_{10} = 4\ 2\ 2\ 1$$
$$\downarrow\downarrow\downarrow\downarrow$$
$$1\ 0\ 1\ 1$$
$$= (1011)_{4221\ BCD}$$

3. 5211 code

$$(7)_{10} = 5\ 2\ 2\ 1$$
$$\downarrow\downarrow\downarrow\downarrow$$
$$1\ 1\ 0\ 0$$
$$= (1100)_{5211\ BCD}$$

4. 5311 code

$$(7)_{10} = 5\ 3\ 1\ 1$$
$$\downarrow\downarrow\downarrow\downarrow$$
$$1\ 0\ 1\ 1$$
$$= (1011)_{5311\ BCD}$$

5. 5421 code

$$(7)_{10} = 5\ 4\ 1\ 1$$
$$\downarrow\downarrow\downarrow\downarrow$$
$$1\ 0\ 1\ 0$$
$$= (1011)_{5421\ BCD}$$

6. 6311 code

$$(7)_{10} = 6\ 3\ 1\ 1$$
$$\downarrow\downarrow\downarrow\downarrow$$
$$1\ 0\ 0\ 1$$

7. 7421 code

$$(7)_{10} = 7\ 4\ 2\ 1$$
$$1\ 0\ 0\ 0$$
$$= (1000)_{7421\ BCD}$$

8. $74\bar{2}\bar{1}$ code

$$(7)_{10} = 7 + 4 - \bar{2} - \bar{1}$$
$$\downarrow\ \ \downarrow\ \ \downarrow\ \ \downarrow$$
$$1\ \ 0\ \ 0\ \ 0$$
$$= (1000)_{74\bar{2}\bar{1}\ BCD}$$

## 1.7 BASIC LOGIC GATES

- The term Logic refers to something which can be reasoned out. In many situations, the problem statements can be expressed in true or false and yes or no formats.
- Since, digital circuits also have two states or binary form, these kind of problem statements can be formulated using logic states or logic functions.
- Because the voltage levels in a digital circuit are assumed to be switched from one value to another, the digital circuits are called logic circuits or switching circuits.
- Logic gate is a logic circuit which obeys a certain set of logic rules. The manner in which a logic circuit responds to an input is referred to as the circuit's logic.
- The name logic gate is derived from the ability of such device to make decisions i.e. produce different outputs in response to different combinations of inputs.
- As mentioned earlier, logic gate is an electronic switching circuit.
- Semiconductor devices such as diode, BJT or MOSFET can be used to build logic gates.
- The inherent characteristics of these devices such as junction capacitance, uni- or bi-polar, diffusion capacitance decides the characteristics of logic gates.

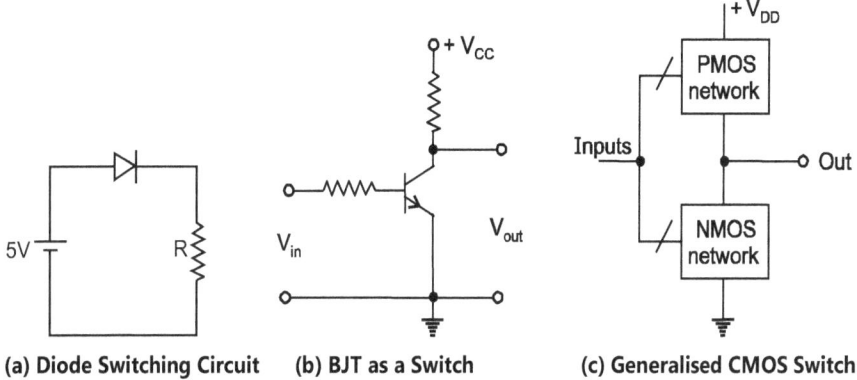

(a) Diode Switching Circuit   (b) BJT as a Switch   (c) Generalised CMOS Switch

Fig. 1.6 : Semiconductor devices as switches

The logic gates can be classified as below :

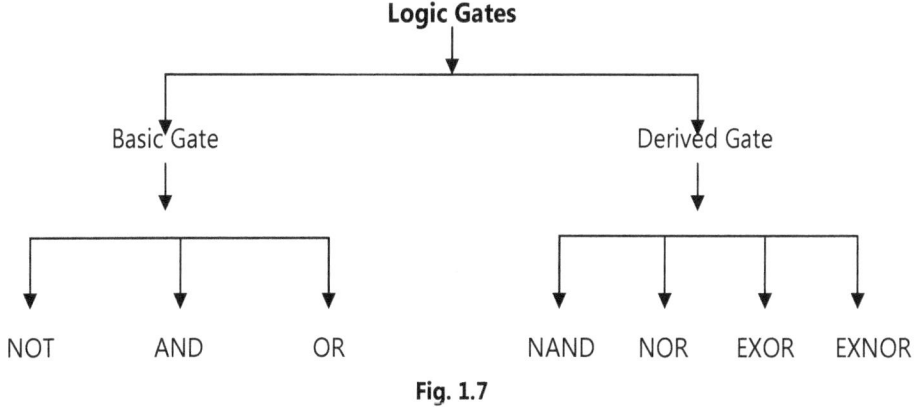

Fig. 1.7

## 1.7.1 NOT Gate (Inverter)

**Logic Statement**
- The output of a NOT circuit takes on the logic '1' state, if and only if the input does not take on the '1' state.

**Truth Table of NOT**

| A | Y |
|---|---|
| 0 | 1 |
| 1 | 0 |

**Logic Symbol of NOT**

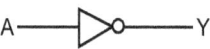

**Fig. 1.8 : Logic symbol of NOT gate**

- The bubble appearing at the output indicates inversion or negation.

**Boolean Equation**

$$Y = \overline{A}$$

- The bar above variable A represents the logical inversion operation.
- Some authors use ' ' ' symbol which is more appropriate.

i.e. $\qquad Y = A'$

## 1.7.2 AND Gate

**Logic Statement**
- The AND gate is an electronic logic circuit in which the output is in logic '1' state only and only when all the inputs are in logic '1' state.

**Truth Table of AND**

| Inputs | | Output |
|---|---|---|
| A | B | Y |
| 0 | 0 | 0 |
| 0 | 1 | 0 |
| 1 | 0 | 0 |
| 1 | 1 | 1 |

**Logic Symbol of AND**

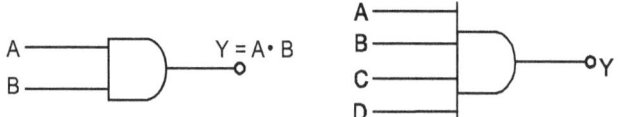

(a) Two Input AND Gate  (b) Four Input AND Gate

**Fig. 1.9 : Logic symbol of AND gate**

**Boolean Equation**

$$Y = A \cdot B$$

The '·' operator is called logic AND operator.

## 1.7.3 OR Gate

### Logic Statement

- The OR gate is an electronic circuit in which the output is in logic 1 state, when any one or more inputs are in logic 1 states.

### Truth Table of OR

| Input | | Output |
|---|---|---|
| A | B | Y |
| 0 | 0 | 0 |
| 0 | 1 | 1 |
| 1 | 0 | 1 |
| 1 | 1 | 1 |

### Logic Symbol of OR

(a) Two Input OR Gate    (b) Four Input OR Gate

Fig. 1.10 : Logic symbol of OR gate

### Boolean Equation

$$Y = A + B$$

- The '+' operator is called logic OR operator.
- It must be noted that logical OR is not equal to addition.

  When A = B = 1 the logical OR gate gives '1' output whereas addition will give output as '0' and carry as '1'.

## 1.7.4 NAND Gate

### Logic Statement

- The NAND gate is an electronic logic circuit in which the output is in logic 1 state, when both or any one of the inputs are in logic 0 state.

### Truth Table of NAND

| Inputs | | Output |
|---|---|---|
| A | B | Y |
| 0 | 0 | 1 |
| 0 | 1 | 1 |
| 1 | 0 | 1 |
| 1 | 1 | 0 |

## Logic Symbol of NAND

(a) Two input NAND gate    (b) Four input NAND gate

Fig. 1.11 : Logic symbol of NAND gate

**Boolean Equation**

$$Y = \overline{(A \cdot B)}$$

## 1.7.5 NOR Gate

**Logic Statement**

- The NOR gate is an electronic logic circuit in which the output is in logic '1' state only when both or more inputs are in logic '0' states.

**Truth Table of NOR**

| Input | | Output |
|---|---|---|
| A | B | Y |
| 0 | 0 | 1 |
| 0 | 1 | 0 |
| 1 | 0 | 0 |
| 1 | 1 | 0 |

**Logic Symbol of NOR**

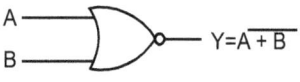
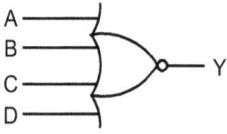

(a) Two input Nor gate    (b) Four input NOR gate

Fig. 1.12 : Logic symbol of NOR gate

**Boolean Equation**

$$Y = \overline{(A + B)}$$

## 1.7.6 Exclusive OR Gate

**Logic Statement**

- The XOR gate is an electronic logic circuit having two or more number of inputs and only one output which recognizes only inputs that have an odd number of logic 1 state.

**Logic Symbol**

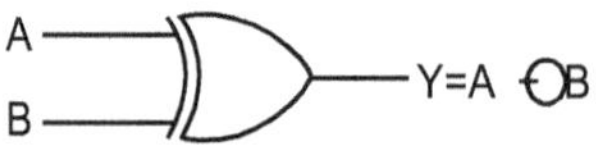

$Y = A \oplus B$

Fig. 1.13 (a) : Logic symbol of EXOR gate

## Boolean Equation

The Boolean equation for XOR gate is written as,

$$Y = \overline{A}B + A\overline{B}$$

or

$$Y = A \oplus B$$

## Timing Diagram (Pulsed Operation)

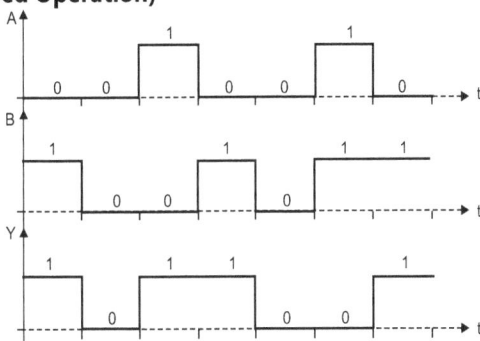

Fig. 1.13 (b) : Timing diagram for EXOR gate

## 1.7.7 Universal Gates – NAND and NOR

### (a) NAND as an Universal Gate

- The NAND gate is an universal gate because all basic gates can be implemented using NAND gates.

| Sr. No. | Gate | NAND Gate Implementation |
|---|---|---|
| 1. | NOT gate | $Y = \overline{A}$ |
| 2. | AND gate | $Y = A \cdot B$ |
| 3. | OR gate | $Y = A + B$ |
| 4. | XOR gate | $\overline{A} \cdot B$ |

- NOR and XNOR can be easily implemented by cascading NOT gate (using NAND) to the output of OR and XOR gates respectively.

### (b) NOR as an Universal Gate

- NOR gate is also an universal gate as we can implement any basic gate using NOR gate.

| Sr. No. | Gate | NOR Implementation |
|---|---|---|
| 1. | NOT gate | $Y = \overline{A}$ |
| 2. | AND gate | $Y = A \cdot B$ |
| 3. | OR gate | $Y = A + B$ |
| 4. | XOR gate | $Y = A \oplus B$ |

- NAND and XNOR gates can be implemented by cascading NOT gate (using NOR) to the output of AND and XOR gates respectively.

## QUESTIONS

1. Explain different types of number systems ?
2. What do you mean by signed magnitude representation of a number ?
3. What are different ways of representing signed binary numbers ? Explain with examples ?
4. Perform addition of $(11001001)_2$ and $(10101111)_2$.
5. Perform the following arithmetic's operations using 2's complement form
   (i) 8 + 12  (ii) −8 + 12  (iii) 8 − 12  (iv) −8 − 12
6. Perform subtraction using 2's complement method.
   (i) 96 − 78  (ii) 57 − 77  (iii) 88 − 99
7. Add the octal numbers : $(777)_8 + (77)_8 = (\ \ )$
8. Perform subtraction using 8's complement form
   (i) $(516)_8 − (413)_8$  (ii) $(316)_8 − (451)_8$
9. Explain different gates.
10. Which gates are known as universal gates ? Justify using examples.
11. What are the different derived gates?

# Unit - II

# BOOLEAN ALGEBRA AND COMBINATIONAL LOGIC DESIGN

## 2.1 INTRODUCTION TO BOOLEAN ALGEBRA

- The rules for manipulation of binary numbers developed by George Boole are known as Boolean algebra.
- A Boolean variable can only take binary values i.e. '1' or '0' just like ordinary algebra.
- Boolean algebra has also its own certain operators like AND ($\cdot$), OR (+), NOT (−) and XOR ($\oplus$).

### 2.1.1 Axioms of Boolean Algebra

- Axioms and postulates of Boolean algebra are a set of logical expressions that we accept without proof and upon which we can built useful theorems or laws.
- Axioms are nothing but logical expressions of the basic three gates i.e. AND, OR and NOT.

Axiom 1 : $0.0 = 0$  
Axiom 2 : $0.1 = 0$  
Axiom 3 : $1.0 = 0$  
Axiom 4 : $1.1 = 1$  
Axiom 5 : $0 + 0 = 0$  
Axiom 6 : $0 + 1 = 1$  
Axiom 7 : $1 + 0 = 1$  
Axiom 8 : $1 + 1 = 1$  
Axiom 9 : $\overline{1} = 0$  
Axiom 10 : $\overline{0} = 1$

### 2.1.2 Laws of Boolean Algebra

| Sr. No. | Category of Law | Laws |
|---|---|---|
| 1. | AND Laws | $A \cdot 0 = 0$<br>$A \cdot 1 = A$<br>$A \cdot A = A$<br>$A \cdot \overline{A} = 0$ |
| 2. | OR Laws | $A + 0 = A$<br>$A + 1 = 1$<br>$A + A = A$<br>$A + \overline{A} = 1$ |
| 3. | NOT or Inversion Laws | $\overline{\overline{A}} = A$ |

| 4. | Commutative laws (allows change of position of variables) | $A + B = B + A$ <br> $A \cdot B = B \cdot A$ |
|---|---|---|
| 5. | Associative laws (allows grouping of variables) | $A + (B + C) = (A + B) + C$ <br> $A \cdot (B \cdot C) = (A \cdot B) \cdot C$ |
| 6. | Distributive Laws (allows factoring or distribution of terms) | $A \cdot (B + C) = A \cdot B + A \cdot C$ <br> $A + (B \cdot C) = (A + B) \cdot (A + C)$ <br> $A + (\overline{A} \cdot B) = A + B$ |
| 7. | Impotence laws (means same value) | $A \cdot A = A$ <br> $A + A = A$ |
| 8. | Identity laws | $A \cdot 1 = A$ <br> $A + 1 = 1$ |
| 9. | Null laws | $A \cdot 0 = 0$ <br> $A + 0 = A$ |
| 10. | Absorption laws | $A + (A \cdot B) = A$ <br> $A (A + B) = A$ |

## 2.1.3 Rules of Boolean Algebra

The rules that are followed in Boolean algebra are given below :

- Capital letters are used for representing variables and functions of variables.
- It will be assumed that the positive logic is used unless until the problem statement specifically mentions negative logic.
- The complement of a variable is represented by a "bar" ( $\overline{\phantom{A}}$ ) over the variable letter.
- The logic AND function is shown by a "dot" (·) between the two variables, e.g. A · B. Many times, this dot is not written i.e. AB.
- Boolean addition is logical OR operation. It is different than mathematical addition. For example,

$$1 + 1 = 1 \text{ in Boolean algebra}$$
$$1 + 1 = 0 \text{ with carry 1 in mathematics}$$

## 2.1.4 DeMorgan's Theorems

- Boolean algebra was initially ignored by both mathematicians and technocrats. Bas Augustus DeMorgan was the first to put Boolean algebra to practice. DeMorgan discovered two important theorems which are known as DeMorgan's theorems.

The two theorems are,

1. $\overline{A + B} = \overline{A} \cdot \overline{B}$

2. $\overline{A \cdot B} = \overline{A} + \overline{B}$

## 2.1.4.1 DeMorgan's First Theorem

- The statement of DeMorgan's first theorem goes like this, "*Complement of a sum of variables is equal to the product of their individual complements*".

$$\overline{A + B} = \overline{A} \cdot \overline{B}$$

**Truth Table Proof :**

| A | B | $\overline{A}$ | $\overline{B}$ | A + B | L.H.S. = $\overline{A + B}$ | R.H.S. = $\overline{A} \cdot \overline{B}$ |
|---|---|---|---|---|---|---|
| 0 | 0 | 1 | 1 | 0 | 1 | 1 |
| 0 | 1 | 1 | 0 | 1 | 0 | 0 |
| 1 | 0 | 0 | 1 | 1 | 0 | 0 |
| 1 | 1 | 0 | 0 | 1 | 0 | 0 |

**Logic Diagram :**

Fig. 2.1 : Logic diagram of DeMorgan's first theorem

Thus, NOR gate is equivalent to a bubbled AND gate.

## 2.1.4.2 DeMorgan's Second Theorem

- The statement of DeMorgan's second theorem goes like this, "*Complement of a product of variables is equal to the sum of their individual complements*".

$$\overline{A + B} = \overline{A} \cdot \overline{B}$$

**Truth Table Proof :**

| A | B | $\overline{A}$ | $\overline{B}$ | A · B | L.H.S. = $\overline{A \cdot B}$ | R.H.S. = $\overline{A} + \overline{B}$ |
|---|---|---|---|---|---|---|
| 0 | 0 | 1 | 1 | 0 | 1 | 1 |
| 0 | 1 | 1 | 0 | 0 | 1 | 1 |
| 1 | 0 | 0 | 1 | 0 | 1 | 1 |
| 1 | 1 | 0 | 0 | 1 | 0 | 0 |

**Logic Diagram :**

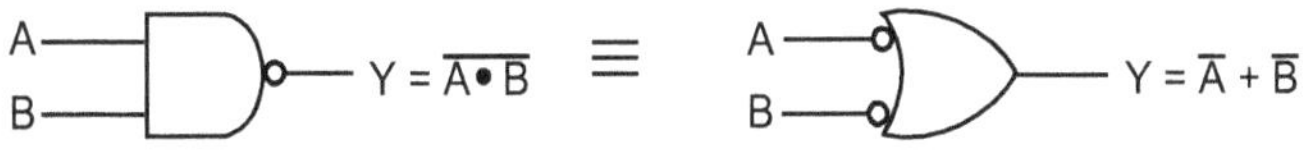

Fig. 2.2 : Logic diagram of DeMorgan's second theorem

- Thus, a NAND gate is equivalent to bubbled OR gate.

**Example 2.1 :** Y = (A + B) (A + C)

**Solution :** Y = (A + B) (A + C)

$= AA + AC + BA + BC$         (Distributive law)

$$= A + AC + AB + BC \qquad (\because AA = A)$$
$$= A(1 + C) + AB + BC$$
$$= A + AB + BC \qquad (\because 1 + C = 1)$$
$$= A(1 + B) + BC \qquad (\because 1 + B = 1)$$
$$= A + BC$$

### 2.1.4.3 Duality Theorem

- The distinction between positive and negative logic gives rise to principle of duality.
- Because an OR gate is the positive logic system becomes AND gate in the negative logic system and vice-versa. Given a Boolean identity, we can produce a dual identity by changing '+' signs to '·' and vice-versa.

|    | Boolean Expression | Dual |
|----|--------------------|------|
| 1. | $A \cdot 0 = 0$    | $A + 1 = 1$ |
| 2. | $A \cdot 1 = A$    | $A + 0 = A$ |
| 3. | $A \cdot A = A$    | $A + A = A$ |
| 4. | $A \cdot \overline{A} = 0$ | $A + \overline{A} = 1$ |
| 5. | $A \cdot B = B \cdot A$ | $A + B = B + A$ |

**Example 2.2 :** $(B + A)(B + D)(A + C)(C + D) = BC + AD$

**Solution :**

$$\begin{aligned}
\text{LHS} &= (B + A)(B + D)(A + C)(C + D) \\
&= (BB + BD + AB + AD)(AC + CC + AD + CD) \qquad \because A \cdot A = A \\
&= (B + BD + AB + AD)(AC + AD + C + CD) \\
&= (B[1 + D + A] + AD)(C[1 + A + D] + AD) \qquad \because A + 1 = 1 \\
&= (B + AD)(C + AD) \\
&= BC + BAD + CAD + AD \cdot AD \qquad \because A \cdot A = A \\
&= BC + AD(B + C + 1) \\
&= BC + AD \qquad \because A + 1 = 1
\end{aligned}$$

$$\text{LHS} = \text{RHS}$$

## 2.2 SUM OF PRODUCTS (SOP) FORM

### 2.2.1 Standard Terms and Standard (or Canonical) Forms

- The object of a Boolean algebra is to describe the behaviour and logic structure.
- The behaviour of the logic circuit can be expressed in standard forms using standard terms.

## 2.2.2 Sum Term or Maximum Term (M)

- The output of OR gate is called sum term.
- In OR gate, the output is logic '1' for maximum number of combinations of inputs.
- So, the output of OR gate is also called Maximum term or Maxterm (M).
- A sum term of any 'n' variable functions containing all the 'n' literals is called a maxterm. The 'n' variables functions have $2^n$ maxterms.
- These are denoted as $M_0, M_1, M_2, \ldots M_n$.
- Each variables taking value '0' appears in uncomplemented form in maxterm and each variable taking '1' value appears in complemented form.

## 2.2.3 Product or Minimum Term (m)

- The output of AND gate is called product term.
- In AND gate, the output is logic '1' for minimum number of combinations of inputs. So, the output of AND gate is also called 'Minimum term or minterm (m).
- A product term of any 'n' variable functions containing all literals is called a minterm. The 'n' variable functions have $2^n$ minterms. These are denoted as $m_0, m_1, m_2, \ldots, m_n$.
- In minterms, each variables taking value '1' appears in uncomplemented form.

**Table 2.1 : Maxterms and minterms of two-variables**

| Decimal Equivalent | Variables | | Minterms | | Maxterms | |
|---|---|---|---|---|---|---|
| | A | B | $m_i$ | Notation | $M_i$ | Notation |
| 0 | 0 | 0 | $\bar{A}\bar{B}$ | $m_0$ | $A + B$ | $M_0$ |
| 1 | 0 | 1 | $\bar{A}B$ | $m_1$ | $A + \bar{B}$ | $M_1$ |
| 2 | 1 | 0 | $A\bar{B}$ | $m_2$ | $\bar{A} + B$ | $M_2$ |
| 3 | 1 | 1 | $AB$ | $m_3$ | $\bar{A} + \bar{B}$ | $M_3$ |

## 2.2.4 Standard (or Canonical) Forms

- If a function is expressed in such a way that each variable is present in each term.

## 2.2.5 Sum of Products (SOP) Form

- The output of AND gate is called product term.
- The output of OR gate is called sum term.
- The output of AND-OR gate circuit is called sum-of-products (SOP) form.
- Consider the equation, $Y = \bar{AB} + AB$

- Each term in the equation is called the fundamental minterm. From table mentioned earlier, the output Y can be written as,

$$Y = m_1 + m_3 = \Sigma m_1, m_3 = \Sigma m_i$$

where, $i = 1, 3 = \Sigma 1, 3$

- The SOP form can be converted to standard SOP form by ANDing the terms in the expression with terms formed by ORing.
- The variable and its complement which are not present in that term.
- Following steps are followed to convert a given SOP form to standard SOP form :
  
  (i) Write down all the terms.
  
  (ii) If one or more variables are missing in any term, expand that term by multiplying it with the sum of each one of the missing variable and its complement.

  For example, $Y = AB + A\bar{B}C$

- The variable C is missing in first term. So, multiply the first term by $(C + \bar{C})$.

$$Y = AB(C + \bar{C}) + A\bar{B}C$$

(iii) Drop out the redundant terms.

**Example 2.3 :** Convert $Y = A\bar{B} + A\bar{C} + \bar{B}C$ into standard SOP form.

**Solution :**
$$Y = A\bar{B} + A\bar{C} + \bar{B}C$$
$$= A\bar{B}(C + \bar{C}) + A\bar{C}(B + \bar{B}) + \bar{B}C(A + \bar{A})$$
$$= A\bar{B}C + A\bar{B}\bar{C} + A\bar{C}B + A\bar{C}\bar{B} + \bar{B}CA + \bar{B}C\bar{A}$$
$$= \underbrace{A\bar{B}C}_{} + A\bar{B}\bar{C} + A\bar{C}B + A\bar{C}\bar{B} + \underbrace{AB\bar{C} + \bar{A}\bar{B}C}_{}$$

Redundant terms

$$= A\bar{B}C + A\bar{B}\bar{C} + A\bar{C}B + A\bar{C}\bar{B} + \bar{A}\bar{B}C$$

**Example 2.4 :** Simplify $Y = \Sigma m (0, 1, 2, 3, 4, 5, 6, 7)$

**Solution :** The given expression has all the minterms of a three variable table.

$$\therefore \quad Y = \underbrace{\bar{A}\bar{B}\bar{C} + \bar{A}\bar{B}C}_{} + \underbrace{\bar{A}B\bar{C} + \bar{A}BC}_{} + \underbrace{A\bar{B}\bar{C} + A\bar{B}C}_{} + \underbrace{AB\bar{C} + ABC}_{}$$

$$= \bar{A}\bar{B}(C + \bar{C}) + \bar{A}B(\bar{C} + C) + A\bar{B}(\bar{C} + C) + AB(\bar{C} + C)$$

$$= \underbrace{\bar{A}\bar{B} + \bar{A}B}_{} + \underbrace{A\bar{B} + AB}_{} \qquad \therefore \quad C + \bar{C} = 1$$

$$= \bar{A}\left(\bar{B}+B\right) + A\left(\bar{B}+B\right)$$

$$= \bar{A} + A$$

$$Y = 1$$

∴ The answer is always 'true' (1) because the given expression contains all possible minterms.

## 2.3 PRODUCT OF SUMS (POS) FORM

### 2.3.1 Product-of-Sums (POS) Form

- The output of OR-AND gate circuit is called Product-Of-Sums (POS) form.
  Consider the equation,

$$Y = (A + B) \cdot (\bar{A} + B)$$

$$Y = M_0, M_2 = \pi\,(0, 2)$$

  where, $\pi$ stands for the product of maxterms.

- The POS form can be converted to standard POS form by ORing the terms in the expression with terms formed by ANDing the variable and its complement which are not present in that term.

- Following steps are followed to convert a POS form to standard POS form.

(i) Write down all the terms.

(ii) If one or more variables are missing in any sum terms, expand that term by adding the products of each of the missing term and its complement.

(iii) Drop out the redundant terms.

**Example 2.5 :** Convert $Y = (A + B) \cdot (A + C) \cdot (B + \bar{C})$ into standard POS form.

**Solution :**

$$Y = (A + B) \cdot (A + C) \cdot (B + \bar{C})$$

$$= (A + B + C \cdot \bar{C}) \cdot (A + B \cdot \bar{B} + C) \cdot (B + \bar{C} + A \cdot \bar{A})$$

We use $X + YZ = (X + Y) \cdot (X + Z)$ law to expand the equation.

$$= (A + B + C)(A + B + \bar{C})(A + C + B)$$

$$(A + B + C)(B + \bar{C} + A)(B + \bar{C} + \bar{A})$$

$$= (A + B + C)(A + B + \bar{C})(A + \bar{B} + C)$$

$$(\bar{A} + B + \bar{C}) \qquad (\because \text{Redundant terms})$$

**Example 2.6 :** Simplify the following three variable expression.
$$Y = \pi M (1, 3, 5, 7)$$

**Solution :**

The given Boolean expression is in POS from. From the table, we can rewrite the Boolean expression as

$$Y = \underbrace{(A + B + \bar{C})}_{N_1} \underbrace{(A + \bar{B} + \bar{C})}_{N_3} \underbrace{(\bar{A} + B + \bar{C})}_{N_5} \underbrace{(\bar{A} + \bar{B} + \bar{C})}_{N_7}$$

$$= (AA + A\bar{B} + A\bar{C} + BA + B\bar{B} + B\bar{C} + \bar{C}A + \bar{C}B + \bar{C}\bar{C})(\bar{A} + B + \bar{C})(\bar{A} + \bar{B} + \bar{C})$$

$$= (A + A\bar{B} + A\bar{C} + AB + 0 + B\bar{C})(\bar{A} + B + \bar{C})(\bar{A} + \bar{B} + \bar{C})$$

$$= (A + (1 + \bar{C}) + A(\bar{B} + B) + \bar{C}B)(\bar{A}(\bar{B} + B) + \bar{A}\bar{C} + \bar{C})$$

$$= (A + A + \bar{C}B)(\bar{A} + \bar{A}\bar{C} + \bar{C})$$

$$= (A + \bar{C}B)(\bar{A} + \bar{C}A)$$

$$= A\bar{A} + A\bar{C}A + \bar{C}B\bar{A} + \bar{C}B\bar{C}A$$

$$= 0 + 0 + \bar{C}B\bar{A} + \bar{C}B\bar{C}A = \bar{A}B\bar{C} + A B\bar{C}$$

$$Y = \bar{A} B \bar{C}$$

## 2.4 REDUCTION TECHNIQUES

### 2.4.1 Boolean Algebra Simplification Technique

- A good digital circuit must have minimum number of logic gates.
- Less number of gates means minimum propagation delay, skew, power dissipation.
- The number of logic gates can be reduced only if the number of terms in the Boolean expression can be reduced.
- There are four methods that are used to simplify or reduce the Boolean equations.
  1. Algebraic (Boolean Laws, DeMorgan's Theorems).
  2. Karnaugh (K) Map.
  3. Variable Entered Mapping (VEM).
  4. Quine-McClauskey (Q-M) Tabular Method.
- The K-map is the simplest and the most commonly used method.

## 2.4.2 Reduction of Boolean Equation using K-map

- The K-map method is a systematic approach for simplifying a Boolean expression.
- This method was proposed by Veitch and then modified by Karnaugh, hence it is called Karnaugh map.
- The basis of K-map method is graphical representation of minterms or maxterms in a chart called Karnaugh map (K-map). K-map contains cells.
- Each cell represents one of the $2^n$ possible product cells that can be formed from n variables.
- Thus, n-variable K-map has 4 cells, 3-variable k-map has 8 cells and 4-variable K-map has 16 cells.
- Product terms are assigned to the cells of a K-map by labelling each row and each column of the map with a variable, with its complements or with a combination of variables and complements. Fig. 2.3 depicts the 2-variable, 3-variable and 4-variable maps.

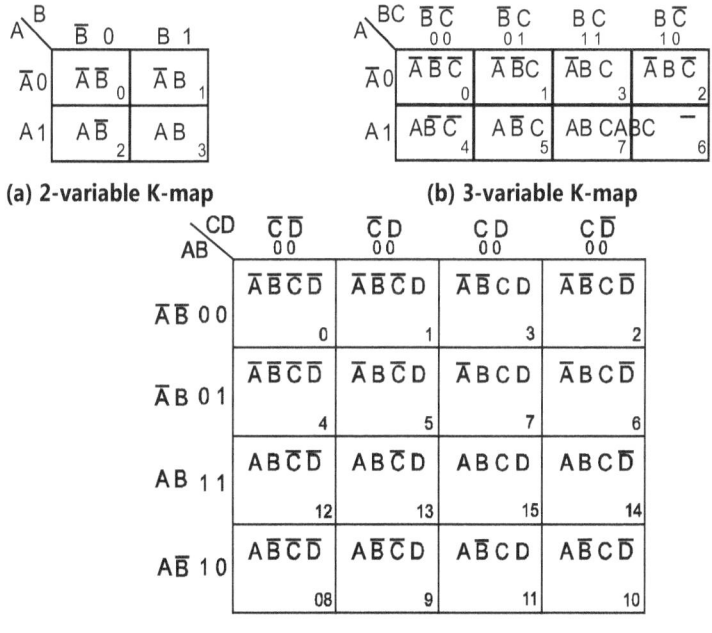

(a) 2-variable K-map

(b) 3-variable K-map

(c) 4-variable K-map

Fig. 2.3

- It is important to note that only one variable changes, when we move from one cell to another along any row or any column.
- Therefore, the third column and the third row in a two-variable K-map have '11' binary representation instead of '10'.
- This peculiar arrangement of K-map has special significance as mentioned below.

- When two inputs change simultaneously then digital circuit output goes in a metastable state.
- Output can swing to either logic '1' or logic '0' state in metastable state.
- This state is to be avoided by prohibiting two inputs from switching simultaneously.
- We know that any logic function can be represented in SOP or POS form. The given Boolean expression can be used to fill entries in the truth table and truth table can be represented on K-map.
- With little practice, it is also possible to fill entries in k-map directly.

### 2.4.3 Representing SOP Equation on K-map

**Example 2.7 :** Plot Boolean expression.

$$Y = \bar{A}B\bar{C}D + AB\bar{C}\bar{D} + AB\bar{C}\bar{D}$$

**Solution :** The Boolean expression has four variables, so we use 4-variable k-map.
- Represent each product term by '1' in corresponding cell.
- Note that number of 1's in K-map is equal to the product terms in the given Boolean expression.
- Fill 0's in all other cells.

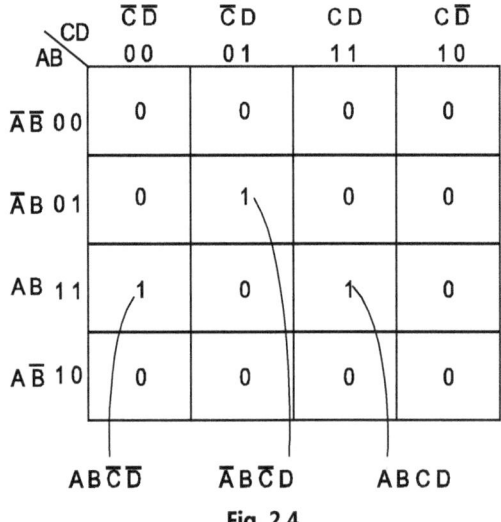

Fig. 2.4

### 2.4.4 Representing POS Equation on K-map

**Example 2.8 :** Plot Boolean expression.

$$Z = (X + \bar{Y})(\bar{X} + \bar{Y})$$

**Solution :** The Boolean expression has two variables, so we use 2-variable K-map.

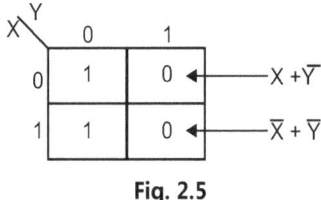

Fig. 2.5

- Represent each sum term by '0' in the corresponding cell.
- Note that number of '0's in K-map is equal to the sum terms in the given Boolean expression.
- Fill '1's in all other cells.

## 2.4.5 K-map Reduction Techniques

- In K-map minterms are represented by 1's and maxterms are represented by 0's.
- The objective of K-map reduction or simplification technique is to reduce the number of logic gates.
- Once the logic or Boolean expression is plotted on K-map, we use grouping technique to simplify the given Boolean expression as follows :

### (a) Grouping Two Adjacent Ones (or Pair) :

- Consider a Boolean expression $Y = ABC + AB\bar{C}$.

  It can be seen from the given Boolean expression that we will require two three-input AND gates and one two-input OR gate to implement the logic equation.

- Now, if we plot the equation in a 3-variable K-map.

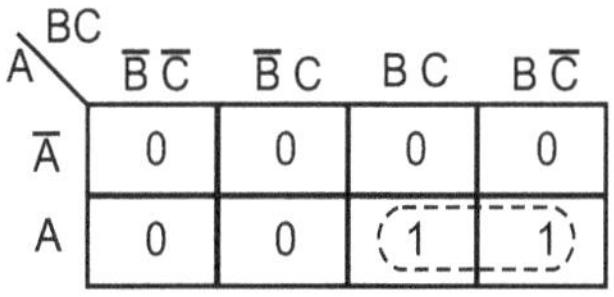

| A \ BC | $\bar{B}\bar{C}$ | $\bar{B}C$ | $BC$ | $B\bar{C}$ |
|---|---|---|---|---|
| $\bar{A}$ | 0 | 0 | 0 | 0 |
| A | 0 | 0 | 1 | 1 |

Fig. 2.6 : Grouping on two adjacent ones

- It can be noticed that when the two adjacent 1's are grouped then only one variable appears in its complemented and uncomplemented form i.e. C and $\bar{C}$.

$$Y = ABC + AB\bar{C}$$
$$= AB(C + \bar{C})$$
$$= AB \qquad (\because C + \bar{C} = 1)$$

- So, these two terms can be combined together to eliminate the variable C.
- Once this third variable is eliminated then it is possible to use two-input AND gate instead of three-input AND.

These adjacent 1's can be also in vertical or any other form as shown in Fig. 2.7.

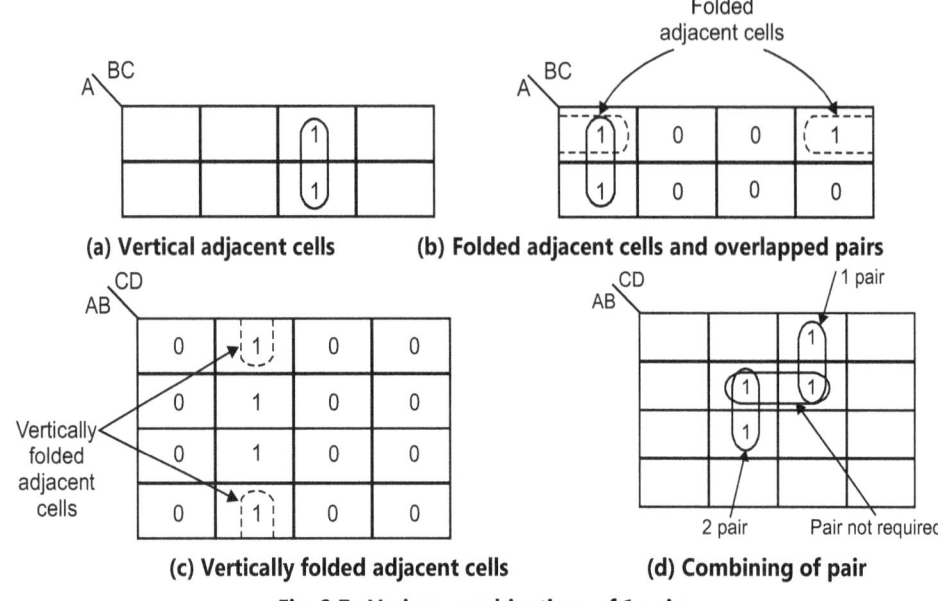

(a) Vertical adjacent cells  (b) Folded adjacent cells and overlapped pairs

(c) Vertically folded adjacent cells  (d) Combining of pair

**Fig. 2.7 : Various combinations of 1 pairs**

### (b) Grouping of Four Adjacent Ones (Quad) :

- We can group four adjacent ones to eliminate two variables out of four variables.
- The several ways to form four adjacent ones or quads are shown in Fig. 2.8.

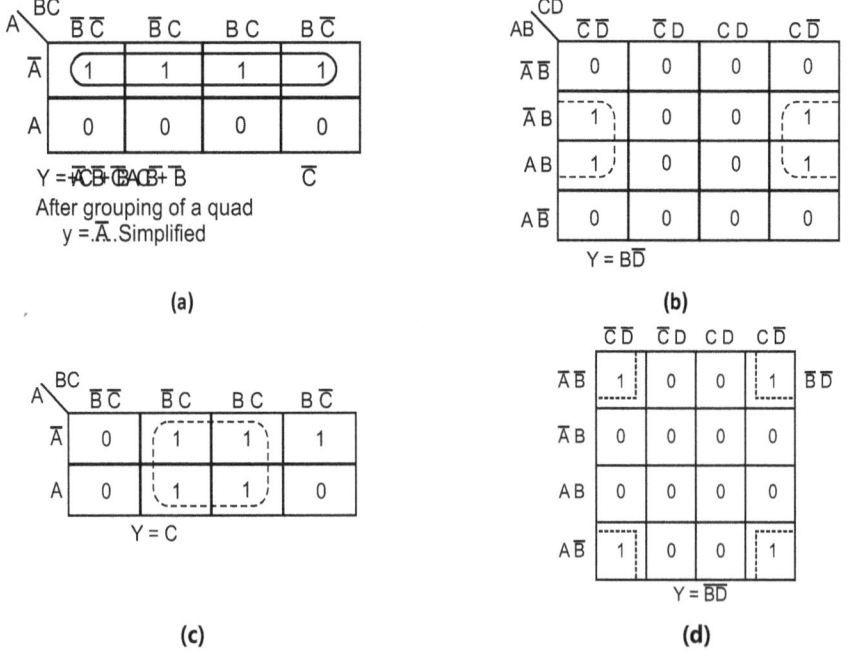

**Fig. 2.8**

**(c) Grouping of Eight Adjacent Ones (Octet) :** We can group four adjacent ones to eliminate three variables out of four variables.

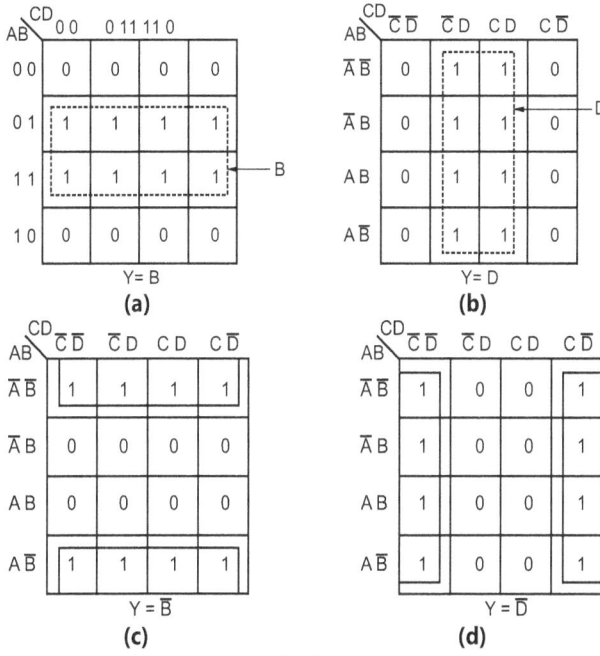

Fig. 2.9

## 2.4.6 Prime Implicant and Essential Prime Implicant

- A group of one or more 1's which are adjacent and can be combined on a Karnaough Map is called an implicant.
- The process of simplication involves grouping of minterms and identifying prime implicants (PI) and essential prime implicants (EPI).

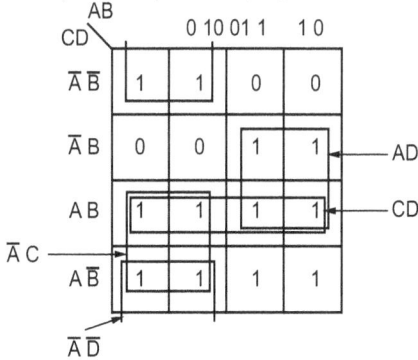

Fig. 2.10

- A prime implicant is a group of minters that cannot be combined with any other minterm or groups. An essential prime implicant is a prime implicant in which one or more minterms are unique i.e. it contains at least one minterm which is not contained in any other prime-implicant.

- A prime implicant is a product term which cannot be further simplified by combination with other terms.

$$\text{Prime implicant} = \overline{AD} + \overline{A}C + \overline{A}D + CD$$

$$\text{Essential prime implicant} = \overline{AD}$$

## 2.4.7 Don't Care Condition

- In some logic circuits, certain input conditions never occur or they are not possible. Therefore, the corresponding output never appears and the output level is not defined. It can be either HIGH or LOW. These output levels are represented as 'Don't Care Conditions' and are indicated by 'X'.
- Don't care conditions can be used to form groups and hence help in simplifying the Boolean expression. See the example below;

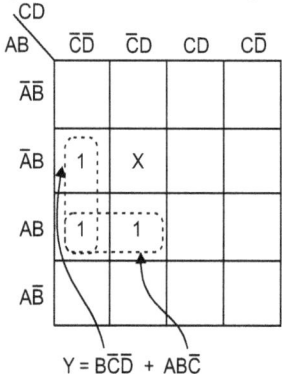
$Y = B\overline{C}\overline{D} + AB\overline{C}$

(a) Without Don't Care Condition

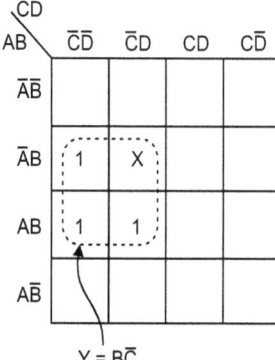
$Y = B\overline{C}$

(b) With Don't Care Condition

**Fig. 2.11 : Use of Don't Care Condition in simlifying the Boolean Expression**

**Example 2.9 :** Simplify the following Boolean expression

$$Y(A,B,C,D) = \Sigma m (1,3,7,11,15) + d (0, 2, 5)$$

**Solution :** Representing all the minterms and don't care conditions on the K – map

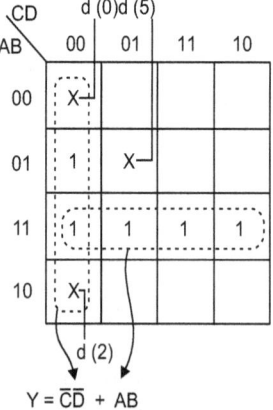

$Y = \overline{CD} + AB$

**Fig. 2.12**

**Example 2.10 :** Simplify the Boolean expression Y = π M (4,5,6,7,8,12) · d (0,13,15,14)

**Solution :** Represent all the maxterms and don't care conditions in the K – map

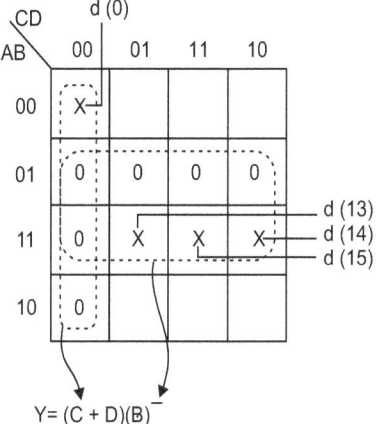

Y= (C + D)(B̄)

**Fig. 2.13**

## 2.4.8 Limitations of Karnaugh Map

- The Map method of simplification is convenient as long as for the number of five and six variables. If the number of variables increases the difficultly to make combination of variables in k-map increases.

# 2.5 HALF ADDER AND FULL ADDER

- Addition is the most basic arithmetic operation in digital circuit.
- The simple addition of two bits has the following truth table.

**Table 2.2 : Truth Table**

| A | B | Sum | Carry |
|---|---|-----|-------|
| 0 | 0 | 0   | 0     |
| 0 | 1 | 1   | 0     |
| 1 | 0 | 1   | 0     |
| 1 | 1 | 0   | 1     |

- Note that when both the inputs are 1's then 'sum' is '0' and one carry is generated, similar to decimal addition.

## 2.5.1 Half-Adder

- The half-adder has two inputs (A, B) and two outputs (sum, carry).
- The block diagram of half-adder is shown in Fig. 2.14.

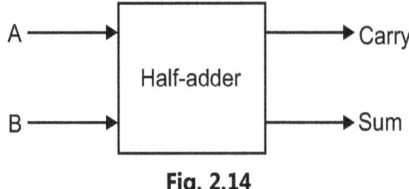

**Fig. 2.14**

- When the circuit has two or more outputs, one K-map is plotted for each output.
- The K-maps for half adder are :

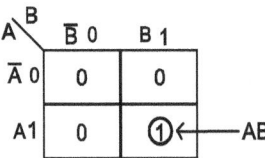

**Fig. 2.15 : K-map for carry**

∴ Carry output = AB

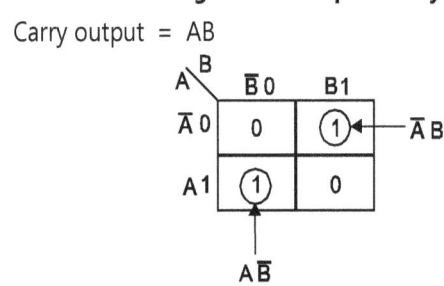

**Fig. 2.16 : K-Map for sum output**

∴ Sum = $\bar{A}B + A\bar{B}$
     = $A \oplus B$
        ↑
       XOR

**Half-Adder Circuit :** The half-adder circuit based on above K-map simplifications is shown in Fig. 2.17.

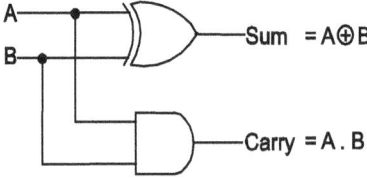

**Fig. 2.17 : Half adder logic diagram**

## 2.5.2 Full-Adder

- Full-adder has an additional input of previous carry in.
- Full-adder is a combinational circuit that forms the arithmetic sum of three input bits i.e. A, B, Cin and produces two outputs, sum, $C_{out}$.

- The logic block diagram of full adder is shown in Fig. 2.18.

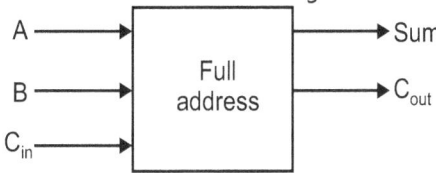

Fig. 2.18 : Block diagram of full-adder

The truth table of full-adder

Table 2.3

| Inputs | | | Outputs | |
|---|---|---|---|---|
| A | B | $C_{in}$ | $C_{out}$ | Sum |
| 0 | 0 | 0 | 0 | 0 |
| 0 | 0 | 1 | 0 | 1 |
| 0 | 1 | 0 | 0 | 1 |
| 0 | 1 | 1 | 1 | 0 |
| 1 | 0 | 0 | 0 | 1 |
| 1 | 0 | 1 | 1 | 0 |
| 1 | 1 | 0 | 1 | 0 |
| 1 | 1 | 1 | 1 | 1 |

- Full-adder truth table is plotted on two K-maps corresponding to two outputs, $C_{out}$ and sum.

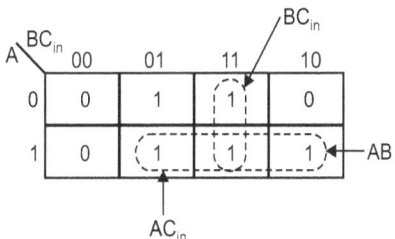

Fig. 2.19 : K-map for $C_{out}$

$C_{out} = AB + AC_{in} + BC_{in}$

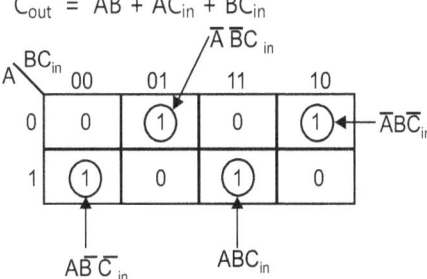

Fig. 2.20 : K-Map for Sum

$Sum = AB\overline{C}in + \overline{A}\overline{B}Cin + AB\overline{C}in + \overline{A}B\overline{C}in$

$$\text{Sum} = \bar{A}\bar{B}\text{Cin} + \bar{A}B\bar{\text{Cin}} + A\bar{B}\bar{\text{Cin}} + AB\text{Cin}$$

$$= \text{Cin}\,(\bar{A}\bar{B} + AB) + \bar{\text{Cin}}\,(\bar{A}B + A\bar{B}) = \text{Cin} \oplus (A \oplus B)$$

- The sum is the XORed output of A, B and Cin inputs.

**Full-Adder Circuit :**

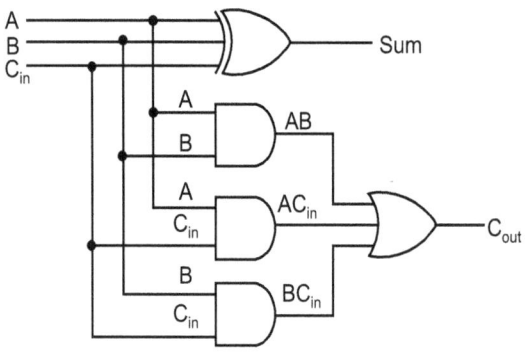

Fig. 2.21 : Full-adder logic diagram

**Full-Adder Circuit using Half-Adder :**

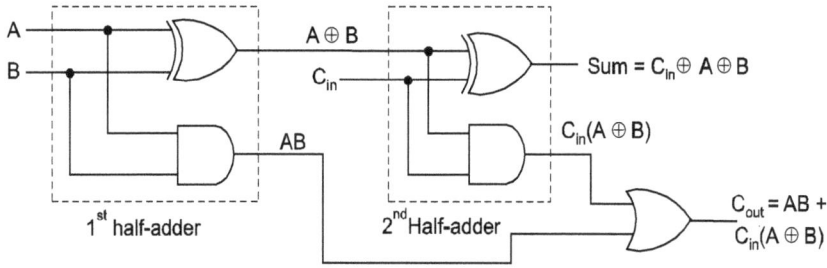

Fig. 2.22 : Full-adder using half adder

For K-map simplification :

$$C_{out} = AB + AC_{in} + BC_{in}$$

$$= AB + C_{in}(A + B) = AB + C_{in}(A\bar{B} + \bar{A}B)$$

$$= AB + C_{in}(A \oplus B)$$

Therefore, the $C_{out}$ is produced by ORing the carry output of the first adder (AB) with sum of output of the first adder (A ⊕ B).

## 2.6 HALF AND FULL SUBTRACTOR

**Subtractor :** The subtraction of two binary numbers is performed by combinational circuits called as half-subtractor and full-subtractor.

## 2.6.1 Half-Subtractor

Half-subtractor is a combinational logic circuit which subtracts two one-bit binary numbers. The truth table and the K-maps for corresponding outputs are as shown in Fig. 2.23 below :

Table 2.4 : Truth Table

| Inputs | | Outputs | |
|---|---|---|---|
| A (Minuend) | B (Subtrahend) | D (Difference) | C (Borrow) |
| 0 | 0 | 0 | 0 |
| 0 | 1 | 1 | 1 |
| 1 | 0 | 1 | 0 |
| 1 | 1 | 0 | 0 |

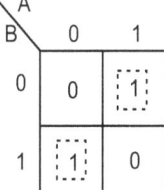   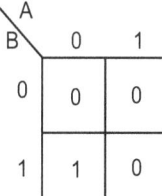

(a) k-map for D (difference)      (b) k-map for C (borrow)

Fig. 2.23 : Truth Table and K-maps of half-subtractor

- From the K-maps for the boolean expressions for the outputs are written as;

$$D = \bar{A}B + A\bar{B} = A \oplus B$$

$$C = \bar{A}B$$

- Therefore, the logic circuit for half subtractor is drawn as;

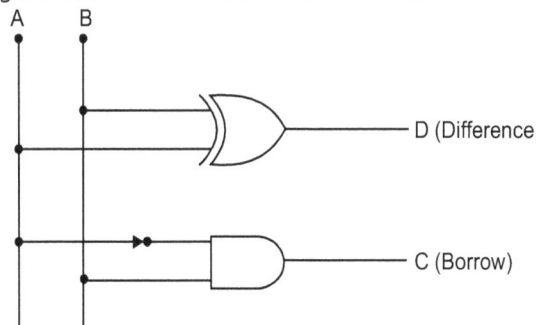

Fig. 2.24 : Half-subtractor

## 2.6.2 Full-Subtractor

Full-subtractor allows to subtract a borrow which may be generated from lower order bit subtraction. A simple block schematic of full subtractor is shown in Fig. 2.25 below :

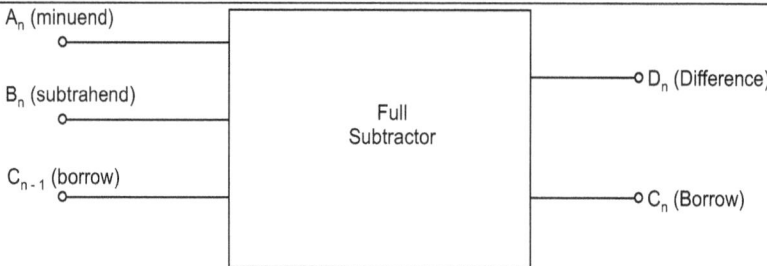

Fig. 2.25

- The truth table and k-maps for the corresponding outputs are shown in Fig. 2.26 below

Table 2.5 : Truth Table

| Inputs | | | Outputs | |
|---|---|---|---|---|
| $A_n$ | $B_n$ | $C_{n-1}$ | $D_n$ | $C_n$ |
| 0 | 0 | 0 | 0 | 0 |
| 0 | 0 | 1 | 1 | 1 |
| 0 | 1 | 0 | 1 | 1 |
| 0 | 1 | 1 | 0 | 1 |
| 1 | 0 | 0 | 1 | 0 |
| 1 | 0 | 1 | 0 | 0 |
| 1 | 1 | 0 | 0 | 0 |
| 1 | 1 | 1 | 1 | 1 |

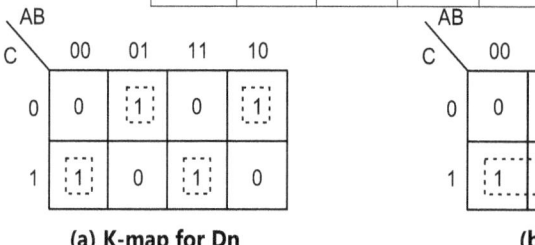

(a) K-map for Dn                    (b) K-map for Cn

Fig. 2.26

- Therefore, the boolean expression for Dn is ≈ B

$$D_1 = \overline{A}_n \overline{B}_n C_{n-1} + \overline{A}_n B_n \overline{C}_{n-1} + A_n \overline{B}_n \overline{C}_{n-1} + A_n B_n C_{n-1}$$

Which becomes exoring of the three inputs after simplification.

$$D_1 = C_{n-1} \oplus A \oplus B$$

The boolean expression for $C_n$ is

$$C_1 = \overline{A}_n B_n + \overline{A}_n C_{n-1} + B_n C_{n-1}$$

- There are two boolean expressions can be used to design a combinational logic circuit for full-subtractor as shown in Fig. 2.27 below :

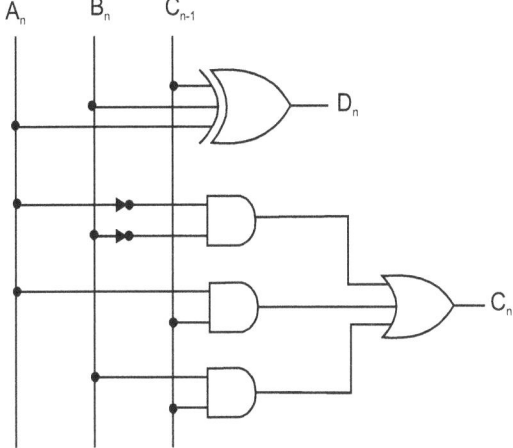

Fig. 2.27 : Full-subtractor

## 2.7 PARALLEL ADDER

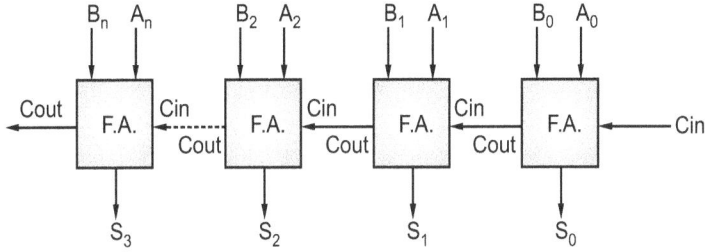

Fig. 2.28 : Block diagram of n-bit parallel adder

- A single full adder is capable of adding two one bit numbers and input carry. In order to add binary numbers with more than one bit, additional full adders must be employed. A 3 bit full adder can be constructed using number of full adder circuit connected in parallel.
- Fig. 2.28 shows the arrangement of parallel adder in that output of one adder i.e. connected to the carry input of the next higher order adder.

## 2.8 PARALLEL SUBTRACTOR

- The subtraction of binary numbers can be done must conveniently by means of complements. i.e. subtraction A-B can be done by taking 2's complement of B and adding it to A.

- The 2's complement can be obtained by taking 1's complement can be obtained by taking 1's complement and adding 1 to LSB in 1's complement of number.
- Logically it can be implemented with inverter of second bit and a one can be added to the sum through the input carry as shown in Fig. 2.29.

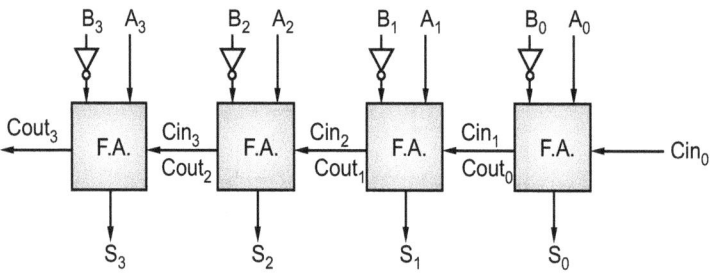

**Fig. 2.29 : 4-bit parallel subtractor**

## 2.9 PARALLEL ADDER / SUBTRACTOR

- The addition and subtraction operations can be combined into one circuit with one common binary adder. This is done by including an exclusive OR gate with each full adder as shown in Fig. 2.30.

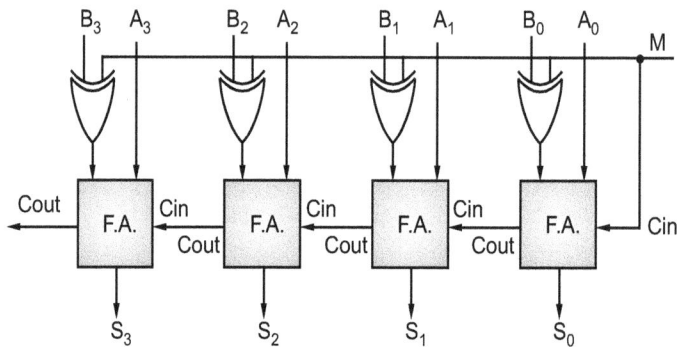

**Fig. 2.30 : 4-bit adder subtractor**

- The ripple adder is ripple carry adder in which the carry output of each full adder stage is connected to the carry input ($C_{in}$) of the next higher order stage. Therefore the sum and carry outputs of any stage cannot be produced until the input carry occurs, this leads to a time delay in addition process. This delay is known as carry propagation delay.
- One method of speeding up this process by eliminating inter stage carry delay is called look ahead carry addition.

## 2.10 CARRY LOOK - AHEAD ADDER

- The delay generated by an N - bit adder is proportional to the length N of the two numbers X and Y that are added because the carry signals have to propagate from one full-adder to the next. For large values of N, the delay becomes unacceptably large so that a special solution needs to be adopted to accelerate the calculation of the carry bits.

- This solution involves a "look- ahead carry generator" which is a block that simultaneously calculates all the carry bits involved. Once these bits are available to the rest of the circuit, each individual three-bit addition ($X_1 + Y_1$ + carry - $in_i$) is implemented by a simple 3 - input XOR gate.

- The design of the look ahead carry generator involves two Boolean functions named Generate and Propagate. For each input bits pair these functions are defined as :

$$G_i = X_i \cdot Y_i$$
$$P_i = X_i + Y_i$$

- The carry bit c-out(i) generated when adding two bits $X_i$ and $Y_i$ is '1' if the corresponding function $G_i$ is '1' or if the C-out (i-1) = '1' and the function $P_i$ = '1' simultaneously. In the first case, the carry bit is activated by the local conditions (the values for $X_i$ and $Y_i$).

- In the second, the carry bit is received from the less significant elementary addition and is propagated further to the more significant elementary addition. Therefore, the carry out bit corresponding to a pair of bits $X_i$ and $Y_i$ is calculated according to the equation :

$$\text{carry\_out}(i) = G_i + P_i \cdot \text{carry\_in}(i-1)$$

- For a four - bit adder the carry -outs are calculated as follows

$$\text{carry\_out0} = G_0 + P_0 \cdot \text{carry\_in}_0$$
$$\text{carry\_out1} = G_1 + P_1 \cdot \text{carry\_out}_0 = G_1 + P_1 G_0 + P_1 P_0 \cdot \text{carry\_in}_0$$
$$\text{carry\_out2} = G_2 + P_2 G_1 + P_2 P_1 G_0 + P_2 P_1 P_0 \cdot \text{carry\_in}_0$$
$$\text{carry\_out3} = G_3 + P_3 G_2 + P_3 P_2 G_1 + P_3 P_2 P_1 G_0 + P_3 P_2 P_1 \cdot \text{carry\_in}_0$$

- The set of equations above are implemented by the circuit below and a complete adder with a look - ahead carry generator is next. The input singnals need to propagate through a maximum of 4 logic gate in such an adder as opposed to 8 and 12 logic gates.

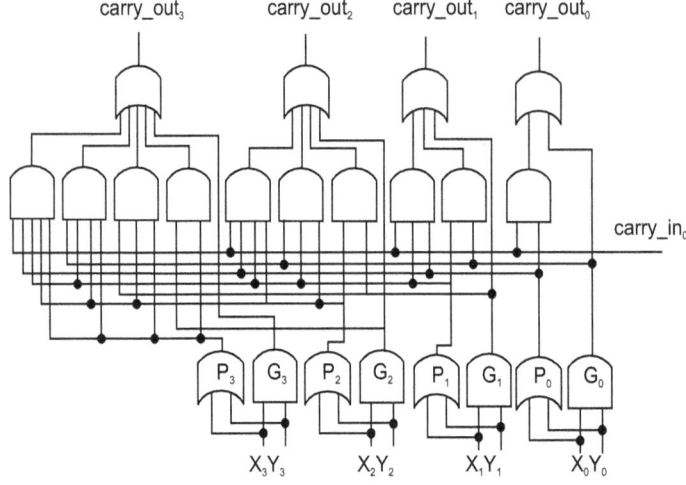

Fig. 2.31: Carry look-ahead adder – carry output

- Sums can be calculated from the following equations, where carry _ out is taken from the carry calculated in the above circuit.

$$\text{sum\_out}_0 = X_0 \oplus Y_0 \oplus \text{carry\_out}_0$$

$$\text{sum\_out}_1 = X_1 \oplus Y_1 \oplus \text{carry\_out}_1$$

$$\text{sum\_out}_2 = X_2 \oplus Y_2 \oplus \text{carry\_out}_2$$

$$\text{sum\_out}_3 = X_3 \oplus Y_3 \oplus \text{carry\_out}_3$$

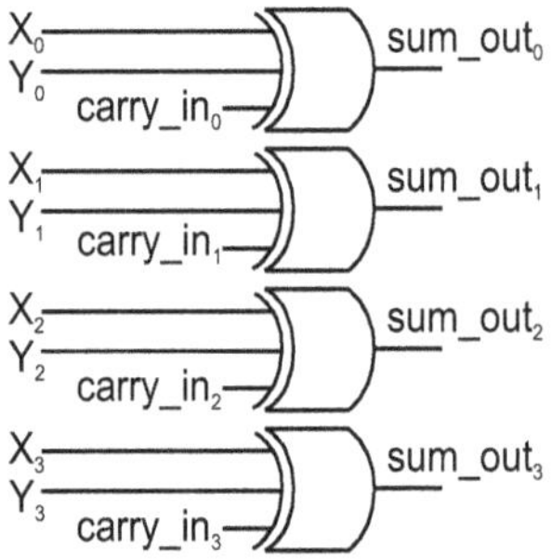

Fig. 2.32 : Carry look-ahead adder – sum output

## 2.11 BCD ADDER

- The digital systems handle the decimal number is the form of binary coded decimal numbers (BCD) A BCD adder is a circuit that adds two BCD digits and produces a sum digit also in BCD.

**To implement BCD adder we require**
1. 4 bit binary adder for initial condition.

2. logic circuit to detect sum greater than 9 and one more 4-bit adder to add $0110_2$ in the sum if sum is greater than 9 or carry is 1.

Table 2.6

| Input | | | | Output |
|---|---|---|---|---|
| $S_3$ | $S_2$ | $S_1$ | $S_0$ | Y |
| 0 | 0 | 0 | 0 | 0 |
| 0 | 0 | 0 | 1 | 0 |
| 0 | 0 | 1 | 0 | 0 |
| 0 | 0 | 1 | 1 | 0 |
| 0 | 1 | 0 | 0 | 0 |
| 0 | 1 | 0 | 1 | 0 |
| 0 | 1 | 1 | 0 | 0 |
| 0 | 1 | 1 | 1 | 0 |
| 1 | 0 | 0 | 0 | 0 |
| 1 | 0 | 0 | 1 | 0 |
| 1 | 0 | 1 | 0 | 1 |
| 1 | 0 | 1 | 1 | 1 |
| 1 | 1 | 0 | 0 | 1 |
| 1 | 1 | 0 | 1 | 1 |
| 1 | 1 | 1 | 0 | 1 |
| 1 | 1 | 1 | 1 | 1 |

- BCD adders can be cascaded to add numbers several digits long by connecting the carry out of a stage to the carry in of the next stage.
- The logic circuit to detect sum greater than 9 can be determined by simplifying the Boolean expression of given truth table Y = 1 indicates sum is greater than 9 we can put one more term $C_{out}$ in the above expression to check whether carry is one. It any one condition is satisfied we need to add (0110) in the sum.

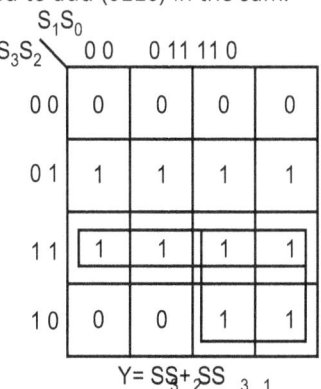

$Y = S_3 S_2 + S_2 S_1$

(a) K-map simplification

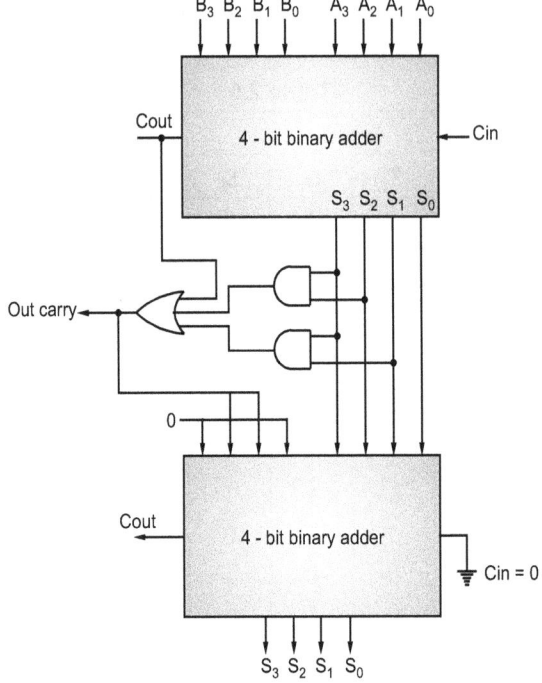

**(b) Block diagram of BCD adder**
**Fig. 2.33**

## 2.12 BCD SUBTRACTOR
- BCD subtraction can be performed using 9's and 10's complement.

### 2.12.1 BCD Subtraction using 9's Complement
The steps for 9's complement method :
- Find the 9's complement of negative number.
- Add two number using BCD addition.
- If carry is generated add carry to the result otherwise find 9's complement of the result.

**Example 2.11 :** Subtract $(2)_{10}$ from $(7)_{10}$ in BCD.
**Step 1 :** Obtain 9's complement of $(2)_{10}$

$$\begin{array}{r} 9 \\ -\ 2 \\ \hline 7 \end{array}$$

**Step 2 :** Add 7 into 9's complement of 3.

$$\begin{array}{rl} & 7 \\ +\ 7 & \text{...9's complement of 2} \\ \hline \text{end around...}\ \boxed{1}\,4 & \text{...sum} \\ +\ 1 & \text{...add carry} \\ \hline 5 & \text{...final result} \end{array}$$

## 2.12.2 BCD Subtractor using 9's Complement

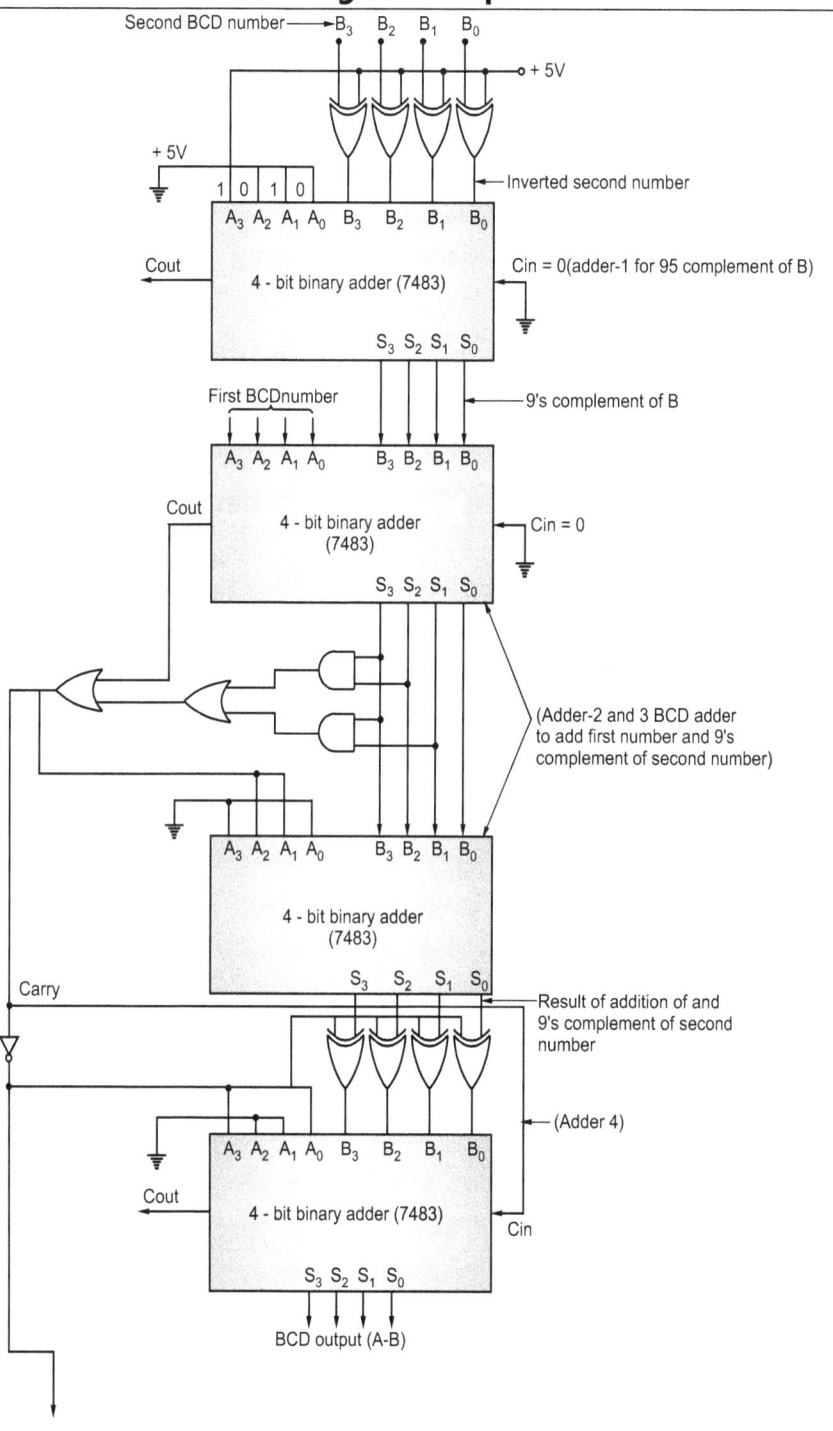

Fig. 2.34

Fig. 2.34 shows the circuit diagram of 4-bit BCD subtractor. It consists of four binary parallel adder (IC 7483).

- Adder 1 is to obtains the 9's complement of second number.
- Adder 2 and 3 are used for the normal 4-bit BCD adder with a facility to add 6 for correction.
- Adder 2 adds the first number with the 9's complement of second number B and adder 3 will correct the sum by adding six (0110) if necessary.
- The output of combinational circuit is used further as a carry. At the output of adder – 3 we get the correct BCD sum of first number and as complement of second number.
- Adder – 4 is used to either add 1 to the output of adder – 3 or take the 9's complement of the output of adder – 3 depending on the status of carry.
- If carry = 1 ; then add 1 to the sum output of adders

    If carry = 0; take as complement of sum output of adder 3.

## 2.12.3 BCD Subtraction using 10's Complement

The 10's complement is obtained by adding 1 to the 9's complement

Steps for 10's complement BCD subtraction given below :

- Obtain the 10's complement of second number
- Add first number with 10's complement of second number.
- Discard is card carry. If carry is 1 then the answer is positive and in its true form
- If carry is not produced the answer is negative so take 10's complement to get final answer.

**Example 2.12 :** Perform the subtraction $(9)_{10} - (4)_{10}$ in BCD using the 10's complement.

**Step 1 :** Obtain the 10's complement of $(4)_{10}$

$$
\begin{array}{r}
9 \\
-4 \\
\hline
5 \\
+1 \\
\hline
6
\end{array}
\quad \text{...9's complement}
$$

...10's complement

**Step 2 :** Add $(9)_{10}$ and 10's complement of second number

$$
\begin{array}{rl}
(9)_{10} \rightarrow & 1001 \\
(6)_{10} \rightarrow & 0110 \\
\hline
& 1111
\end{array}
\quad \leftarrow \text{invalid BCD number}
$$

**Step 3 :** add $(6)_{10}$ to invalid BCD number

$$
\begin{array}{r}
1111 \\
0110 \\
\hline
\end{array}
$$

Discard final carry → $\boxed{1}\,0101$  ← true BCD form

## 2.12.4 4-bit BCD Subtraction using 10's Complement

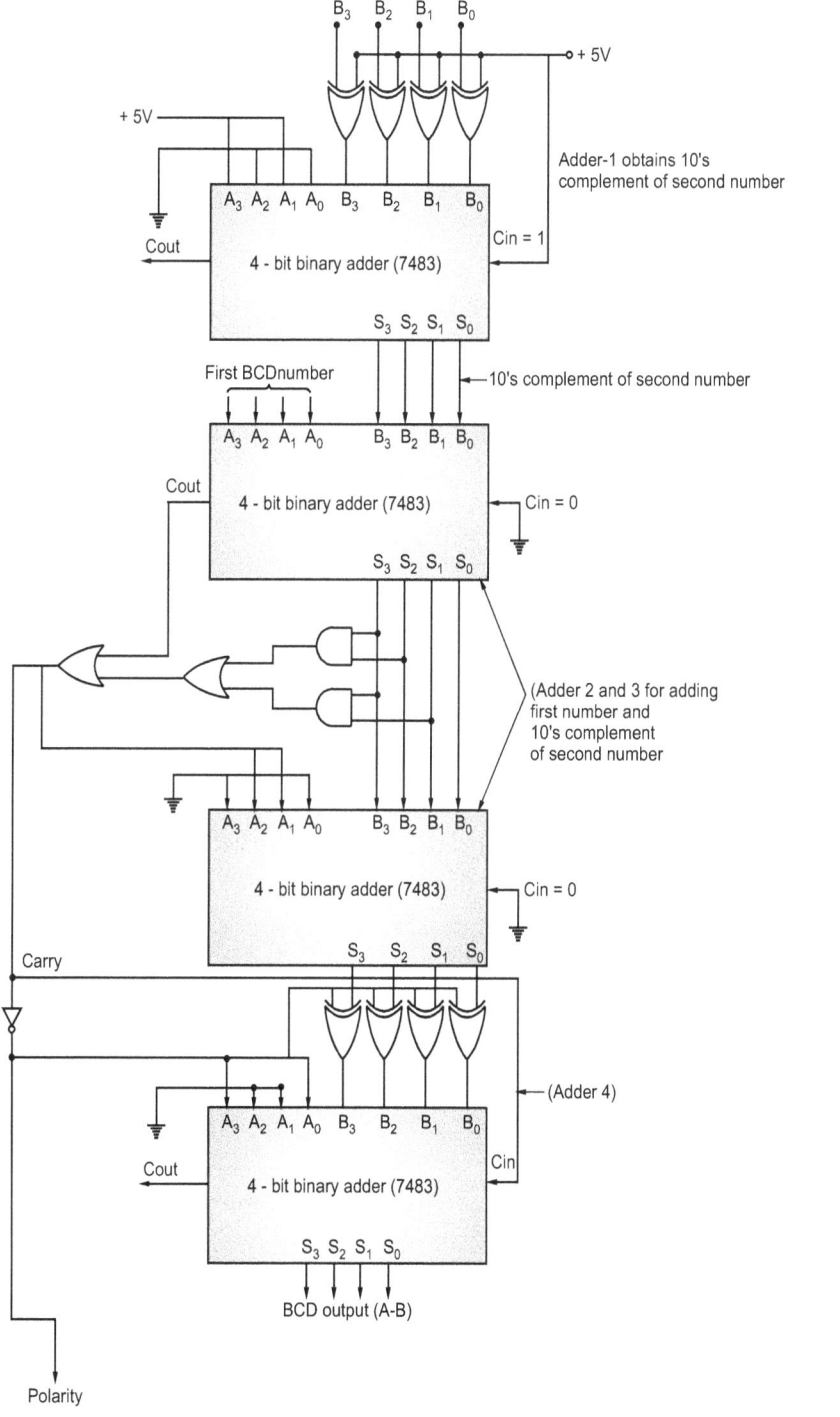

**Fig. 2.35**

The circuit consist of 4 adders. (See Fig. 2.35)

1. **Adder 1 :**

Performs the 10's complement of second number. The second numbers inverted using the EX-OR gates and then $C_{in} = 1$ is added to it to obtain 2's complement of second number.

- $A_3 A_2 A_1 A_0 = 1010$ i.e. $(10)_{10}$ adder 1 adds 1010 and 2's complement of number B. i.e. adder 1 performs subtraction to obtain 10's complement of B.
- In that way we get 10's complement of second number.

2. **Adder 2 and 3 :**

- Adder 2 and 3 together forms the addition of BCD number. Adder 2 adds number A to 10's complement of B.
- If the correction is necessary adder 3 adds 6 (0110) to BCD answer.
- The output of the combinational circuit is treated as a carry and it passed to adder 4.

3. **Adder 4 :**

- If carry = 0 then due to inverter used $A_3 A_2 A_1 A_0 = 1010$ i.e. $C(10)_{10}$ and carry input $C_{in} = 1$. Also the EXOR gates will acts as inverter.
- It carry = 1 then adder 4 will pass the adder – 3 output unchanged.

## 2.13 MULTIPLEXERS

- The literal meaning of word 'multiplex' is 'many into one'. A multiplexer circuit may have several inputs and only one output.
- Multiplexer is a special combinational logic circuit which accepts many inputs and allows only one of them to get through to the output at any instance of time.
- Therefore, multiplexer output is a particular data input which is selected with the help of control signal called 'select'.
- Multiplexers are important block of many important digital circuits such as microprocessor and microcontroller. The symbolic representation of multiplexer is shown in Fig. 2.30.

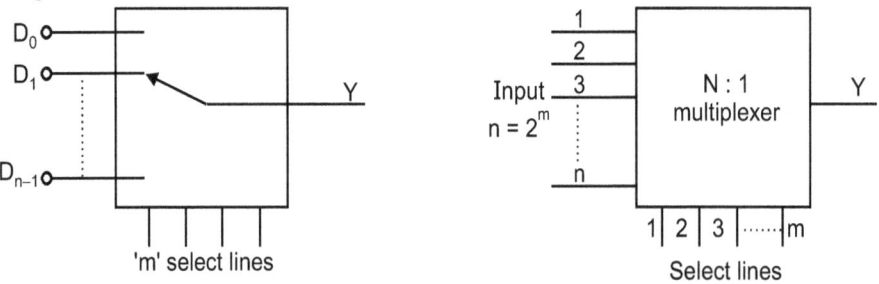

**Fig. 2.36 : Symbolic representation of N : 1 multiplexer**

## 2 : 1 Multiplexer :

- There are two data inputs $D_0$ and $D_1$ in 2 : 1 multiplexer.
- It has only one output. The number of select lines (m) is equal to 1.
- Every multiplexer has one more additional input called 'Enable' or 'Strobe' which is an active low input. This input is always kept at ground potential or logic '0'.
- Table shows truth table and logic circuit diagram of 2 : 1 multiplexer.

**Table 2.7 : Truth Table of 2 : 1 multiplexer**

| $S_0$ | Y |
|---|---|
| 0 | $D_0$ |
| 1 | $D_1$ |

$$Y = \bar{S_0}D_0 + S_0D_1$$

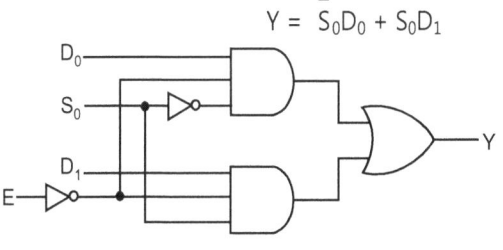
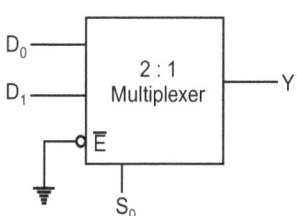

Fig. 2.37 : Logic circuit of 2 : 1 multiplexer          Fig. 2.38 : Logic symbol of 2 : 1 mux.

## 4 : 1 Multiplexer :

- 4 : 1 Multiplexer circuit has four data inputs and one output.
- The number of select lines required to control four data inputs is two.
- These two select lines are called $S_0$ and $S_1$.
- The Boolean expression for Y output is,

$$Y_1 = \bar{S_1}\bar{S_0}D_0 + \bar{S_1}S_0D_1 + S_1\bar{S_0}D_2 + S_1S_0D_3$$

Table 2.8 shows truth table and logic circuit diagram of 4 : 1 multiplexer.

**Table 2.8 : Truth table of 4 : 1 multiplexer**

| Inputs | | Output |
|---|---|---|
| $S_1$ | $S_0$ | Y |
| 0 | 0 | $D_0$ |
| 0 | 1 | $D_1$ |
| 1 | 0 | $D_2$ |
| 1 | 1 | $D_3$ |

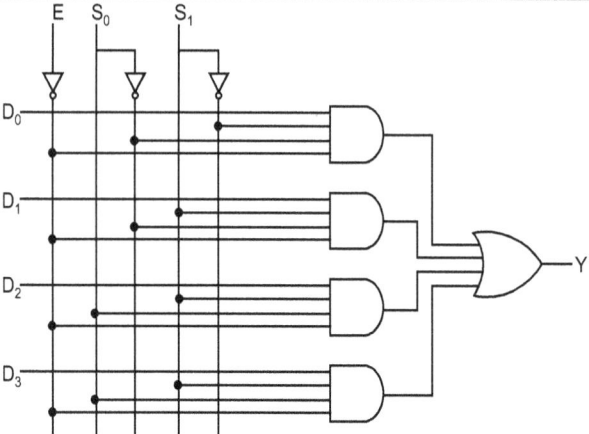

**Fig. 2.39 (a) : Logic Circuit Diagram of 4 : 1 Multiplexer**

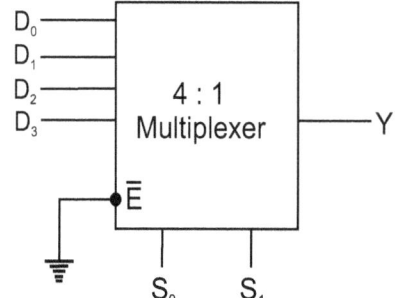

**Fig. 2.39 (b) : Logic block diagram of 4 : 1 multiplexer**

## Multiplexer ICs

- The list of popular and commercially available multiplexer ICs.

**Table 2.9**

| IC No. | Description | Output/Input |
|---|---|---|
| 74150 | 16 : 1 Multiplexer | Inverted input |
| 74151A | 8 : 1 Multiplexer | Complementary output |
| 74152 | 8 : 1 Multiplexer | Inverted input |
| 74153 | Dual 4 : 1 Multiplexer | Same as input |
| 74157 | Quad 2 : 1 Multiplexer | Same as input |
| 74158 | Quad 2 : 1 Multiplexer | Inverted input |
| 74352 | Dual 4 : 1 Multiplexer | Inverted input |

## Multiplexer Tree :

Fig. 2.40 shows design of 8 : 1 multiplexer using two 4 : 1 multiplexers and one 2 : 1 multiplexer.

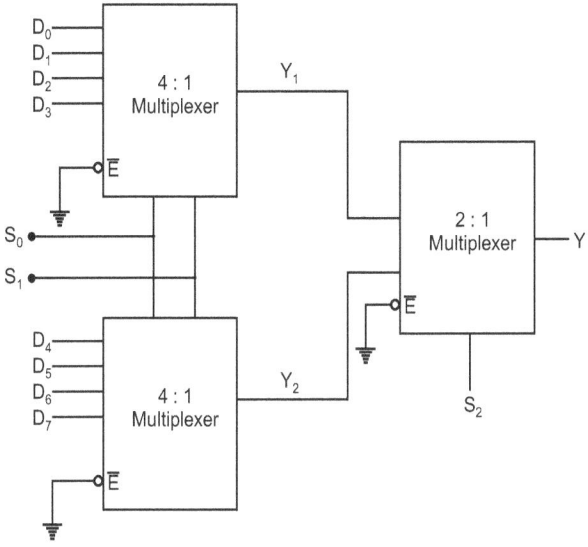

Fig. 2.40 : 8 : 1 multiplexer

## 2.13.1 IC 74153 Dual 4 to 1 multiplexer

IC 74153 is dual 4 to 1 multiplexer Fig. 2.41 shows the symbol of IC 74153.

It contains two identical and independent 4 to 1 multiplexers. Each multiplexer has separate enable inputs. The table 2.10 shows the truth table for IC 74153.

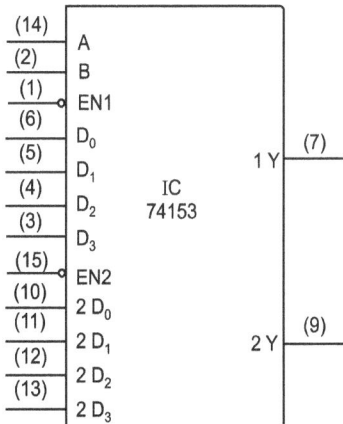

Fig. 2.41 : Logic symbol for 74153

Table : 2.10 Truth table for (74153 dual multiplexer)

| Inputs | | | | outputs | |
|---|---|---|---|---|---|
| EN1 | EN2 | B | A | Y | 2Y |
| 0 | 0 | 0 | 0 | $D_0$ | $D_0$ |
| 0 | 0 | 0 | 1 | $D_1$ | $D_1$ |

| | | | | | |
|---|---|---|---|---|---|
| 0 | 0 | 1 | 0 | D₂ | D₂ |
| 0 | 0 | 1 | 1 | D₃ | D₃ |
| 0 | 1 | 0 | 0 | D₀ | 0 |
| 0 | 1 | 0 | 1 | D₁ | 0 |
| 0 | 1 | 1 | 0 | D₂ | 0 |
| 0 | 1 | 1 | 1 | D₃ | 0 |
| 1 | 0 | 0 | 0 | 0 | D₀ |
| 1 | 0 | 0 | 1 | 0 | D₁ |
| 1 | 0 | 1 | 0 | 0 | D₂ |
| 1 | 0 | 1 | 1 | 0 | D₃ |
| 1 | 1 | X | X | 0 | 0 |

### 2.13.2 IC 74151 Multiplexer

IC 74151 is a 8 to 1 multiplexer. It has eight inputs. It provides two outputs one is active high and other is active low. Fig. 2.42 shows the logic symbol for IC 74151. As shown in the logic symbol there are three select inputs C,B and which select one of the eight inputs. IC 74151 is provided with active low enble input.

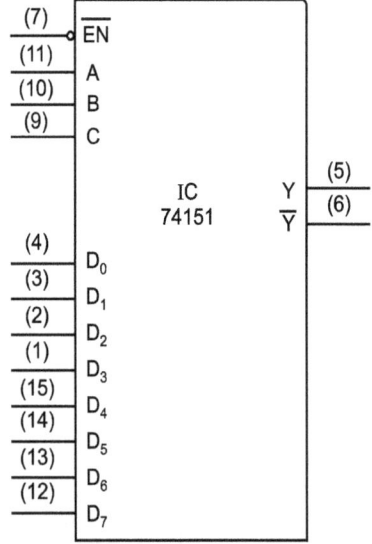

**Fig. 2.42 : Logic symbol for 74151 8 to 1 multiplexer.**

The truth table 2.11 shown below.

Table 2.11

| Input | | | Enable | Outputs | |
|---|---|---|---|---|---|
| Select | | | | | |
| C | B | A | $\overline{EN}$ | Y | $\overline{Y}$ |
| X | X | X | 1 | 0 | 1 |
| 0 | 0 | 0 | 0 | $D_0$ | $\overline{D_0}$ |
| 0 | 0 | 1 | 0 | $D_1$ | $\overline{D_1}$ |
| 0 | 1 | 0 | 0 | $D_2$ | $\overline{D_2}$ |
| 0 | 1 | 1 | 0 | $D_3$ | $\overline{D_3}$ |
| 1 | 0 | 0 | 0 | $D_4$ | $\overline{D_4}$ |
| 1 | 0 | 1 | 0 | $D_5$ | $\overline{D_5}$ |
| 1 | 1 | 0 | 0 | $D_6$ | $\overline{D_6}$ |
| 1 | 1 | 1 | 0 | $D_7$ | $\overline{D_7}$ |

**Example 2.13 :** Implement the following expression using a multiplexer
$$Y = \Sigma m (0, 1, 2, 6, 7).$$

**Solution :**

**Given :** Boolean expression is,
$$Y (A, B, C) = \Sigma m (0, 1, 2, 6, 7)$$

It is a three-variable Boolean function and hence a multiplexer will require three select inputs. The inputs of multiplexer corresponding to given minterms are connected to $V_{CC}$. Other inputs are grounded.

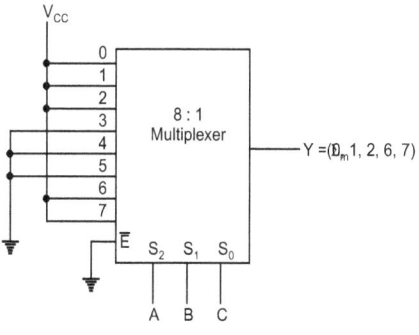

Fig. 2.43

# DIGITAL SYSTEM & MICROPROCESSOR (S.E. IT SEM – III SU)    BOOLEAN ALGEBRA AND...

### Application of Multiplexer
- They are used in time multiplexing system.
- They are used infrequency multiplexing systems.
- It is also used implement combinational logic circuit.
- They are used in data acquisition systems.

**Example 2.14 :** Implement the following expression using a multiplexer

$$Y(A, B, C) = \pi M(0, 1, 4, 5)$$

**Solution :** Given Boolean function is a three variable function expressed in terms of maxterms. The inputs of multiplexer corresponding to given maxterms are connected to ground and other inputs are connected to Vcc. The enable input is grounded.

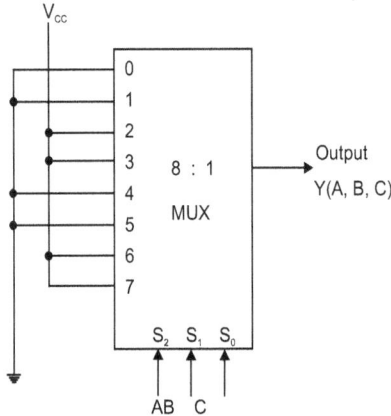

**Fig. 2.44 : Multiplexer based circuit design**

**Example 2.15 :** Implement the following Boolean expression Y = (A + B)

$$(\bar{A} + B + C)(A + \bar{B})$$ using multiplexer

**Solution :** Convert the given Boolean expression into standard POS form

$$\therefore \quad Y = (A + B + C\bar{C})(\bar{A} + B + C)(A + \bar{B} + C\bar{C})$$

$$= (A + B + C)(\bar{A} + B + C)(A + \bar{B} + C)(A + \bar{B} + \bar{C})$$

But $\quad A + B + C = 000 = 0$

$A + B + \bar{C} = 001 = 1$

$\bar{A} + B + C = 100 = 4$

$A + \bar{B} + C = 010 = 2$

$A + \bar{B} + \bar{C} = 011 = 3$

$\therefore$ The Boolean expression becomes $Y(A, B, C) = \pi M(0, 1, 2, 3, 4)$

Therefore, the inputs corresponding to given maxterms are connected to ground. Other inputs are connected to Vcc. The enable pin is grounded.

Unit II | 2.36

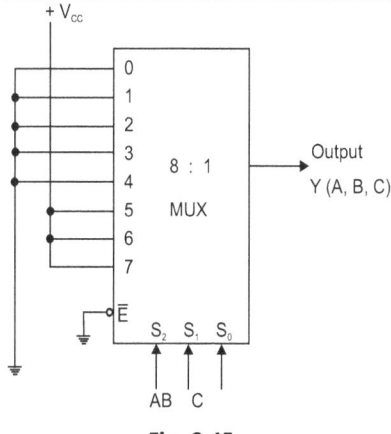

Fig. 2.45

**Example 2.16 :** Implement following using multiplexer
 (a) Half-adder  (b) Half-subtractor

**Solution : (a) Half - adder :** The truth table for half adder is given below

| Inputs | | Outputs | |
|---|---|---|---|
| A | B | S | C |
| 0 | 0 | 0 | 0 |
| 0 | 1 | 1 | 0 |
| 1 | 0 | 1 | 0 |
| 1 | 1 | 0 | 1 |

Therefore, Boolean expressions for the outputs are;

$$\text{Sum (A, B)} = \Sigma m\,(1, 2)$$
$$\text{Carry (A, B)} = \Sigma m\,(3)$$

Hence the logic diagram of half adder using two 4 : 1 multiplexers is;

**(b) Half-Subtractor :** The truth table for half subtractor is

| Inputs | | Outputs | |
|---|---|---|---|
| A | B | S | C |
| 0 | 0 | 0 | 0 |
| 0 | 1 | 1 | 1 |
| 1 | 0 | 1 | 0 |
| 1 | 1 | 0 | 0 |

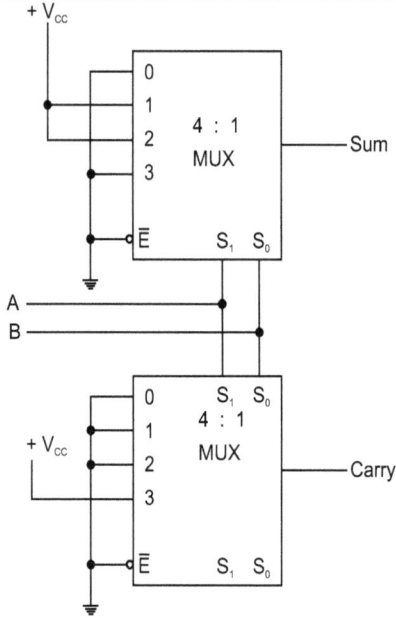

Fig. 2.46 : Half-adder using 4 : 1 multiplexer

The Boolean expressions are

∴ D (A, B) = Σ m (1, 2)

C (A, B) = Σ m (1)

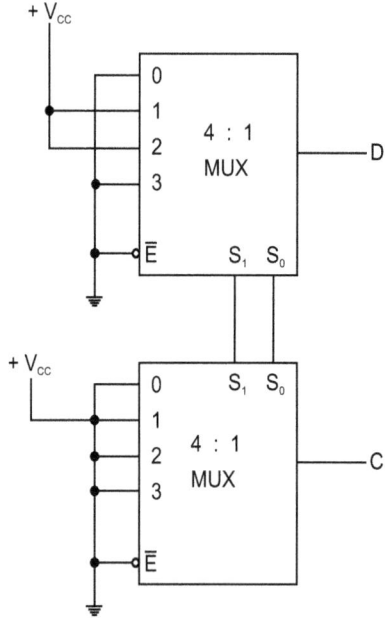

Fig. 2.47 : Half Subtractor using 4 : 1 Multiplexer

## 2.14 DEMULTIPLEXER

- Demultiplexer is a combinational logic circuit having one input and several outputs.
- Demultiplexer means 'One into many'.
- It accepts a single input and sends it to one of the output lines.
- The output line is selected by control or select signals. For n-output demultiplexer, number of select lines is m, where $n = 2^m$.
- Fig. 2.48 depicts 1 : n demultiplexer.

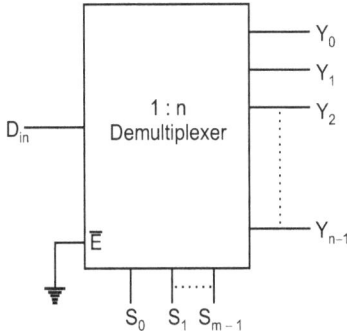

**Fig. 2.48 : Block Diagram of 1 : n Demultiplexer**

- This 1 : n demultiplexer is also known as binary-to-decimal decoder with binary inputs applied at the select lines, and the decoded output will be obtained on the output line.
- Consider an example 1 : 4 demultiplexer.
- The number of select input lines is 2.
- The truth table of 1 : 4 demultiplexer is given below :

**Table 2.12**

| Select Inputs | | Outputs | | | |
|---|---|---|---|---|---|
| $S_0$ | $S_1$ | $Y_0$ | $Y_1$ | $Y_2$ | $Y_3$ |
| 0 | 0 | 1 | 0 | 0 | 0 |
| 0 | 1 | 0 | 1 | 0 | 0 |
| 1 | 0 | 0 | 0 | 1 | 0 |
| 1 | 1 | 0 | 0 | 0 | 1 |

- The logic expression for different outputs can be written as,

$$Y_0 = \bar{S_0}\bar{S_1},\ Y_1 = \bar{S_0}S_1,\ Y_2 = S_0\bar{S_1},\ Y_3 = S_0S_1$$

- The logic circuit diagram of 1 : 4 demultiplexer is shown in Fig. 2.48.

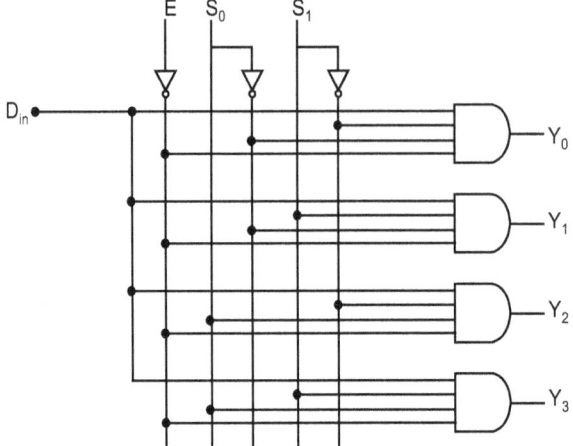

Fig. 2.49 : 1 : 4 Demultiplexer

**Demultiplexer Tree :**
- Demultiplexer tree can be built hierarchically by lower hierarchial demultiplexer.
- Many commercially available demultiplexer ICs are listed below.

| IC | Description | Output/Input |
|---|---|---|
| 74139 | Dual 1 : 4 | Inverted input |
| 74138 | Dual 1 : 8 | Inverted input |
| 74154 | Dual 1 : 16 | Same as input |

- Let us consider example of implementing 1 : 8 demultiplexer using two 1 : 4 demultiplexers.

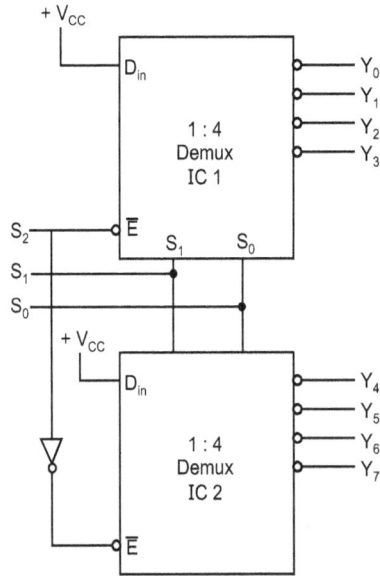

Fig. 2.50 : 1 : 8 Demultiplexer

- Note that 1 : 4 demultiplexer has inverted output. Whenever $S_2$ is logic '0', the $IC_1$ is selected and $IC_2$ is disabled. Depending upon the status of $S_1$ and $S_0$ lines the data in will be fed to one of the outputs $Y_0, Y_1, Y_2$ or $Y_3$.
- To send the output on $Y_4$ or $Y_5$ or $Y_6$ or $Y_7$ line, the status of pin $S_2$ is to be made high. Based on the logic status of $S_0$ and $S_1$ the data in will be fed to corresponding output line.
- The truth table of the above 1 : 8 multiplexer circuit having initial inverted input is given below.

**Example 2.17 :** Implement the following function using demultiplexer :

$$f_1 (A, B, C) = \Sigma m (0, 3, 7)$$
$$f_2 (A, B, C) = \Sigma m (1, 2, 5)$$

It can be implemented using 1 : 8 Demux.

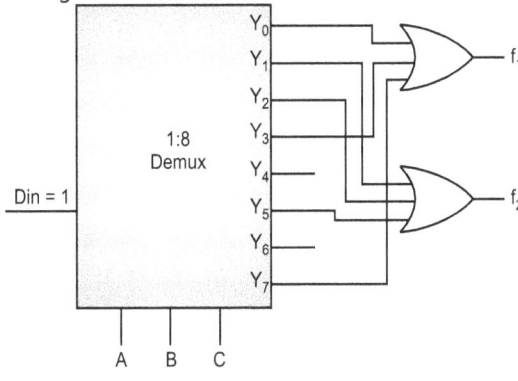

**Fig. 2.51**

## 2.15 DECODER

- A decoder is multiple input, multiple output logic circuit which converts coded inputs into coded outputs, where the input and output codes are different.

Fig. 2.52 shows the structure of the decoder circuit.

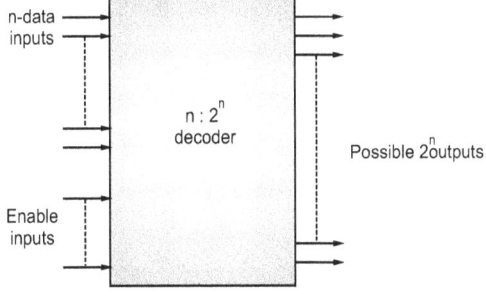

**Fig. 2.52 : Structure of decoder**

- As shown in Fig. 2.52 the encoded information is presented as n inputs producing $2^n$ possible outputs. The $2^n$ output values are from 0 through $2^n - 1$.
- A decoder is provided with enable inputs to activate decoded output based on data inputs. When any one enable input is unasserted, all outputs of decoder are disabled.

**Table 2.13**

| Inputs | | | Selected IC | Outputs | | | | | | | |
|---|---|---|---|---|---|---|---|---|---|---|---|
| $S_2$ | $S_1$ | $S_0$ | | $Y_7$ | $Y_6$ | $Y_5$ | $Y_4$ | $Y_3$ | $Y_2$ | $Y_1$ | $Y_0$ |
| 0 | 0 | 0 | IC1 | 1 | 1 | 1 | 1 | 1 | 1 | 1 | 0 |
| 0 | 0 | 1 | IC1 | 1 | 1 | 1 | 1 | 1 | 1 | 0 | 1 |
| 0 | 1 | 0 | IC1 | 1 | 1 | 1 | 1 | 1 | 0 | 1 | 1 |
| 0 | 1 | 1 | IC1 | 1 | 1 | 1 | 1 | 0 | 1 | 1 | 1 |
| 1 | 0 | 0 | IC2 | 1 | 1 | 1 | 0 | 1 | 1 | 1 | 1 |
| 1 | 0 | 1 | IC2 | 1 | 1 | 0 | 1 | 1 | 1 | 1 | 1 |
| 1 | 1 | 0 | IC2 | 1 | 0 | 1 | 1 | 1 | 1 | 1 | 1 |
| 1 | 1 | 1 | IC2 | 0 | 1 | 1 | 1 | 1 | 1 | 1 | 1 |

**Example 2.18 :** Design full - adder using 3 : 8 decoder

**Solution :** The truth table of full - adder is

| Inputs | | | Outputs | |
|---|---|---|---|---|
| A | B | $C_{n-1}$ | $S_n$ | $C_n$ |
| 0 | 0 | 0 | 0 | 0 |
| 0 | 0 | 1 | 1 | 0 |
| 0 | 1 | 0 | 1 | 0 |
| 0 | 1 | 1 | 0 | 1 |
| 1 | 0 | 0 | 1 | 0 |
| 1 | 0 | 1 | 0 | 1 |
| 1 | 1 | 0 | 0 | 1 |
| 1 | 1 | 1 | 1 | 1 |

Therefore, the expressions for $S_n$ and $C_n$ are

$$S_n = \Sigma m (1, 2, 4, 7)$$
$$C_n = \Sigma m (3, 5, 6, 7)$$

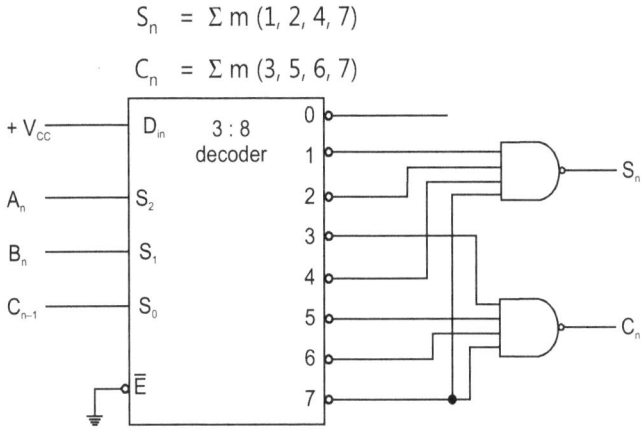

Fig. 2.53 : Full-adder using 3 : 8 decoder

**Example 2.19 :**

Design 1 : 16 demultiplexer using

(a) 1 : 8 demultiplexer

(b) 1 : 4 demultiplexer

**Solution :** 1 : 8 demultiplexer is also known as 3 : 8 decoder. The MSB input $S_3$ of 4 - bit input i.e. $S_3$ $S_2$ $S_1$ $S_0$ is used to select one of these two 3 : 8 decoders. $S_3$ is connected to enable pin.

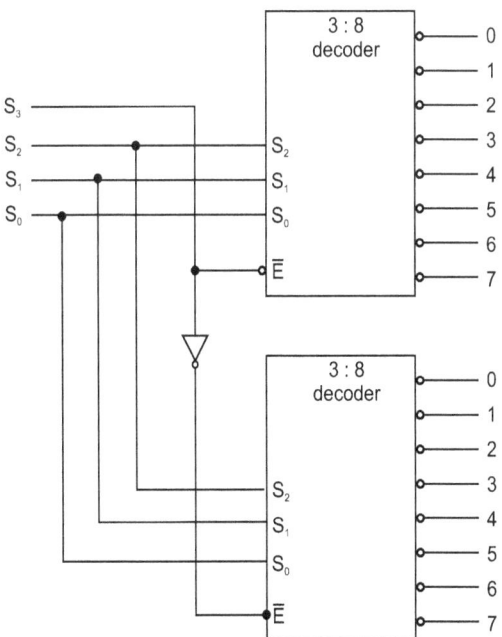

Fig. 2.54 : Demultiplexer using two 1 : 8 demultiplexers

(b)

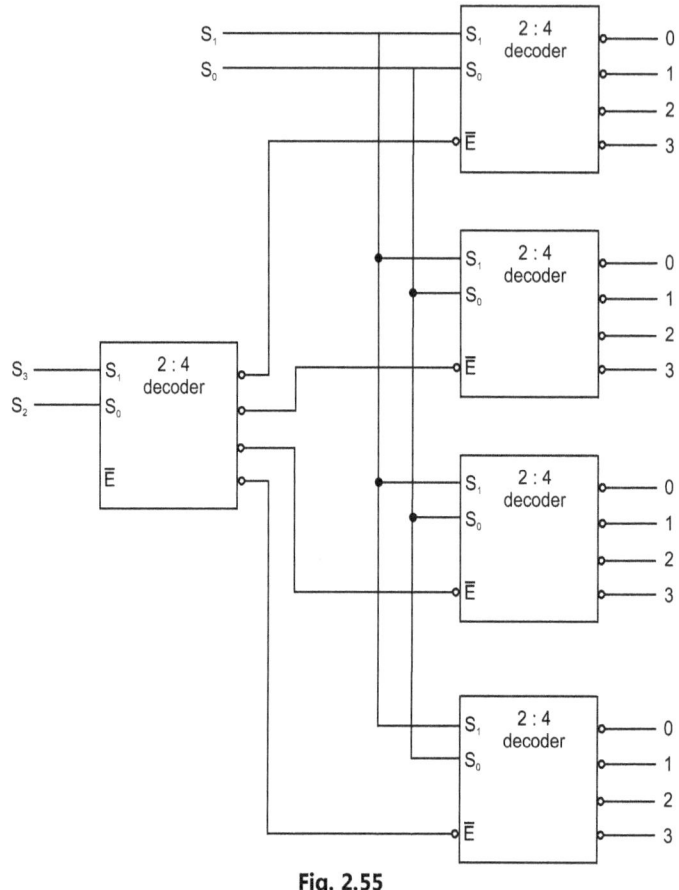

Fig. 2.55

**Example 2.20 :** (a) Implement the following using 3 : 8 decoder

$$Y_0 (A, B, C) = \Sigma m (0, 1, 2, 4)7, \quad Y_1 (A, B, C) = \Sigma m (1, 3, 5, 7)$$
$$Y_2 (A, B, C) = \Sigma m (4, 5, 6, 7)$$

(b) Design some using NAND gates

**Solution :** (a) Since the expressions for Y are in terms of minterms, we use OR gates. Because the outputs of decoder are active low, the inputs to OR gates are inverted.

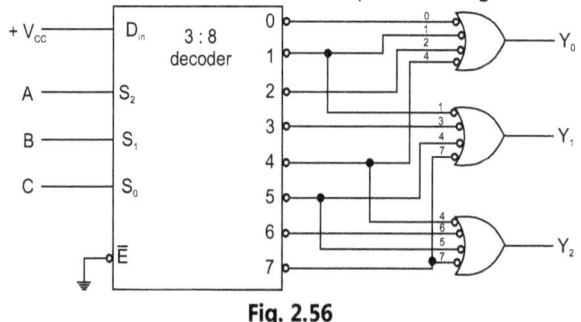

Fig. 2.56

(b) Inverted input OR gate is equivalent to NAND gate.

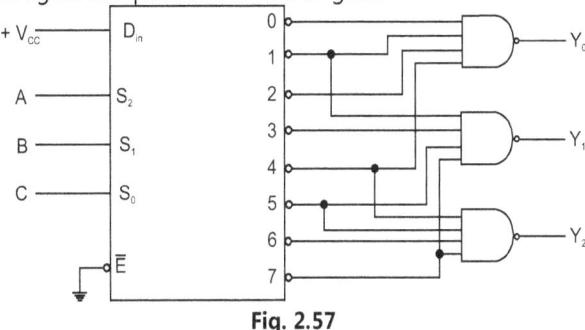

Fig. 2.57

## 2.15.1 IC 74138 (3 :8 decoder)

IC 74138 is commercial IC for 3 to 8 decoder. It accepts three binary inputs (A, B and C) and when enabled provides eight individual active low outputs ($Y_0$-$Y_7$). The device has three enable inputs two active low ($\overline{G_2}$, $\overline{G_3}$) and one active high ($G_1$). Fig. 2.58 shows logic symbol of 74138 and function table also shown in table 2.14

Table 2.14

| Inputs | | | | | | Outputs | | | | | | | |
|---|---|---|---|---|---|---|---|---|---|---|---|---|---|
| $\overline{G_3}$ | $\overline{G_2}$ | $G_1$ | C | B | A | $\overline{Y_7}$ | $\overline{Y_6}$ | $\overline{Y_5}$ | $\overline{Y_4}$ | $\overline{Y_3}$ | $\overline{Y_2}$ | $\overline{Y_1}$ | $\overline{Y_0}$ |
| 1 | X | X | X | X | X | 1 | 1 | 1 | 1 | 1 | 01 | 1 | 1 |
| X | 1 | X | X | X | X | 1 | 1 | 1 | 1 | 1 | 1 | 1 | 1 |
| X | 1 | 0 | X | X | X | 1 | 1 | 1 | 1 | 1 | 1 | 1 | 1 |
| 0 | 0 | 1 | 0 | 0 | 0 | 1 | 1 | 1 | 1 | 1 | 1 | 1 | 0 |
| 0 | 0 | 1 | 0 | 0 | 1 | 1 | 1 | 1 | 1 | 1 | 1 | 0 | 1 |
| 0 | 0 | 1 | 0 | 1 | 0 | 1 | 1 | 1 | 1 | 1 | 0 | 1 | 1 |
| 0 | 0 | 1 | 0 | 1 | 1 | 1 | 1 | 1 | 1 | 0 | 1 | 1 | 1 |
| 0 | 0 | 1 | 1 | 0 | 0 | 1 | 1 | 1 | 0 | 1 | 1 | 1 | 1 |
| 0 | 0 | 1 | 1 | 0 | 1 | 1 | 1 | 0 | 1 | 1 | 1 | 1 | 1 |
| 0 | 0 | 1 | 1 | 1 | 0 | 1 | 0 | 1 | 1 | 1 | 1 | 1 | 1 |
| 0 | 0 | 1 | 1 | 1 | 1 | 0 | 1 | 1 | 1 | 1 | 1 | 1 | 1 |

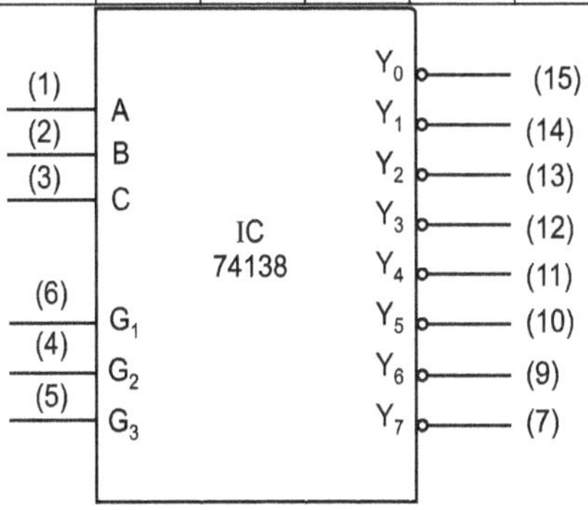

Fig. 2.58 : Logic symbol

## 2.16 BCD CODE

Each digit of decimal number is represented by four bits. For example digit '5' is represented as '0101'. The BCD code is also called as 8-4-2-1 code where 8,4,2 and 1 represent weights of binary symbol in the respective positions. The examples of BCD codes are given below ;

| Decimal | 4 | 2 | 8 | 6 |
|---|---|---|---|---|
| BCD | 0100 | 0010 | 1000 | 0110 |

BCD code for 0 to 9 digits are given as;

| Decimal digit | BCD code |
|---|---|
| 0 | 0000 |
| 1 | 0001 |
| 2 | 0010 |
| 3 | 0011 |
| 4 | 0100 |
| 5 | 0101 |
| 6 | 0110 |
| 7 | 0111 |
| 8 | 1000 |
| 9 | 1001 |

The remaining 4 digit binary representations i.e. 1010, 1011, 1100, 1101, 1110 and 1111 are invalid BCD codes.

### 2.16.1 Seven Segment Code

In many electronic systems seven segments are used for displaying quantities. The binary codes cannot be used to drive seven segment displays. The generalised seven segment display is shown below in Fig. 2.59. It uses seven LED segments. These LED's can be either common - anode connected or common cathode connected.

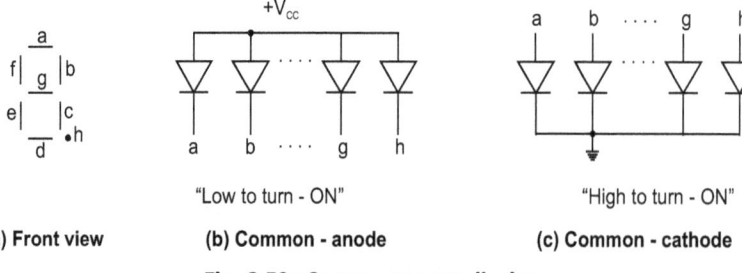

(a) Front view  (b) Common - anode  (c) Common - cathode

"Low to turn - ON"   "High to turn - ON"

**Fig. 2.59 : Seven segment display**

### Table 2.15 : Common anode seven segment code

| Decimal | | a | b | c | d | e | f | g | h | Hex code |
|---|---|---|---|---|---|---|---|---|---|---|
| 0 | 0 | 0 | 0 | 0 | 0 | 0 | 0 | 1 | 1 | 03 |
| 1 | 1 | 1 | 0 | 0 | 1 | 1 | 1 | 1 | 1 | 5F |
| 2 | 2 | 0 | 0 | 1 | 0 | 0 | 1 | 0 | 1 | 25 |
| 3 | 3 | 0 | 0 | 0 | 0 | 1 | 1 | 0 | 1 | 0D |
| 4 | 4 | 1 | 0 | 0 | 1 | 1 | 0 | 0 | 1 | 99 |
| 5 | 5 | 0 | 1 | 0 | 0 | 1 | 0 | 0 | 1 | 49 |
| 6 | 6 | 0 | 1 | 0 | 0 | 0 | 0 | 0 | 1 | 41 |
| 7 | 7 | 0 | 0 | 0 | 1 | 1 | 1 | 1 | 1 | 1F |
| 8 | 8 | 0 | 0 | 0 | 0 | 0 | 0 | 0 | 1 | 01 |
| 9 | 9 | 0 | 0 | 0 | 0 | 1 | 0 | 0 | 1 | 09 |

### Table 2.16 : Common cathode seven segment code

| Decimal | | a | b | c | d | e | f | g | h | Hex code |
|---|---|---|---|---|---|---|---|---|---|---|
| 0 | 0 | 1 | 1 | 1 | 1 | 1 | 1 | 0 | 0 | FC |
| 1 | 1 | 0 | 1 | 1 | 0 | 0 | 0 | 0 | 0 | 60 |
| 2 | 2 | 1 | 1 | 0 | 1 | 1 | 0 | 1 | 0 | DA |
| 3 | 3 | 1 | 1 | 1 | 1 | 0 | 0 | 1 | 0 | F2 |
| 4 | 4 | 0 | 1 | 1 | 0 | 0 | 1 | 1 | 0 | 66 |
| 5 | 5 | 1 | 0 | 1 | 1 | 0 | 1 | 1 | 0 | B6 |
| 6 | 6 | 1 | 0 | 1 | 1 | 1 | 1 | 1 | 0 | BE |
| 7 | 7 | 1 | 1 | 1 | 0 | 0 | 0 | 0 | 0 | E0 |
| 8 | 8 | 1 | 1 | 1 | 1 | 1 | 1 | 1 | 0 | FE |
| 9 | 9 | 1 | 1 | 1 | 1 | 0 | 1 | 1 | 0 | F6 |

## 2.16.2 BCD to Seven Segment Code Converter

**(a) Common cathode type seven segment :** The truth table for BCD to seven segment (common anode type) is given below.

| Decimal digit | BCD Code | | | | Seven segment code (common anode) | | | | | | |
|---|---|---|---|---|---|---|---|---|---|---|---|
| | $B_3$ | $B_2$ | $B_1$ | $B_0$ | a | b | c | d | e | f | g | h |
| 0 | 0 | 0 | 0 | 0 | 0 | 0 | 0 | 0 | 0 | 0 | 1 | 1 |
| 1 | 0 | 0 | 0 | 1 | 1 | 0 | 0 | 1 | 1 | 1 | 1 | 1 |
| 2 | 0 | 0 | 1 | 0 | 0 | 0 | 1 | 0 | 0 | 1 | 0 | 1 |
| 3 | 0 | 0 | 1 | 1 | 0 | 0 | 0 | 0 | 1 | 1 | 0 | 1 |
| 4 | 0 | 1 | 0 | 0 | 1 | 0 | 0 | 1 | 1 | 0 | 0 | 1 |
| 5 | 0 | 1 | 0 | 1 | 0 | 1 | 0 | 0 | 1 | 0 | 0 | 1 |
| 6 | 0 | 1 | 1 | 0 | 0 | 1 | 0 | 0 | 0 | 0 | 0 | 1 |
| 7 | 0 | 1 | 1 | 1 | 0 | 0 | 0 | 1 | 1 | 1 | 1 | 1 |
| 8 | 1 | 0 | 0 | 0 | 0 | 0 | 0 | 0 | 0 | 0 | 0 | 1 |
| 9 | 1 | 0 | 0 | 1 | 0 | 0 | 0 | 0 | 1 | 0 | 0 | 1 |

From the truth the we write K – maps for seven segment outputs.

K – map a :

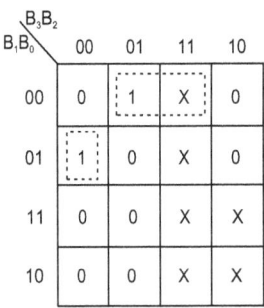

$$a = \bar{B}_1 \bar{B}_0 B_2 + \bar{B}_1 B_0 \bar{B}_3 \bar{B}_2$$

$$\therefore \quad a = \bar{B}_0 \bar{B}_1 B_2 + B_0 \bar{B}_1 \bar{B}_2 \bar{B}_3$$

K – Map for b :

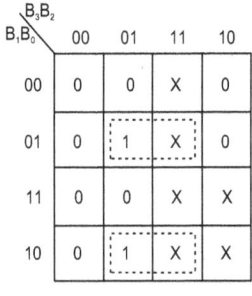

$$b = \bar{B}_1 B_0 B_2 + B_1 \bar{B}_0 B_2$$

$$\therefore \quad b = B_0 \bar{B}_1 B_2 + \bar{B}_0 B_1 B_2$$

**K – Map for c :**

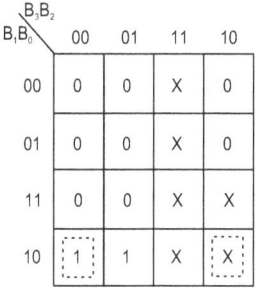

$$c = B_1 \bar{B}_0 \bar{B}_2 = \bar{B}_0 B_1 \bar{B}_2$$

**K – Map for d :**

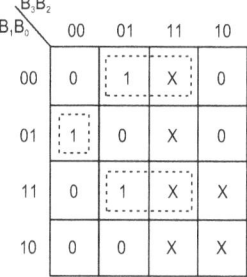

$$d = \bar{B}_1 B_0 \bar{B}_3 \bar{B}_2 + \bar{B}_1 \bar{B}_0 B_2 + B_1 B_0 B_2$$

$$\therefore d = B_0 \bar{B}_1 \bar{B}_2 \bar{B}_3 + \bar{B}_0 \bar{B}_1 B_2 + B_0 B_1 B_2$$

**K – Map for e :**

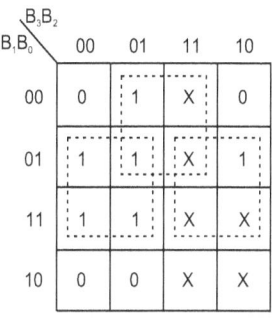

$$e = B_0 + \bar{B}_1 B_2$$

**K – Map for f :**

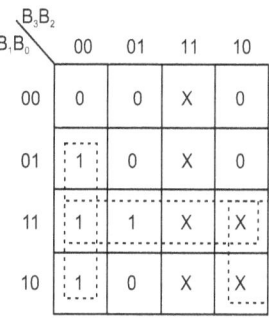

$$f = B_0 B_1 + B_0 \bar{B}_2 \bar{B}_3 + B_1 \bar{B}_2$$

**K – Map for g :**

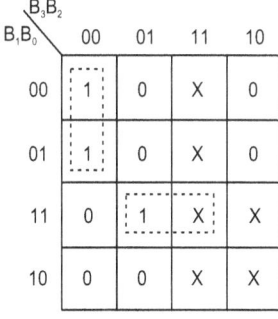

$$g = \bar{B}_1 \bar{B}_2 \bar{B}_3 + B_0 B_1 B_2$$

**K – Map for h :**

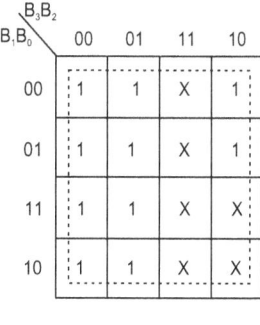

$$h = 1$$

**Fig. 2.60**

Therefore, the logic diagram for BCD to seven segment common (anode code) converter is

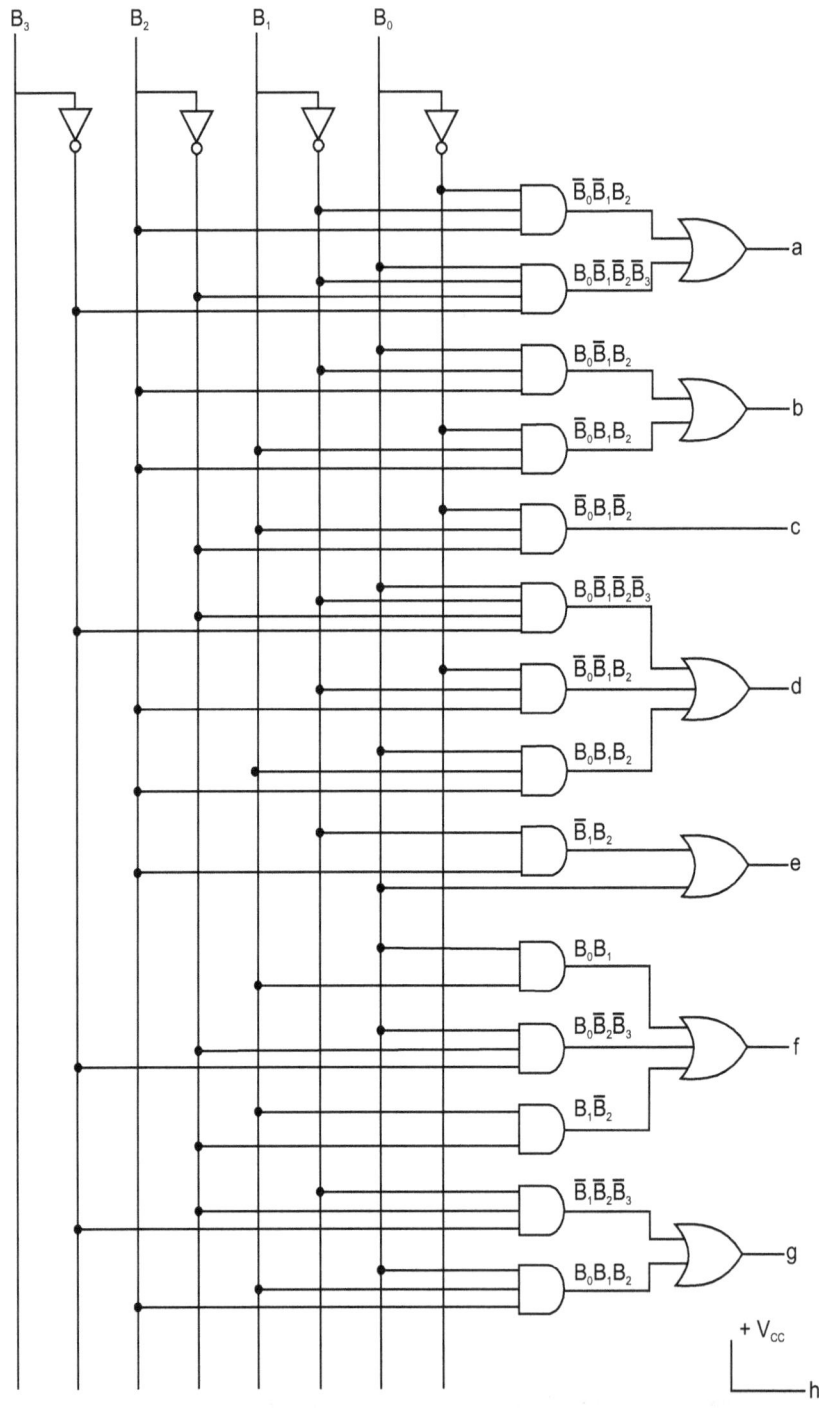

**Fig. 2.61 : Logic diagram for BCD to seven segment (common anode) code converter**

## 2.16.3 Common Cathode type Seven Segment

The truth table for common cathode type seven segment outputs is given below;

| Decimal digit | BCD Code | | | | Seven segment code | | | | | | |
|---|---|---|---|---|---|---|---|---|---|---|---|
| | $B_3$ | $B_2$ | $B_1$ | $B_0$ | a | b | c | d | e | f | g | h |
| 0 | 0 | 0 | 0 | 0 | 1 | 1 | 1 | 1 | 1 | 1 | 0 | 0 |
| 1 | 0 | 0 | 0 | 1 | 0 | 1 | 1 | 0 | 0 | 0 | 0 | 0 |
| 2 | 0 | 0 | 1 | 0 | 1 | 1 | 0 | 1 | 1 | 0 | 1 | 0 |
| 3 | 0 | 0 | 1 | 1 | 1 | 1 | 1 | 1 | 0 | 0 | 1 | 0 |
| 4 | 0 | 1 | 0 | 0 | 0 | 1 | 1 | 0 | 0 | 1 | 1 | 0 |
| 5 | 0 | 1 | 0 | 1 | 1 | 0 | 1 | 1 | 0 | 1 | 1 | 0 |
| 6 | 0 | 1 | 1 | 0 | 1 | 0 | 1 | 1 | 1 | 1 | 1 | 0 |
| 7 | 0 | 1 | 1 | 1 | 1 | 1 | 1 | 0 | 0 | 0 | 0 | 0 |
| 8 | 1 | 0 | 0 | 0 | 1 | 1 | 1 | 1 | 1 | 1 | 1 | 0 |
| 9 | 1 | 0 | 0 | 1 | 1 | 1 | 1 | 1 | 0 | 1 | 1 | 0 |

The K – maps for all the seven segment outputs can be written as.

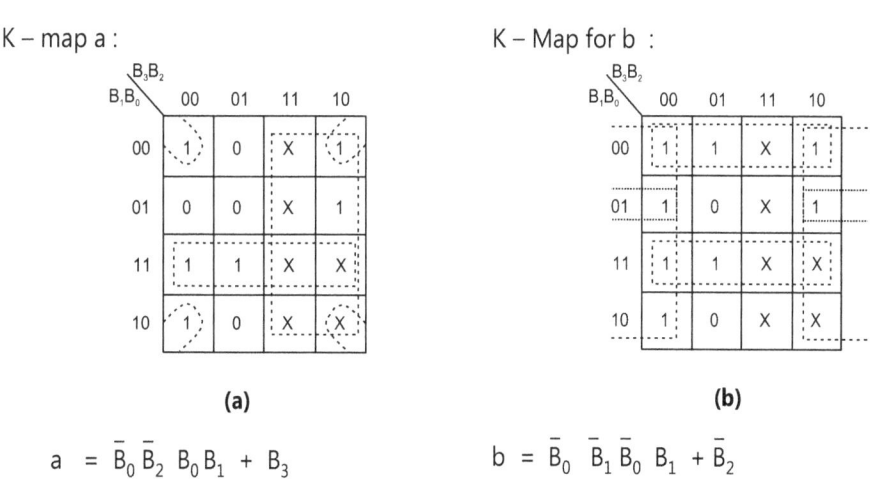

(a)  (b)

$a = \bar{B}_0 \bar{B}_2 \, B_0 B_1 + B_3$     $b = \bar{B}_0 \bar{B}_1 \, B_0 B_1 + \bar{B}_2$

**K – Map for c :**

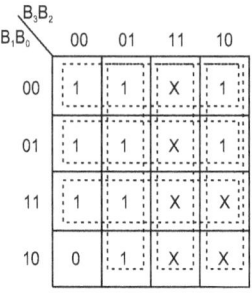

(c)

$$c = B_3 B_2 \overline{B_1} + \overline{B_0}$$

**K – Map for d :**

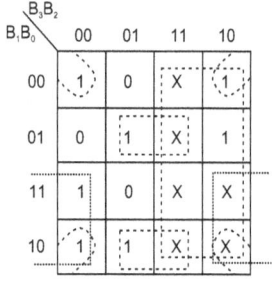

(d)

$$d = \overline{B_3} + \overline{B_0}\, \overline{B_2} + \overline{B_1}\, \overline{B_2} + \overline{B_0}\, B_1 B_2 + \overline{B_0}\, b_1 B_2$$

**K – Map for e :**

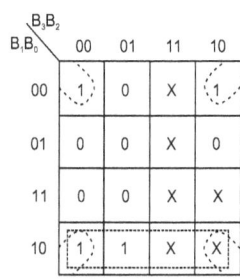

(e)

$$e = \overline{B_0}\, \overline{B_1} + \overline{B_0}\, \overline{B_2}$$

**K – Map for f :**

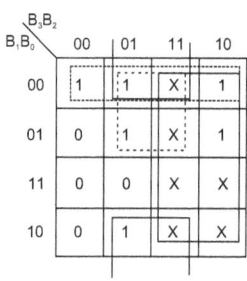

(f)

$$f = B_3 + \overline{B_1}\, B_2 + \overline{B_0}\, B_2 + \overline{B_0}\, \overline{B_0}$$

**K – Map for g :**

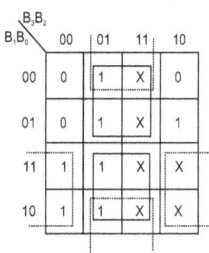

(g)

$$g = B_1\, \overline{B_2} + \overline{B_1}\, B_2 + \overline{B_0}\, B_2 + B_3$$

**K – Map for h :**

| $B_1B_0$ \ $B_3B_2$ | 00 | 01 | 11 | 10 |
|---|---|---|---|---|
| 00 | 0 | 0 | X | 0 |
| 01 | 0 | 0 | X | 0 |
| 11 | 0 | 0 | X | X |
| 10 | 0 | 0 | X | X |

(h)

$$h = 0$$

**Fig. 2.62**

Therefore, the logic diagram to convert BCD code into seven segment (common cathode) code is;

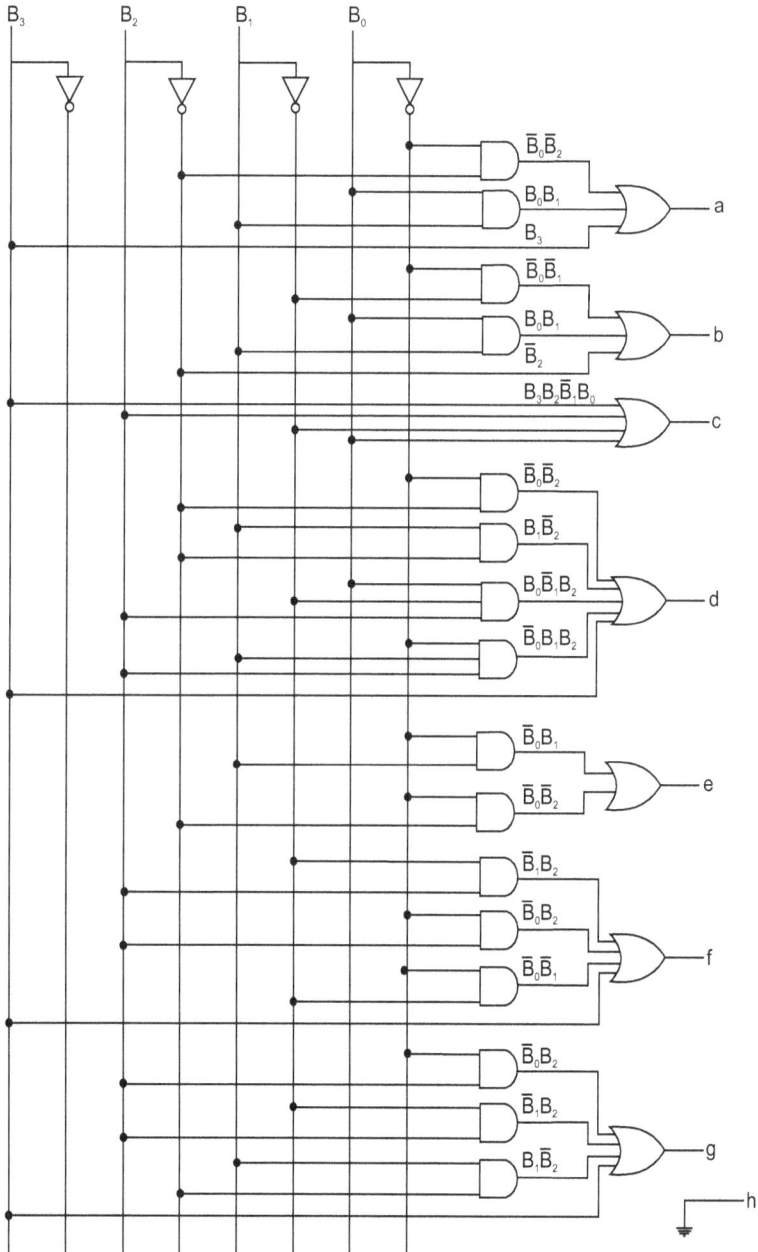

**Fig. 2.63 : Logic diagram for BCD to seven segment (common cathode) code converter**

## Questions

1. State and prove any two theorem of Boolean algebra.
2. What are DeMorgan's theorem ? How will define them in terms of your own words ?
3. What is the sum of product form?
4. What is the product of sum form?
5. List out the reduction techniques.
6. Simplify following logical expression using K-maps.

   $y = \overline{A}\overline{B}\overline{C} + \overline{A}\overline{B}C + \overline{A}B\overline{C} + A\overline{B}\overline{C} + AB\overline{C}$

7. Solve the following using minimization technique.

   $z = f(A, B, C, D) = \Sigma (0, 2, 4, 7, 11, 13, 15)$

8. Simplify the following function

   $f_1(A, B, C, D) = \Sigma m (0, 3, 5, 6, 9, 10, 12, 15)$

9. What is the limitation of K-map?
10. Design a half-adder and full-adder circuits using K-maps.
11. Design a half and full subtractor circuit using K-map.
12. Design a 4-bit parallel adder using full-adders.
13. Explain with suitable example rules for BCD addition and design 1-digit BCD adder using IC 74LS83.
14. Draw and explain the basic IC 7483. How will you make two digit BCD adder ? Explain the logic of the circuit.
15. Draw and explain 4-bit BCD adder using IC 7483. Explain any two BCD addition operations.
16. How to convert 4-bit binary adder to BCD adder ? Explain with the help of circuit diagram.
17. How will make 3-digit BCD adder using 4-bit binary adder as a basic building block ? Explain with the help of suitable diagram.
18. Draw and explain 4-bit BCD adder using IC 7483. Also explain with reference to your design addition of $(9 + 5)_{BCD}$ and $(7 + 2)_{BCD}$.
19. Draw and explain 4-bit BCD adder using IC 7483. Also explain with example addition of numbers with carry.
20. Draw and explain 4-bit BCD subtractor using IC 7483.
21. What is the use of 7483 chip ? Draw and explain 9's complement used in BCD subtractor using 7483.
22. Draw and explain 4-bit BCD subtractor using IC 7483.
23. Design 16 : 1 multiplexer using 4 : 1 multiplexers.

# Unit - III

# SEQUENTIAL LOGIC DESIGN

## 3.1 SEQUENTIAL CIRCUITS

- In many applications it is required to generate digital outputs in accordance with the sequence in which the input signals are applied.
- Thus, these applications require that the outputs to be generated are not only dependent on present input conditions. The outputs also depend upon the past history of these inputs.
- The past history is provided by storing it in memory elements and providing a feedback from the output back to the input. Such circuits are known as sequential circuits
- Block diagram of a sequential circuit is shown in Fig. 3.1.

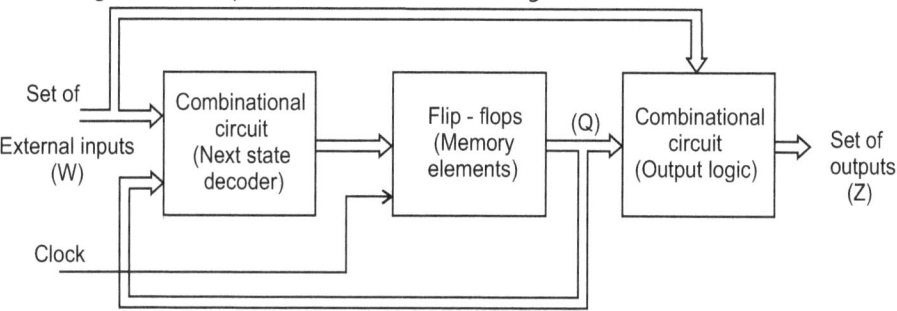

**Fig. 3.1 : Block diagram of sequential circuit**

- As shown in above Fig. 3.1, the circuit accepts a set of external inputs W and produces a set of outputs Z.
- The values of the outputs of the flip–flops are known as the state Q of the circuit.
- Upon application of clock pulse, the flip flop outputs change their state (circuit goes to next state).
- As shown in Fig. 3.1 the next state of the circuit is decided by the combinational circuit (next state decoder) that provides the inputs to the flip–flops.
- The combinational logic that provides the inputs to the flip–flops, derives its input from two sources (1) set of external inputs (W) and (2) the present state Q of the circuit (outputs of the flip–flops).
- Thus, changes in state depend upon the external inputs as well the present state of the circuit.
- As shown in Fig. 3.1, the outputs of the sequential circuit are generated by another combinational circuit (output logic). The outputs are generated from the present state Q of the circuit and the set of primary inputs W.

- Sequential circuits are also known as finite state machines (FSMs) as the functional behaviour of these circuits can be represented using finite number of states.
- Sequential circuits are broadly classified into two categories:
  (1) Moore type sequential circuits and (2) Mealy type sequential circuits.

## 3.2 COMPARISON OF COMBINATIONAL AND SEQUENTIAL CIRCUIT

| Combinational Circuit | Sequential Circuit |
|---|---|
| 1. The outputs depend on the combination of inputs. | 1. The outputs depend on the past history of inputs as well as the present input states. |
| 2. Memory is not required. | 2. Memory is required to store previous states of the inputs. |
| 3. The delay between outputs and inputs is less, so the combinational circuit is faster. | 3. Sequential circuit is slower due to propagational delay of additional memory element. |
| 4. Combinational circuits are concurrent in nature. | 4. Sequential circuit is not entirely concurrent. |
| 5. Easier to design. | 5. Complex to design. Timings can be critical. |
| 6. Block diagram : <br><br> Input → Combinational Logic circuit (gates) → Output <br><br> Fig. 3.2 (a) | 6. Block diagram : <br><br> Inputs → Combinational logic cicuit → Outputs, with Memory feedback <br><br> Fig. 3.2 (b) |

## 3.3 SEQUENTIAL CIRCUIT TYPES

### (A) Synchronous Circuit :
- The change in inputs can affect memory element upon the activation of clock signal.
- Memory elements are clocked flip-flops.
- The maximum operational speed of synchronous circuit is governed by the clock speed, which in turn, is decided by the propagation delays of the logic gates.

## (B) Asynchronous Circuit :

- The change in inputs can occur at any instant of time.
- Memory elements are unclocked flip-flops or time delay elements.
- Asynchronous circuits can operate faster than synchronous circuits because the clock is absent.

# 3.4 ONE BIT MEMORY CELL (BASIC BISTABLE ELEMENTS)

- One bit memory cell, as the name suggests can store 'one' bit (logic 0 or logic 1) information.
- It can be built using NAND or NOR gates.
- A one bit memory cell using NAND gates is as shown in Fig. 3.3.

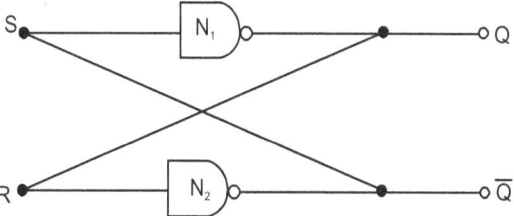

**Fig. 3.3 : One bit memory cell**

- The above circuit is also known as 'S-R' (Set-Reset) latch.
- This circuit has two stable states : '1 state' (Output Q = 1) and '0 state' (output Q = 0).
- The '1 state' is also called as 'set state' and the '0 state' is known as 'reset state'.
- The digital information gets locked or latched in this circuit. Therefore it is known as S-R i.e. set-reset latch.

**Operation of the circuit :**

- Two NAND gates ($N_1$ & $N_2$) are used as inverters. The output of $N_1$ is connected to the input of $N_2$ (R) and the output of $N_2$ is connected to the input of $N_1$ (S).
- Let us assume that the output of $N_1$ is logic 1 (Q = 1). This is the input of $N_2$ i.e. R=1. Therefore the output of $N_2$ becomes logic 0 ($\bar{Q}$ = 0).
- The output of $N_2$ is the input of $N_1$ i.e. S become 0 and consequently output of $N_1$ become 1 (Q=1), which confirms our assumption.
- Let us now assume that the output of $N_1$ is logic 0 (Q = 0). This is the input of $N_2$ i.e. R = 0. Therefore the output of $N_2$ becomes logic 1 ($\bar{Q}$ = 1).
- The output of $N_2$ is the input of $N_1$ i.e. S becomes 1 and consequently output of $N_1$ becomes 0 (Q = 0) which confirms our assumption.

## Drawback:

- In the above circuit there is no way to enter the desired digital information. When the power is turned on, the circuit switches to one of the stable states i.e. 1 state or 0 state and it is not possible to predict it.
- To overcome this drawback, a modified circuit with 2 input NAND gates and two additional inverters are used. The desired digital information can be entered in this circuit.

## 3.5 LATCH VS FLIP-FLOP

- The main difference between latches and flip-flops is the method used for changing their state.
- Latches are controlled by enable signal, and they are level triggered, either positive level triggered or negative level triggered.
- Flip-flops are pulse or clock edge triggered instead of level triggered.

## 3.6 LEVEL TRIGGERED AND EDGE TRIGGERED

**(A) Level Triggered :** In level triggering the output state change according to input (s) when active level (i.e. positive or negative) is maintained at the enable input.

Two types of level triggered

1. **Positive level triggered :** The output of flip flop respond to the input changes when its enable input is 1 (high).

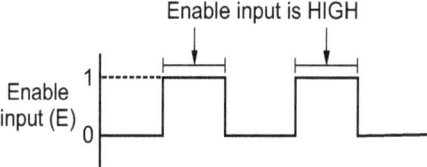

Fig. 3.4(a) : **Positive level triggered**

2. **Negative level triggered :** The output of flip-flop respond to the input changes when its input is 0 (low).

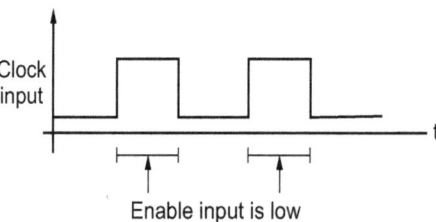

Fig. 3.4(b): **Negative level triggered**

- S-R flip flop and JK flip flop are known as level triggered flip flops as their output changes according to applied inputs as long as clock is present.
- As these flip flops respond when CLK=1 they are further called as positive level triggered flip flops.

- We know that level triggered JK flip flop has the drawback of race around condition. And to overcome that drawback we use master slave JK flip flop which is called as pulse triggered flip flop.
- In a pulse triggered flip flop like MS JK flip flop, output changes according to applied inputs, when a pulse is applied at the clock input. The state of this flip flop changes at the negative transition of the clock.
- Thus, in MS JK flip flop the race around condition is eliminated as the fed back output is blocked at the master when the CLK = 0.
- But in certain systems there is a possibility that the inputs of flip flop may change during the presence of the clock pulse. This causes uncertainty in the output of flip flop. This uncertainty can be eliminated by using edge triggered flip flops.

**(B) Edge Triggered :** In edge triggered flip flops output changes according to applied inputs only at the positive or negative edge of the clock pulse.

- Based on the type of edge there are two types of edge triggered flip flops : (1) positive edge triggered and (2) negative edge triggered.
- In case of positive edge triggered flip flop output changes only when the clock pulse changes from 0 to 1. While in case of negative edge triggered flip flop output responds only when the clock pulse changes from 1 to 0. The positive and negative edge of the clock is shown in Fig. 3.5.

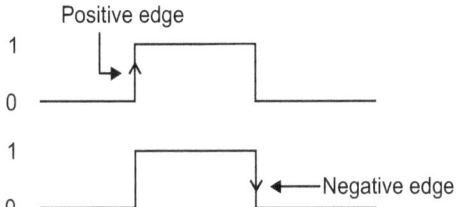

**Fig. 3.5 : Positive & negative edge of the clock**

- Thus, the state of the flip flop changes during very short interval of time in which clock changes from 0 to 1 or 1 to 0 and the uncertainty in the output gets completely eliminated.
- The logic symbol of positive edge triggered and negative edge triggered JK flip flop is shown in Fig. 3.6.

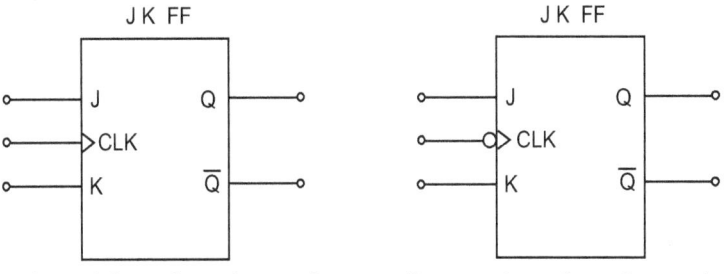

**(i) Positive edge triggered**     **(ii) Negative edge triggered**

**Fig. 3.6 : Edge triggered JK flip flop**

- Note that the logic symbol of negative edge triggered JK flip flop is same as that of MS JK flip flop without preset and clear inputs.
- Also in case of positive edge triggered JK flip flop bubble is absent.

## 3.7 BASIC LATCH

- A latch is an electronic logic circuit that has two inputs and one output. One of the inputs is called the SET input, the other is called the RESET input.
- A latch is with 2 input NAND gates $N_1$ and $N_2$; two additional inverters $N_3$ and $N_4$ is shown in Fig. 3.7.

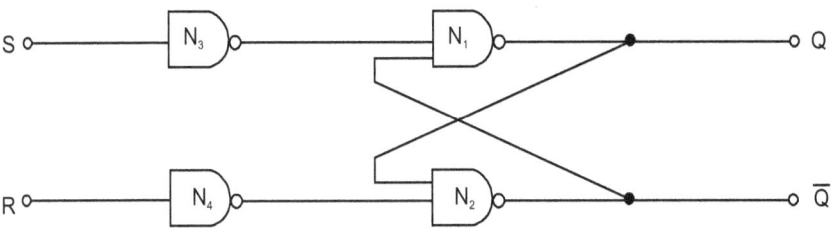

**Fig. 3.7 : Memory cell with provision for entering data**

- If S = R = 0, the circuit will behave exactly as the previous circuit shown in Fig. 3.3.
- If S = 1 & R = 0 then the output of $N_4$ will be 0 and the output of $N_4$ will be 1. As one of the inputs of $N_1$ is 0, its output will be certainly 1 (Q = 1).
- When Q become 1, both inputs of $N_2$ become 1 causing its output to go low ($\bar{Q}$ = 0). This is known as 1 state or set state of the circuit, which is achieved with the input pattern S = 1 and R = 0.
- If S = 0 and R = 1, then the output of $N_4$ will be 0 and the output of $N_4$ will be 1. As one of the inputs of $N_2$ becomes 0, its output will be certainly 1 ($\bar{Q}$ = 1).
- When $\bar{Q}$ becomes 1, both inputs of $N_1$ become 1 causing its output to go low (Q = 0). This is known as 0 state or reset state of the circuit which is achieved with the input pattern S = 0 and R = 1.
- In this way, user can enter desired information in the one bit memory cell.
- Uptil now we have seen that the outputs Q and $\bar{Q}$ are always complementary. If we apply the input S = 1 and R = 1, then the output of $N_4$ and $N_4$ become 0. This makes one input of both $N_1$ and $N_2$ as 0, which in turn cause both outputs Q and $\bar{Q}$ to become 1.
- Both Q and $\bar{Q}$ getting same state is not allowed and therefore the condition of inputs S = R = 1 is prohibited.

## 3.7.1 SR Latch using NAND Gate

- The simplest way to make any basic single bit set-reset SR latch is to connect together a pair of cross-coupled 2-input NAND gates as shown, to form a set-reset bistable also known as an active low SR NAND gate latch, so that there is feedback from each output to one of the other NAND gate inputs.
- This device consists of two inputs, one called the Set, S and the other called the Reset, R with two corresponding outputs Q and its inverse or complement $\bar{Q}$ (not-Q) as shown below in Fig. 3.8.

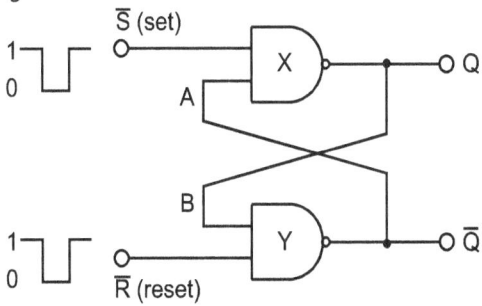

Fig. 3.8 : SR Latch using NAND gate

- **When S = 0, R = 0 :**

  The input R is at logic level "0" (R = 0) and input S is at logic level "1" (S = 1), the NAND gate Y has at least one of its inputs at logic "0" therefore, its output $\bar{Q}$ must be at a logic level "1" (NAND Gate principles). Output $\bar{Q}$ is also fed back to input "A" and so both inputs to NAND gate X are at logic level "1", and therefore its output Q must be at logic level "0".

- **When S = 1, R = 1 :**

  The NAND gate Y inputs are now R = "1" and B = "0". Since one of its inputs is still at logic level "0" the output at $\bar{Q}$ still remains HIGH at logic level "1" and there is no change of state. Therefore, the flip-flop circuit is said to be "Latched" or "Set" with $\bar{Q}$ = "1" and Q = "0".

- **When S = 0, R = 1 :**

  $\bar{Q}$ is at logic level "0", ($\bar{Q}$ = "0") its inverse output at Q is at logic level "1", ($\bar{Q}$ = "1"), and is given by R = "1" and S = "0". As gate X has one of its inputs at logic "0" its output $\bar{Q}$ must equal logic level "1" (again NAND gate principles). Output $\bar{Q}$ is fed back to input "B", so both inputs to NAND gate Y are at logic "1", therefore, $\bar{Q}$ = "0".

- **When S = 1, R = 1 :**

  If the set input, S now changes state to logic "1" with input R remaining at logic "1", output $\bar{Q}$ still remains LOW at logic level "0" and there is no change of state. Therefore, the flip-flop circuits "Reset" state has also been latched and we can define this "set/reset" action in the following truth table 3.1.

  **Table 3.1 : Truth table of latch using NAND gate**

  | State | S | R | Q | $\bar{Q}$ | Description |
  |---|---|---|---|---|---|
  | Set | 1 | 0 | 0 | 1 | Set Q » 1 |
  |  | 1 | 1 | 0 | 1 | no change |
  | Reset | 0 | 1 | 1 | 0 | Reset Q » 0 |
  |  | 1 | 1 | 1 | 0 | no change |
  | Invalid | 0 | 0 | 1 | 1 | Invalid Condition |

- It can be seen that when both inputs S = "1" and R = "1" the outputs $\bar{Q}$ and $\bar{Q}$ can be at either logic level "1" or "0", depending upon the state of the inputs S or R before this input condition existed. Therefore the condition of S = R = "1" does not change the state of the outputs $\bar{Q}$ and $\bar{Q}$.

- The input state of S=0 and R=0 is an undesirable or invalid condition and must be avoided. The condition of S = R = "0" causes both outputs $\bar{Q}$ and $\bar{Q}$ to be high together at logic level "1" when we would normally want $\bar{Q}$ to be the inverse of $\bar{Q}$. The result is that the flip-flop looses control of $\bar{Q}$ and $\bar{Q}$, and if the two inputs are now switched "high" again after this condition to logic "1", the flip-flop becomes unstable and switches to an unknown data state based upon the unbalance as shown in the following switching diagram.

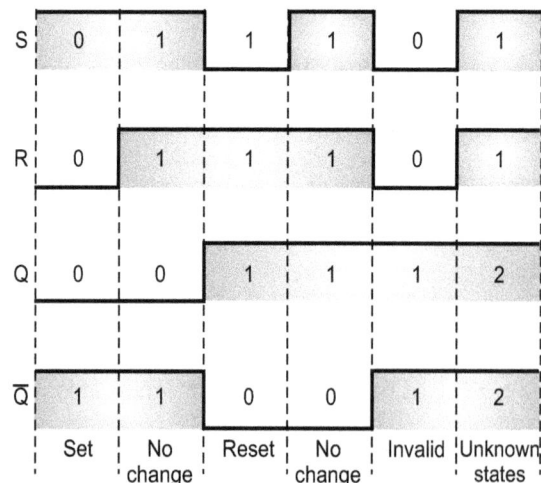

**Fig. 3.9 : S-R latch using NAND gate Switching Diagram**

- Then, a bistable SR flip-flop or SR latch is activated or set by a logic "1" applied to its S input and deactivated or reset by a logic "1" applied to its R. The SR flip-flop is said to be in an "invalid" condition (Meta-stable) if both the set and reset inputs are activated simultaneously.

## 3.7.2 SR Latch using NOR Gate

- RS latch have two inputs, S and R. S is called set and R is called reset.
- The S input is used to produce HIGH on Q ( i.e. store binary 1 in flip-flop). The R input is used to produce low on Q (i.e. store binary 0 in flip-flop). $\bar{Q}$ is Q complementary output, so it always holds the opposite value of Q.
- The output of the S-R latch depends on current as well as previous inputs or state, and its state (value stored) can change as soon as its inputs change. The circuit and the truth table of RS latch is shown below.

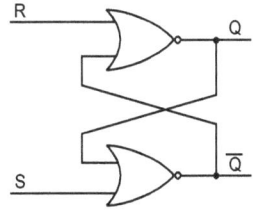

**Fig. 3.10**

**Table 3.2 : Truth table SR latch using NOR gate**

| S | R | Q | Q+ |
|---|---|---|----|
| 0 | 0 | 0 | 0 |
| 0 | 0 | 1 | 1 |
| 0 | 1 | X | 0 |
| 1 | 0 | X | 1 |
| 1 | 1 | X | 0 |

- The operation has to be analyzed with the 4 inputs combinations together with the 2 possible previous states.

- **When S = 0 and R = 0 :** If we assume Q = 1 and $\bar{Q}$ = 0 as initial condition, then output Q after input is applied would be Q = 1 and $\bar{Q}$ = 0. Assuming Q = 0 and $\bar{Q}$ = 1 as initial condition, then output Q after the input applied would be Q = 0 and $\bar{Q}$ = 1. So it is clear that when both S and R inputs are low, the output is retained as before the application of inputs. (i.e. there is no state change).

- **When S = 1 and R = 0 :** If we assume Q = 1 and $\bar{Q}$ = 0 as initial condition, then output Q after input is applied would be Q = 1 and $\bar{Q}$ = 0. Assuming Q = 0 and Q = 1 as initial condition, then output Q after the input applied would be $Q = 1$ and $\bar{Q} = 0$. So in simple words when S is HIGH and R is low, output Q is high.

- **When S = 0 and R = 1 :** If we assume $Q = 1$ and $\bar{Q} = 0$ as initial condition, then output Q after input is applied would be $Q = 0$ and $\bar{Q} = 1$. Assuming $Q = 0$ and $\bar{Q} = 1$ as initial condition, then output Q after the input applied would be $Q = = 0$ and $\bar{Q} = 1$. So in simple words when S is LOW and R is HIGH, output Q is LOW.

- **When S = 1 and R =1 :** No matter what state Q and $\bar{Q}$ are in, application of 1 at input of NOR gate always results in 0 at output of NOR gate, which results in both Q and $\bar{Q}$ set to LOW (i.e. $Q = \bar{Q}$). LOW in both the outputs basically is wrong, so this case is invalid.
- The waveform below shows the operation of NOR gates based RS Latch.

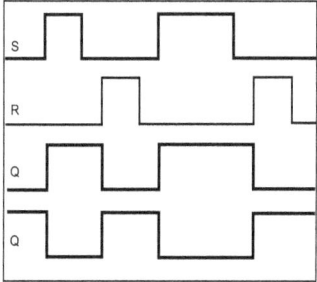

**Fig. 3.11 : Waveform of SR latch using NOR gates**

## 3.7.3 D Latch

- The SR latch seen earlier contains ambiguous state; to eliminate this condition we can ensure that S and R are never equal. This is done by connecting S and R together with an inverter.
- Thus we have D Latch this is same as the RS latch, with the only difference that there is only one input, instead of two (R and S). This input is called D or Data input.
- D latch is called D transparent latch for the reasons explained earlier. Delay flip-flop or delay latch is another name used. Below is the truth table and circuit of D latch.

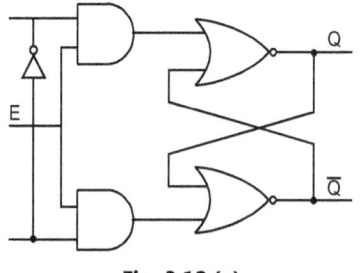

**Fig. 3.12 (a)**

**Table 3.3 : Truth table of D latch**

| D | Q | Q+ |
|---|---|----|
| 1 | X | 1  |
| 0 | X | 0  |

- Below is the D latch waveform, which is similar to the RS latch one, but with R removed.

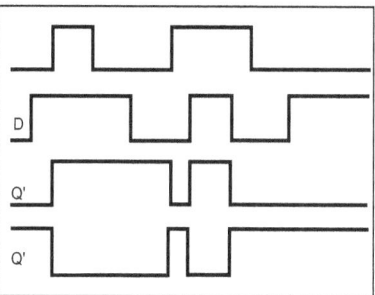

**Fig. 3.12 (b) : D latch waveform**

## 3.8 CLOCKED S-R FLIP-FLOP

- It is often required to enter the desired digital information in the memory cell, in synchronism with a train of pulses known as clock. The circuit of clocked S-R flip flop is as shown in Fig. 3.13.

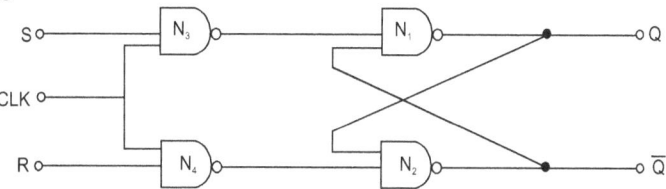

**Fig. 3.13 : Clocked S-R flip flop**

- In above circuit, when CLK = 0, output of both $N_4$ and $N_4$ is certainly 1. In this case, both S and R inputs have no effect on output Q.
- When CLK = 1, the operation of this circuit is exactly the same as that of SR latch.
- For S = R = 0, then output Q does not change i.e. if it is 0 it remains 0 and if it is 1, it remains 1. Thus, there is no change in the output for this input condition.
- For S = 1 and R = 0, the output Q becomes 1 in SR latch. This is known as the set state of the circuit.
- For S = 0 and R = 1 the output Q becomes 0 in SR latch. This is known as the reset state of the circuit.
- For S = R = 1, both the outputs Q and $\bar{Q}$ try to become 1 which is not allowed and therefore this input condition is prohibited.
- Thus, the above circuit responds to S and R inputs, only when CLK = 1.

DIGITAL SYSTEM & MICROPROCESSOR (S.E. IT SEM – III SU)     SEQUENTIAL LOGIC DESIGN

- The operation of the circuit for CLK = 1 can be tabulated as shown in table 3.4.

Table 3.4 : Truth table of clocked SR flip-flop

| Inputs | | Output |
|---|---|---|
| S | R | Q |
| 0 | 0 | No change |
| 0 | 1 | 0 (Reset) |
| 1 | 0 | 1 (Set) |
| 1 | 1 | Prohibited |

- If we represent $Q_n$ as the output of present state of the circuit and $S_n$, $R_n$ as the inputs of the present state, then $Q_{n+1}$ becomes the output of the next state of the circuit.
- The above table 3.4 can be redrawn in terms of present state and next state as table 3.5.

Table 3.5 : Truth table of S-R flip flop

| Inputs | | Output |
|---|---|---|
| $S_n$ | $R_n$ | $Q_{n+1}$ |
| 0 | 0 | $Q_n$ |
| 0 | 1 | 0 |
| 1 | 0 | 1 |
| 1 | 1 | Prohibited |

- The table 3.5 is the truth table of clocked S-R flip flop.
- The truth table of a flip flop is also referred to as the characteristic table as it specifies the operational characteristic of the flip flop.
- Logic symbol of clocked S-R flip flop is as shown in Fig. 3.14.

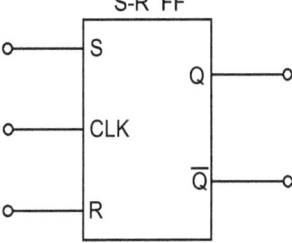

Fig. 3.14 : Logic symbol of clocked S-R flip flop

## 3.9 CLOCKED S-R FLIP FLOP WITH PRESET AND CLEAR INPUTS

- The circuit of clocked S-R flip flop shown in Fig. 3.15 switches to either set state or reset state when the power is turned on i.e. the state of the circuit is uncertain.
- In many applications it is required to define the initial state of the flip flop when the power is turned on.
- This is accomplished by using the preset and clear inputs.

- Preset and clear inputs are known as asynchronous inputs as they do not work in synchronism with the clock.
- Clocked S-R flip flop with preset and clear inputs can be obtained by using $N_1$ and $N_2$ NAND gates as 4 input gates as shown in Fig. 3.15.

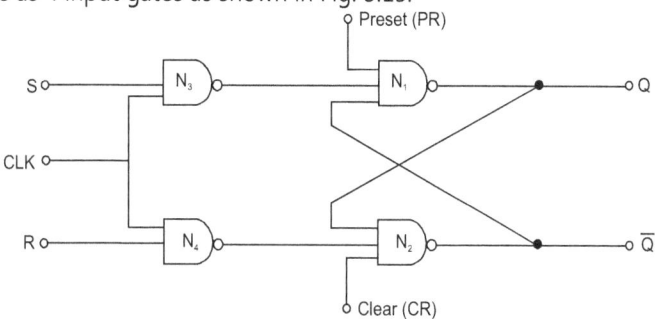

**Fig 3.15 : Clocked S-R flip flop with preset and clear inputs.**

- In When PR = CR = 1, above circuit operates in accordance with the truth table of clocked S-R flip flop given in table 3.5.
- When CR = 0 and PR = 1, one of the inputs of $N_2$ is 0, therefore its output is certainly high ($\bar{Q}$ = 1). Consequently all three inputs of $N_1$ are high which make Q = 0. Thus, CR = 0 resets or clears the flip flop.
- Similarly when CR = 1 and PR = 0, one of the inputs of $N_1$ is 0, therefore its output is certainly high (Q = 1). Consequently all three inputs of $N_2$ are high which make $\bar{Q}$ = 0. Thus, PR = 0 sets the flip flop.
- Both preset & clear inputs are known as active low inputs as they perform the intended operation of setting or clearing the flip flop, when they are low.
- Once the desired initial state of the flip flop is achieved using preset & clear inputs, these inputs are connected to logic 1 while the normal operation of the flip flop takes place.
- The condition PR = CR = 0 must not be used, since this leads to an uncertain state.
- The logic symbol of this flip flop is as shown in Fig. 3.16. Preset and clear inputs are shown as bubbled inputs indicating that they are active low inputs.

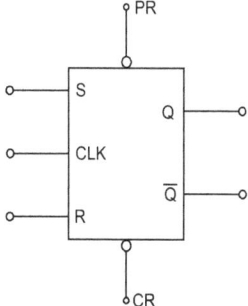

**Fig 3.16 : Logic symbol of clocked S-R flip flop with preset and clear inputs.**

## 3.10 JK FLIP FLOP

- We know that in case of clocked S-R flip flop, for the input condition S = R = 1 both the outputs Q and $\bar{Q}$ try to become 1, which is not allowed and therefore this input condition is prohibited.
- This drawback can be eliminated by converting S-R flip flop into a JK flip flop.
- The data input J is ANDed with $\bar{Q}$ to obtain S input and the data input K is ANDed with Q to obtain R input as shown in Fig. 3.17.

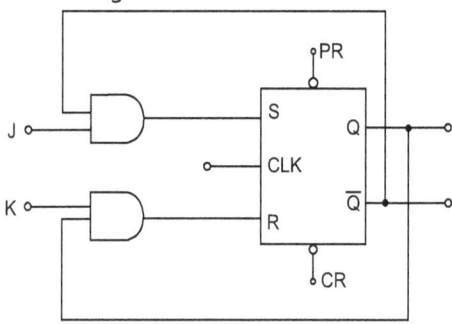

**Fig. 3.17 : JK flip flop constructed using S-R flip flop**

- When J = K = 0, output of both AND gates is 0. Therefore, S and R both become 0. So next state output $Q_{n+1}$ remains same as that of present state output $Q_n$.
- When J = 0 & K = 1, the output of upper AND gate is 0, so S = 0. If the present state output $Q_n$ = 0, the output of lower AND gate is also 0 & R becomes 0.
- For the input condition S = R = 0 the next state output remains unchanged. But if the present state output $Q_n$ = 1, the output of lower AND gate becomes 1 i.e. R becomes 1.
- With S = 0 and R = 1 input combination the next state output $Q_{n+1}$ is reset. Thus for J = 0 & K = 1 input condition, irrespective of the present state $Q_n$, the next state output $Q_{n+1}$ be is 0 i.e. the flip flop is reset.
- Similarly for J = 1 and K = 0 input condition, the next state output $Q_{n+1}$ is certainly 1 i.e. the flip flop is set.

**Race around condition**

- The race around condition occurs for the input combination J = K = 1.
- Let us assume that initially the output Q is 0. With this the output of lower AND gate becomes 0 and upper AND gate becomes 1. Therefore S becomes 1 & R becomes 0. This input combination of S-R causes output Q to become 1.Thus the output changes from 0 to 1 after the time interval Δt equal to the propagation delay through AND gate and S-R flip flop. Now we have J = K = 1 and output Q = 1.
- After another time interval Δt, the output Q will change back to 0 and the cycle repeats till CLK=1.

- At the end of the clock pulse the output Q is uncertain and this situation is known as race around condition. It is shown in Fig. 3.18.

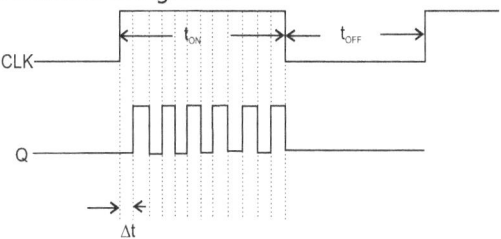

Fig. 3.18 : Timing diagram showing race around condition

- The race around condition can be eliminated if $t_{ON}$ is made smaller than the propagation delay $\Delta t$.
- It can also be eliminated using the master slave JK (MS JK) flip flop.
- The operation of JK flip flop can be expressed with the truth table 3.6.

Table 3.6 : Truth table of JK flip flop

| Inputs | | Output |
|---|---|---|
| $J_n$ | $K_n$ | $Q_{n+1}$ |
| 0 | 0 | $Q_n$ |
| 0 | 1 | 0 |
| 1 | 0 | 1 |
| 1 | 1 | $\overline{Q_n}$ |

- The logic symbol of JK flip flop is shown in Fig. 3.19.

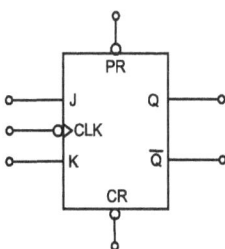

Fig. 3.19 : Logic symbol of JK flip flop

## 3.11 MASTER SLAVE JK (MS JK) FLIP FLOP

- Master slave JK flip flop is a cascade of two S-R flip flops as shown in Fig. 3.20.
- As shown in Fig. 3.20, outputs of slave are fed back to the inputs of master. Also clock is directly applied to the master while it is inverted and then applied to the slave.

- When CLK=1, the master is enabled and the slave is disabled. The outputs of master $Q_m$ and $\bar{Q}_m$ respond to the inputs J and K according to the table 3.6. As long as CLK=1, Q & $\bar{Q}$ outputs do not change as the slave is disabled and therefore the fed back inputs of master also do not change.

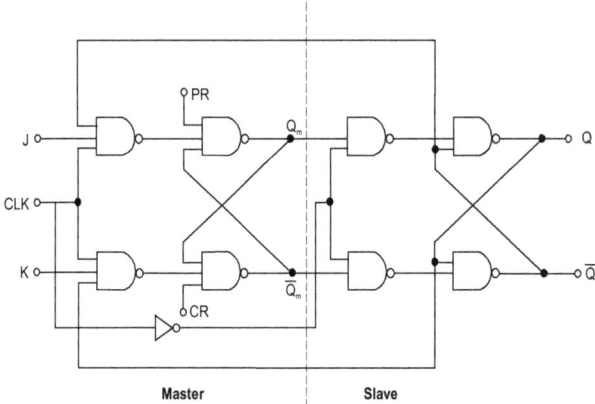

**Fig. 3.20 : Master slave JK flip flop**

- When CLK= 0, the slave is enabled and the master gets disabled. The outputs Q and $\bar{Q}$ change according to the outputs of the master $Q_m$ and $\bar{Q}_m$. As long as CLK = 0, $Q_m$ and $\bar{Q}_m$ outputs do not change as the master is disabled and therefore Q and $\bar{Q}$ outputs also retain their new values. Thus the race around condition gets eliminated.
- The state of the master slave JK flip flop shown in Fig. 3.21, changes at the negative transition of the clock pulse.
- The logic symbol of master slave JK flip flop is shown in Fig. 3.21.

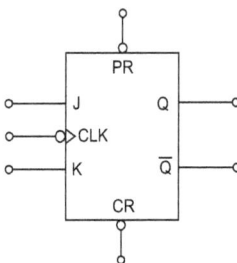

**Fig. 3.21 : Logic symbol of MS JK flip flop**

- The symbol '>' at the CLK input indicates that output changes when the clock makes a transition.
- The bubble indicates that the output changes when there is a negative transition of the clock (i.e. when the clock changes from 1 to 0).

## 3.12 D FLIP FLOP

- It has only one input called as data input (D).
- It is also known as data flip flop or delay flip flop.
- If we use only middle two rows of the truth table of S-R flip flop or JK flip flop we obtain D flip flop.
- The middle two rows of both truth tables indicate that the two inputs S, R or J, K are always complement of each other.
- Thus a D flip flop can be constructed from S-R flip flop or JK flip flop by connecting a NOT gate in between the two inputs as shown in Fig. 3.22.

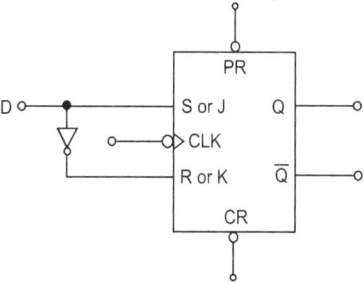

**Fig. 3.22 : D flip flop using S-R flip flop or JK flip flop**

- The truth table of D flip flop is as shown in table 3.7.

**Table 3.7 : Truth table of D flip flop**

| Input | Output |
|---|---|
| $D_n$ | $Q_{n+1}$ |
| 0 | 0 |
| 1 | 1 |

- Here $D_n$ represents the present state input and $Q_{n+1}$ represents the next state output.
- From truth table, it is clear that output is same as that of input therefore it is known as 'data' flip flop.
- The input data appears at the output at the end of the clock pulse. Thus transfer of data from input to the output is delayed by clock pulse and hence it is also called as 'delay' flip flop.
- The logic symbol of D flip flop is shown in Fig. 3.23.

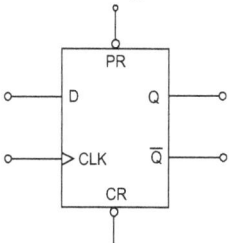

**Fig. 3.23 : Logic symbol of D flip flop**

## 3.13 T FLIP FLOP

- It has only one input called as toggle input (T). It is known as toggle flip flop.
- A T flip flop can be constructed from JK flip flop, just by connecting J and K input terminals together as shown in Fig. 3.24.

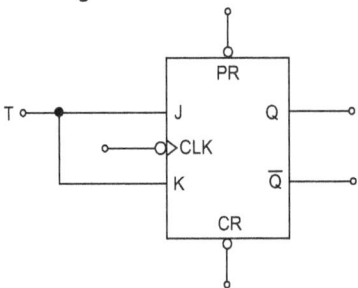

Fig. 3.24 : T flip flop using JK flip flop.

- The truth table of T flip flop is as below.

Table 3.8 : Truth table of T flip flop

| Input | Output |
|---|---|
| $T_n$ | $Q_{n+1}$ |
| 0 | $Q_n$ |
| 1 | $\bar{Q}_n$ |

- Here $T_n$ represents the present state input, $Q_n$ represents the present state output and $Q_{n+1}$ represents the next state output.
- From truth table it is clear that, for T = 1, it acts as toggle switch. The output Q changes for every active transition of the clock signal. Therefore it is called as toggle flip flop.
- S-R flip flop can not be converted into T flip flop since S = R = 1 input condition is not allowed.
- The logic symbol of T flip flop is shown in Fig. 3.25.

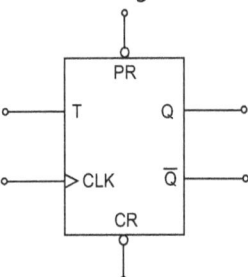

Fig. 3.25 : Logic symbol of T flip flop

## 3.14 DIFFERENT REPRESENTATION OF FLIP FLOP

- There are various ways in which a flip flop represented. Each represented type is used for a different application.
- Different types of representation of flip flop are :
  1. Characteristics equations.
  2. Flip flop as finite state machine.
  4. Excitation tables

## 3.15 EXCITATION TABLE OF FLIP FLOP

- In the design of sequential circuits, it is often required to find input conditions so that desired next state of the circuit is obtained from the present state of the circuit.
- These input conditions can be obtained using the excitation table of a flip flop.
- The truth table of a flip flop specifies its operational characteristic while the excitation table of a flip flop gives an idea regarding the present input conditions along with present state, to obtain the desired next state.
- Construction of excitation table is discussed below.

### 3.15.1 Excitation Table of S-R Flip-Flop

- Let the present state of the S-R flip flop be $Q_n = 0$ and the desired next state be $Q_{n+1} = 0$.
- As there is no change in the state of the flip flop (present state & next state is same), from the first row of the truth table of S-R flip flop we obtain the input condition as $S_n = 0$ and $R_n = 0$.
- Similarly from the third row of the truth table of S-R flip flop, it is clear that whatever may be the present state, the next state of the flip flop is certainly 0 for the input condition $S_n = 0$ and $R_n = 1$.
- By combining these two input conditions we conclude that, $S_n$ input must be 0 while $R_n$ input can be 0 or 1 i.e. $R_n$ input can be X (don't care), to obtain next state $Q_{n+1} = 0$ from the present state $Q_n = 0$. This gives first row of the excitation table of S-R flip flop.
- Similarly input conditions can be found for remaining three combinations of present state & next state. The excitation table is given in table 3.9.

Table 3.9 : Excitation table of S-R flip flop

| Present State | Next State | Flip flop inputs | |
|---|---|---|---|
| $Q_n$ | $Q_{n+1}$ | $S_n$ | $R_n$ |
| 0 | 0 | 0 | X |
| 0 | 1 | 1 | 0 |
| 1 | 0 | 0 | 1 |
| 1 | 1 | X | 0 |

## 3.15.2 Excitation Table of JK, D & T Flip Flop

- In the similar manner excitation table of JK, D & T flip flops can be prepared by using their truth tables. Table 3.10, table 3.11 and table 3.12 are the excitation table of JK, D & T flip flop respectively.

**Table 3.10 : Excitation table of JK flip flop**

| Present State | Next State | Flip flop input | |
|---|---|---|---|
| $Q_n$ | $Q_{n+1}$ | $S_n$ | $R_n$ |
| 0 | 0 | 0 | X |
| 0 | 1 | 1 | X |
| 1 | 0 | X | 1 |
| 1 | 1 | X | 0 |

**Table 3.11 : Excitation table of D flip flop**

| Present State | Next State | Flip flop input |
|---|---|---|
| $Q_n$ | $Q_{n+1}$ | $D_n$ |
| 0 | 0 | 0 |
| 0 | 1 | 1 |
| 1 | 0 | 0 |
| 1 | 1 | 1 |

**Table 3.12 : Excitation table of T flip flop**

| Present State | Next State | Flip flop inputs |
|---|---|---|
| $Q_n$ | $Q_{n+1}$ | $T_n$ |
| 0 | 0 | 0 |
| 0 | 1 | 1 |
| 1 | 0 | 1 |
| 1 | 1 | 0 |

**Example 3.1 :** Prepare the truth table for the circuit shown in Fig. 3.26 and show that it acts as T type flip flop.

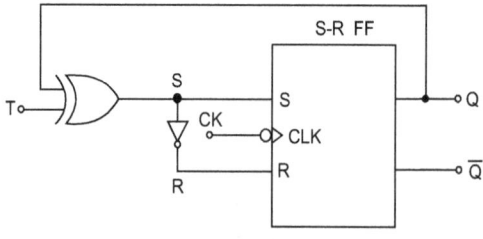

Fig. 3.26

## Solution :

- Let us assume that initially Q=0 & T=0. Therefore output of EX-OR is also 0- which leads S=0 & R=1. From the truth table of S-R flip flop, for this input condition, next state output is 0. This gives first row of the truth table for the circuit.
- Now let us assume that Q=1 and T=0.Therefore output of EX-OR is 1 which leads S = 1 & R = 0. From the truth table of S-R flip flop for this input condition, next state output is 1. This gives second row of the truth table for the circuit.
- Proceeding in a similar manner, we can obtain the remaining two rows of the truth table. The complete truth table is given in table 3.13.

### Table 3.13

| Data Input | Present State | Next State |
|---|---|---|
| T | $Q_n$ | $Q_{n+1}$ |
| 0 | 0 | 0 |
| 0 | 1 | 1 |
| 1 | 0 | 1 |
| 1 | 1 | 0 |

- From the first two rows of the table 3.13, it is clear that when T=0, the next state output $Q_{n+1}$ is same as that of present state output $Q_n$. From the last two rows of the table 3.13, it is clear that, when T=1, the next state output $Q_{n+1}$ is complement of the present state output $Q_n$. this can be represented in a tabular form as shown in table 3.14.

### Table 3.14

| Data input | Next state output |
|---|---|
| $T_n$ | $Q_{n+1}$ |
| 0 | $Q_n$ |
| 1 | $\bar{Q}_n$ |

- The table 3.14 is the truth table of T type flip flop. Thus, the given circuit is same as that of T type flip flop.

**Example 3.2 :** Analyze the circuit shown in Fig. 3.27 and prove that it is equivalent to T flip flop.

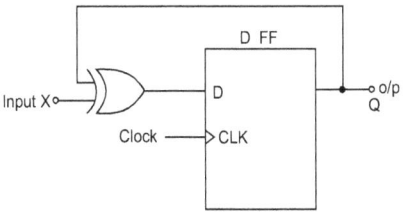

**Fig. 3.27**

**Solution :**

- Let us assume that initially X=0 & Q=0. Therefore output of EX-OR gate is also 0 which leads D=0. From the truth table of D flip flop, for this input condition next state output is 0. This gives first row of the truth table for the circuit.
- Now let us assume that Q=1 & X=0. Therefore, output of EX-OR gate is 1 which leads D=1. From the truth table of D flip flop, for this input condition next state output is 1. This gives second row of the truth table for the circuit.
- Proceeding in a similar manner we can obtain the remaining two rows of the truth table. The complete truth table is given table 3.15.

**Table 3.15**

| Data input X | Present state $Q_n$ | Next state $Q_{n+1}$ |
|---|---|---|
| 0 | 0 | 0 |
| 0 | 1 | 1 |
| 1 | 0 | 1 |
| 1 | 1 | 0 |

- From the first two rows of the above table, it is clear that when X=0 the next state output $Q_{n+1}$ is same as that of present state output $Q_n$.
- From the last two rows of the above table it is clear that, when X=1, the next state output $Q_{n+1}$ is complement of the present state output $Q_n$. This can be represented in tabular form as shown in table 3.16.

**Table 3.16**

| Data input $X_n$ | Next state output $Q_{n+1}$ |
|---|---|
| 0 | $Q_n$ |
| 1 | $\overline{Q}_n$ |

- The table 3.16 is the truth table of T-type flip flop. Thus the given circuit is equivalent to T type flip flop.

## 3.16 CONVERSION OF FLIP FLOPS

- Conversion of Flip flops is based upon the block diagram as shown in Fig. 3.28.

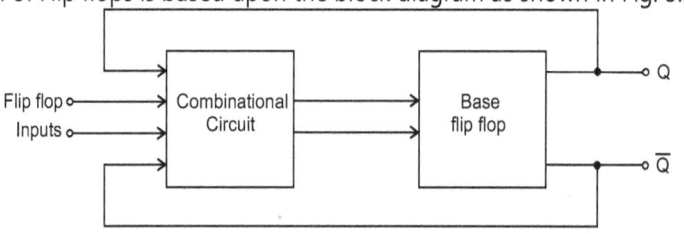

**Fig. 3.28 : Block diagram used for flip flop conversion.**

- Base flip flop shown in the Fig. 3.28 is the flip flop to be converted. Here we need to design a combinational circuit for converting the base flip flop into desired one.
- For designing the combinational circuit we have to use the excitation tables of both, base flip flop & desired flip flop. From that we construct a truth table with desired flip flop data inputs, present state Q, as inputs and base flip flop data inputs as outputs.
- Then we write separate K-maps for individual outputs and obtain the simplified expressions. Based on these expressions we get the combinational circuit required for conversion.

## 3.16.1 Convert S-R Flip Flop to JK Flip Flop

- Here the base flip flop is S-R & desired flip flop is JK.
- We first construct a truth table in which inputs are - desired flip flop data inputs i.e. J, K and present state Q. In the truth table outputs are - based flip flop data inputs i.e. S,R.
- Using the excitation table of both flip flops we construct the truth table 3.17.
- The first row of excitation table of JK flip flop for Q=0 is JK=0X. Therefore in the truth table for first two rows we get inputs as JK=00 and JK=01 for Q=0.
- The first row of excitation table of S-R flip flop for Q=0 is S-R=0X. Therefore in the truth table for first two rows we get the outputs as S-R=0X.
- Proceeding in this manner we obtain the truth table 3.17.
- In this table cell number for the K-map is also written so that it becomes easy while representing the truth table in the K-map.
- Fig. 3.29 in the right bottom corner of K-map cell indicates the cell numbers.

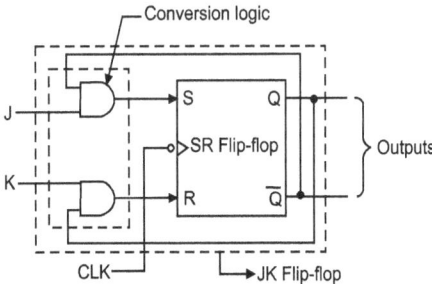

**Fig. 3.29 : S-R to JK conversion**

**Table 3.17 : Truth table for S-R to JK conversion**

| Cell no. | Desired FF data inputs | | Present state | Base FF data inputs | |
|---|---|---|---|---|---|
| | J | K | Q | S | R |
| 0 | 0 | 0 | 0 | 0 | × |
| 2 | 0 | 1 | 0 | 0 | × |
| 4 | 1 | 0 | 0 | 1 | 0 |
| 6 | 1 | 1 | 0 | 1 | 0 |

| 4 | 0 | 1 | 1 | 0 | 1 |
| 7 | 1 | 1 | 1 | 0 | 1 |
| 1 | 0 | 0 | 1 | × | 0 |
| 5 | 1 | 0 | 1 | × | 0 |

- Now we write separate K-maps for S & R outputs according to the cell numbers.

(1) For S ⇒

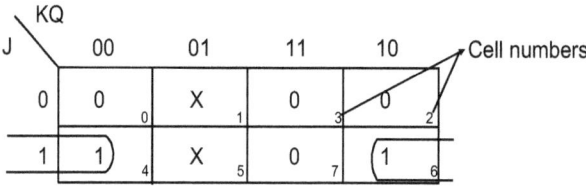

∴ $S = J\bar{Q}$ ...3.1

(2) For R ⇒

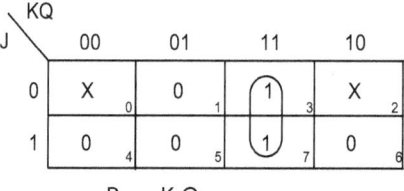

∴ $R = KQ$ ...3.2

- The resulting conversion diagram is as shown in Fig. 3.29.

## 3.16.2 Convert S-R flip flop to D flip flop

- Using the directions given for S-R to JK conversion we construct the truth table 3.18 for S-R to D conversion.

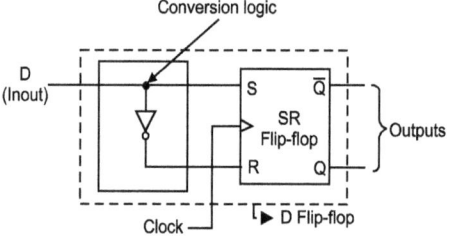

Fig. 3.30 : S-R to D conversion

Table 3.18 : Truth table for S-R to D conversion

| Cell No | Desired FF data input | Present State | Base FF Data inputs | |
|---|---|---|---|---|
| | D | Q | S | R |
| 0 | 0 | 0 | 0 | × |

| 2 | 1 | 0 | 1 | 0 |
|---|---|---|---|---|
| 1 | 0 | 1 | 0 | 1 |
| 4 | 1 | 1 | × | 0 |

- K map for S ⇒

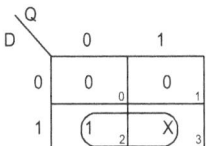

∴            S = D                         ...3.3

- K map for R ⇒

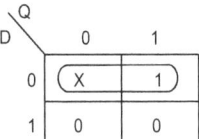

∴            R = $\bar{D}$                         ...3.4

- The resulting conversion diagram is as shown in Fig. 3.30.

### 3.16.3 Convert S-R Flip Flop into T Flip Flop

- Converting SR flip flop to T flip flop is same as SR to D flip flop conversion.

### 3.16.4 Convert JK Flip Flop into T Flip Flop

- We construct the truth table 3.19 for JK to T conversion.

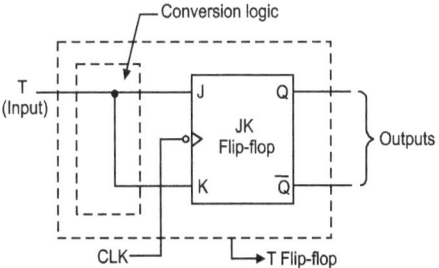

**Fig. 3.31 : JK to T flip flop conversion**

**Table 3.19 : Truth table for JK to T conversion**

| Cell No | Desired FF data input | Present State | Base FF data input | |
|---|---|---|---|---|
| | T | Q | J | K |
| 0 | 0 | 0 | 0 | × |
| 2 | 1 | 0 | 1 | × |
| 4 | 1 | 1 | × | 1 |
| 1 | 0 | 1 | × | 0 |

- K maps for J ⇒

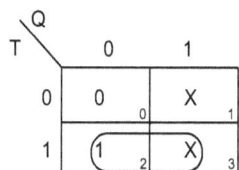

∴           J = T                                                   ...3.5

- K maps for K ⇒

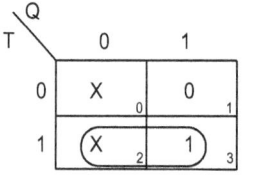

∴           K = T                                                   ...3.6

- The resulting conversion diagram is as known in Fig. 3.31.

## 3.16.5 Convert JK Flip Flop into D Flip Flop

- Using the directions given in JK to T flip flop conversion we construct the truth table 3.20 for JK to D conversion.

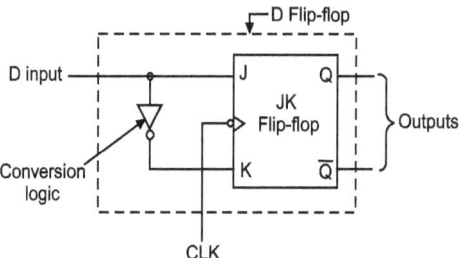

**Fig. 3.32 : JK to D flip flop conversion**

**Table 3.20 : Truth table for JK to D conversion**

| Cell No | Desired FF Data Input | Present State | Base FF Data Input | |
|---|---|---|---|---|
| | D | Q | J | K |
| 0 | 0 | 0 | 0 | × |
| 2 | 1 | 0 | 1 | × |
| 1 | 0 | 1 | × | 1 |
| 4 | 1 | 1 | × | 0 |

- k map for J

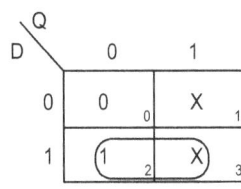

∴  $J = D$  ...3.7

- k map for K

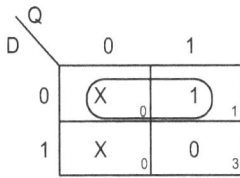

∴  $K = \bar{D}$  ...3.8
- . The resulting conversion diagram is as shown in Fig. 3.32.

## 3.17 APPLICATIONS OF FLIP-FLOPS
### 3.17.1 Bounce Elimination Switch

- Mechanical switches are used as a means to give input to any digital circuit.
- These switches are associated with a problem that when the arm of the switch is thrown from one position to another, it chatters many times initially. Then it comes to rest in the position of contact. This problem is known as switch bouncing or switch chattering.
- The bouncing of the switch causes variations in the corresponding input which can cause errors in the output of the circuit. For example, suppose a switch makes transition from 1 to 0. But before going to final value 0, it oscillates between 0 and 1. This chattering may lead the sequential circuit to enter into undesired state and produce undesired outputs.
- Therefore, it is required that the effect switch bouncing is to be nullified at the output. Out of the various techniques available for this, one is to use bounce elimination switch.
- The bounce elimination switch using $\bar{S}\,\bar{R}$ latch is as shown in Fig. 3.33.

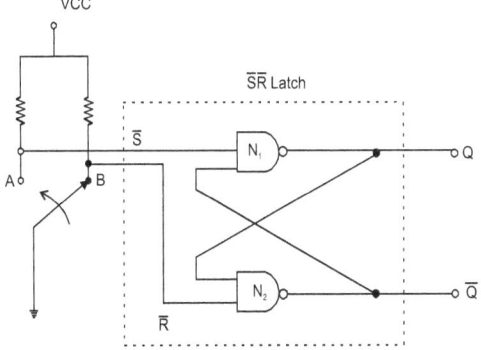

**Fig. 3.33: Bounce Elimination Switch**

- Initially, the switch is at position B, therefore $\bar{R} = 0$ and $\bar{S} = 1$. As $\bar{R} = 0$, output of $N_2$ is 1 ($\bar{Q} = 1$) which makes both inputs of $N_1$ logic 1 and its output $Q = 0$. So initially when the switch is at position B, output of $\bar{S}\bar{R}$ latch is stable i.e. $Q = 0$ and $\bar{Q} = 1$. It is shown in the form of waveforms in Fig. 3.33.

- At instant $t = t_1$, the switch is thrown from position B to A. Certain delay is associated with the switch, therefore it reaches at A at $t = t_2$. Between the instants $t_2$ and $t_1$, both $\bar{S}$, $\bar{R}$ are at logic 1. But still the output of the latch is stable i.e. $Q = 0$ and $\bar{Q} = 1$ as shown in Fig. 3.33

- When the switch makes contact at A for the first time at instant $t_2$, $\bar{S}$ becomes 0 and $\bar{R}$ becomes 1. As $\bar{S} = 0$ output of $N_1$ i.e. $Q = 1$. It makes both inputs of $N_2$ logic 1 and its output $\bar{Q} = 0$. Thus at instant $t_2$ when the switch makes contact at A for the first time, the output of $\bar{S}\bar{R}$ latch moves to another stable state i.e. $Q = 1$ and $\bar{Q} = 0$. It is as shown in Fig. 3.33.

- After the instant $t_2$, the switch chatters and therefore $\bar{S}$ swings between 0 and 1 at instants $t_4$, $t_4$, $t_5$ as shown. Though $\bar{S}$ swings between 0 and 1, it does not affect the output of $N_1$, it remains same i.e. $Q = 1$.

- Thus, the mechanical switch has the drawback that it chatters, but it is when combined with $\bar{S}\bar{R}$ latch, it becomes a chatterless switch.

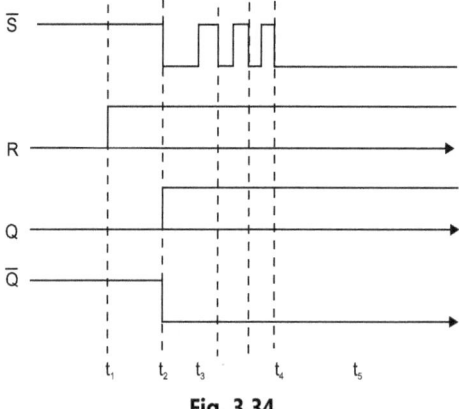

Fig. 3.34

## 3.18 REGISTERS

- Registers are used for storing the digital information. A register that stores N-bit information is called as N-bit register.

- Flip-flops are used for the construction of registers. As flip-flop can store 1-bit information, a N-bit register consists of N flip-flops.
- D type flip-flops are most widely used in the registers. Also JK flip-flop and SR flip-flop when converted to D flip-flop can be used in the registers.
- A 4-bit register is shown in Fig. 3.35.

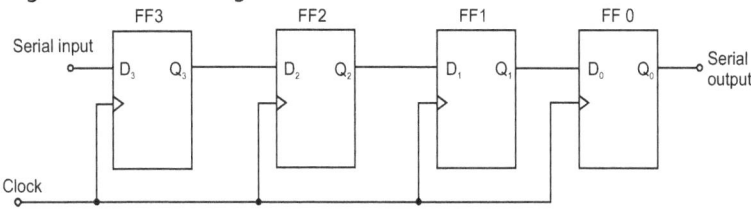

**Fig. 3.35 : 4-bit register**

- As shown in Fig. 3.35 four positive edge triggered D type flip flops are used.
- The data to be stored in the register must be available in serial form in this case.
- The serial data is applied at the serial input bit by bit starting from least significant bit along with the clock pulses.
- As $Q_4$ is connected to $D_2$, $Q_2$ is connected to $D_1$ and $Q_1$ is connected to $D_0$, the data gets shifted from one flip-flop to another. After four clock pulses the 4-bit information gets stored in the register.

## 3.19 BUFFER REGISTER

- An 'n' bit registers has group of 'n' flip flop and capable to store any binary information, which contains 'n' numbers of bits.
- This type of register is also called storage registers.
- These are used for temporary storage of data.

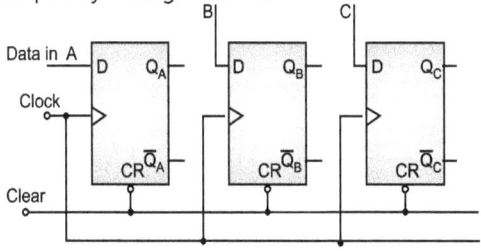

**Fig. 3.36 : Buffer register**

## 3.20 SHIFT REGISTER

- The data can be entered in serial or parallel form and can be retrieved in the serial or parallel form. The serial form means bit by bit (one bit at time) and parallel means all the bits are simultaneously retrieved. On the basis of data entered (write) and retrieved (read), the registers are classified as,

- Serial In Serial Out
- Serial In Parallel Out
- Parallel In Serial Out
- Parallel In Parallel Out
- Registers, in which data are entered or/and retrieved in serial form, are referred to as shift register.

## 3.20.1 Serial In Serial Out Shift Register

- In serial in serial out shift register, data is entered and retrieved in serial fashion with clock.
- The logic diagram of 4-bit serial in serial out shift register using J-K flip-flop is shown Fig. 3.37.

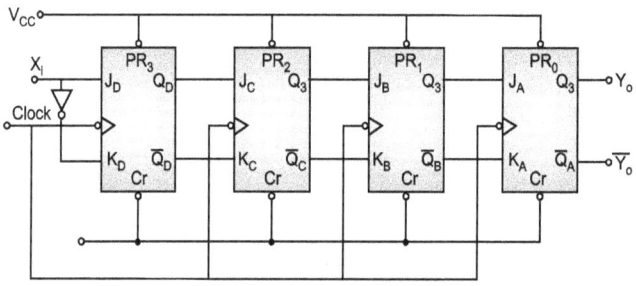

**Fig. 3.37**

- In Fig. 3.37, $X_i$ is input and $Y_O$ is output of serial in serial out shift register.
- The process of entering the digital data starts with the least significant bits. The data input is entered with falling edge of clock pulse, hence number of clock pulses required to enter the data is equal to the length of digital data or size of shift register. The data is read, bit by bit at output $Y_O$ with clock pulse.
- Let us consider the data 0111 is applied to the input. How the data was entered in shift register is given in Table 3.21 and waveforms of shift register for serial input are shown in Fig. 3.38.

**Table 3.21**

| CLK No. | $X_i$ | $Q_D$ | $Q_C$ | $Q_B$ | $Q_A$ |
|---|---|---|---|---|---|
| 0 | 1 (LSB) | 0 | 0 | 0 | 0 |
| 1 | 1 | 1 | 0 | 0 | 0 |
| 2 | 1 | 1 | 1 | 0 | 0 |
| 4 | 0 | 1 | 1 | 1 | 0 |
| 4 |   | 0 | 1 | 1 | 1 |

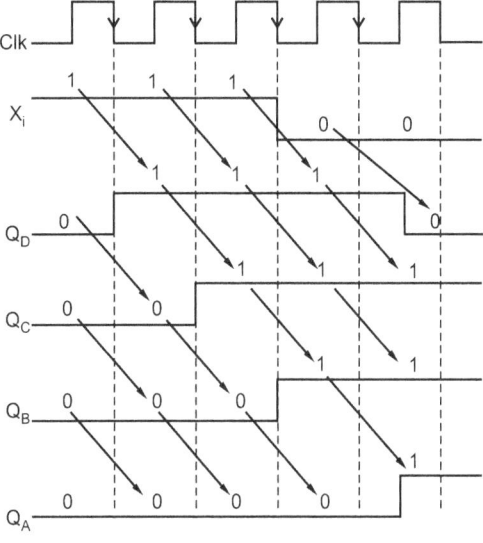

Fig. 3.38

**Operation :**

The input of flip-flop D is $X_i$, flip-flop of C is $Q_D$, flip-flop of B is $Q_C$ and flip-flop of A is $Q_B$. All flip-flops operate as D flip-flop and input applied is 0111.

Initially shift register is cleared.

$$Q_D\ Q_C\ Q_B\ Q_A = 0000 \text{ and input } X_i = 1$$

- At negative edge of first clock pulse, the input data is entered into the flip-flop and at the end of first clock pulse,

$$Q_D\ Q_C\ Q_B\ Q_A = 1000 \text{ and input } X_i = 1$$

- At negative edge of second clock pulse, the inputs are entered and at the end of second clock pulse,

$$Q_D\ Q_C\ Q_B\ Q_A = 1100 \text{ and input } X_i = 1$$

- At negative edge of third clock pulse, the inputs are entered and at the end of third clock pulse,

$$Q_D\ Q_C\ Q_B\ Q_A = 1110 \text{ and input } X_i = 0$$

- At negative edge of fourth clock pulse, the inputs are entered and at the end of fourth clock pulse,

$$Q_D\ Q_C\ Q_B\ Q_A = 0111$$

**Disadvantages :**

- n clock pulses are required to enter the n-bit data.
- n clock pulses are required to read the n-bit data.
- Once the data is read, it will be lost.

## 3.20.2 Serial in Parallel Out Shift Register

- In serial in parallel out shift register, data is entered into the register in serial fashion same as serial in serial out shift register and read from the shift register in parallel fashion. In serial output shift register, clock pulses are required to read the data and once the data is read, it will be lost, but in parallel out shift register, clock pulse(s) is not required to read the data and data is not lost after the read operation.
- The logic diagram of four-bits serial in parallel out shift register using D flip-flop is shown in Fig. 3.39.

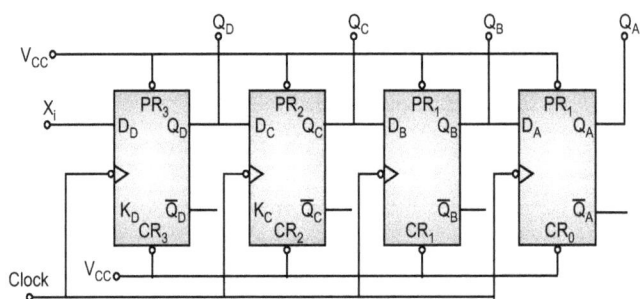

**Fig. 3.39**

where $X_i$ is serial input for shift register and $Q_D$ $Q_C$ $Q_B$ $Q_A$ are the parallel outputs of shift register.

## 3.20.3 Parallel In Serial Out Shift Register

- In parallel in serial out shift register, the data is entered in parallel fashion and data is read in serial fashion. There are two types of parallel loading :
  1. Asynchronous loading,
  2. Synchronous loading.

1. **Asynchronous Loading :**
- In asynchronous loading, the preset inputs are used to load the data simultaneously. The logic diagram of four bit parallel in serial out shift register with asynchronous loading is shown in Fig. 3.40.

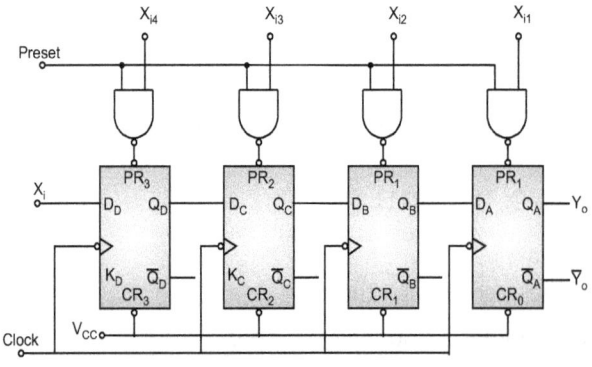

**Fig. 3.40**

- Initially, connecting the clear input to ground clears the flip-flops. The inputs are given to the parallel inputs ($X_{i1}$, $X_{i2}$, $X_{i4}$ and $X_{i4}$) and preset is connected to logic '0', the output of NAND gate is complement of input, the preset input is active low, flip-flop is set for '0' and unchanged for '1'. The data are written into the registers. The inputs are written into the registers without clock pulse. Such parallel loading is known as asynchronous loading. The data is read from output lines $Y_O$ bit by bit by applying the clock pulse. Once, data is read, it will be lost.
- For example, let us assume the data stored in a shift register is 0101 and it will be read from the output line $Y_O$. How the data is read from the shift register is given in Table 3.22 and waveforms of shift register for serial out are shown in Fig. 3.41

Table 3.22

| CLK No. | $Q_D$ | $Q_C$ | $Q_B$ | $Q_A$ | $Y_O$ |
|---|---|---|---|---|---|
| 0 | 1 | 1 | 0 | 1 | 1 |
| 1 | 0 | 1 | 1 | 0 | 0 |
| 2 | 0 | 0 | 1 | 1 | 1 |
| 4 | 0 | 0 | 0 | 1 | 1 |
| 4 | 0 | 0 | 0 | 0 | 0 |

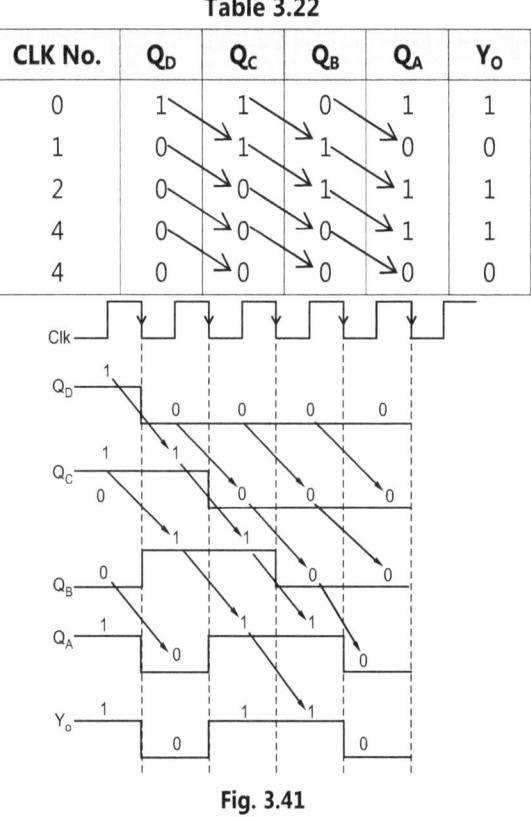

Fig. 3.41

**Operation :**

The input of flip-flop D is '0', flip-flop of C is $Q_D$, flip-flop of B is $Q_C$ and flip-flop of A is $Q_B$. All flip-flops operate as D flip-flop.

Initially data stored in a shift register is 1101.

$$Q_D\ Q_C\ Q_B\ Q_A = 1101 \text{ and output } Y_O = 1$$

- At negative edge of first clock pulse,

$$Q_D\ Q_C\ Q_B\ Q_A = 0110 \text{ and output } Y_O = 0$$

- At negative edge of second clock pulse,

    $Q_D Q_C Q_B Q_A$ = 0011 and output $Y_O$ = 1
- At negative edge of third clock pulse,

    $Q_D Q_C Q_B Q_A$ = 0001 and output $Y_O$ = 1
- At negative edge of fourth clock pulse,

    $Q_D Q_C Q_B Q_A$ = 0000 and output $Y_O$ = 0

In n-bit parallel in parallel out shift register, n clock pulses are required to read the data and once the data is read, it will be lost.

## 2. Synchronous Loading :

- In synchronous loading, the input data is entered in parallel form with clock pulse. The logic diagram of four bit parallel in serial out shift register in synchronous mode is shown in Fig. 3.42.

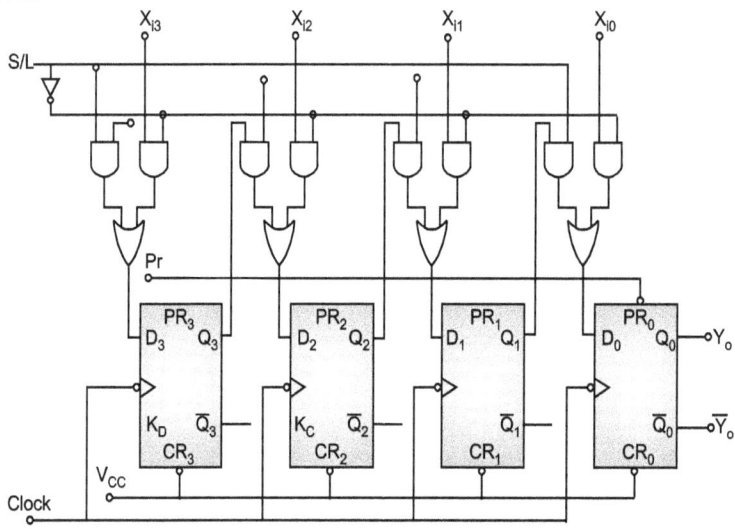

Fig. 3.42

- $\overline{Shift/ Load}$ control signal is used to control the operation of the shift register. When $\overline{Shift/ Load}$ is at logic '1', the data is read from $Y_O$ bit-by-bit with clock pulse. When $\overline{Shift/ Load}$ is at logic '0', the data inputs $X_{i1}$, $X_{i2}$, $X_{i4}$ and $X_{i4}$ load simultaneously with clock pulse. Such type of loading is referred as synchronous loading.
- For example : Consider data inputs are 0101.
- When $\overline{Shift/ Load}$ signal is 0, the outputs of gates $G_1$, $G_4$, $G_5$ and $G_7$ are 0 and outputs of gates $G_2$, $G_4$, $G_6$ and $G_8$ are same to the inputs 0101. The outputs of OR gates are 0101, and these are inputs to D flip-flops. It is loaded into register with falling of the clock pulse.

- When Shift/Load is 0, the outputs of gates $G_2$, $G_4$, $G_6$ and $G_8$ are 0 and the outputs of gates $G_1$, $G_4$, $G_5$ and $G_7$ are 0 $Q_4$ $Q_2$ $Q_1$. The outputs of OR gates are 0 $Q_4$ $Q_2$ $Q_1$, and these are the input to D flip-flops. It is loaded into the register with falling edge of clock pulse. It shows that data is shifted in register and we get output at $Y_O$.

## 3.20.4 Parallel In Parallel Out Shift Register

- In parallel in parallel out shift register, data is entered as well as read in parallel fashion. There are two types of parallel loading : (1) Asynchronous loading and (2) Synchronous loading. The logic diagram of four-bit asynchronous loading parallel in and parallel out is shown in Fig. 3.43 and synchronous loading parallel in parallel out is shown in Fig. 3.44.

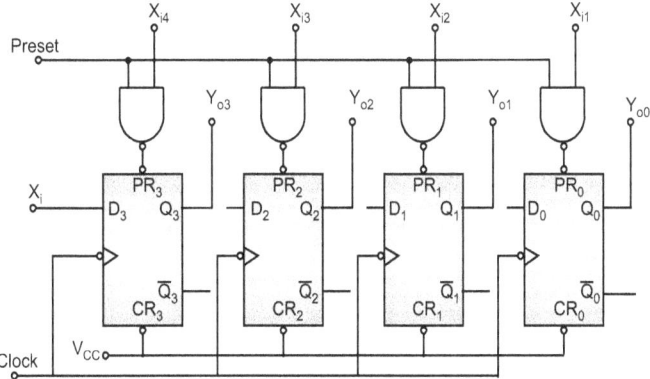

Fig. 3.43

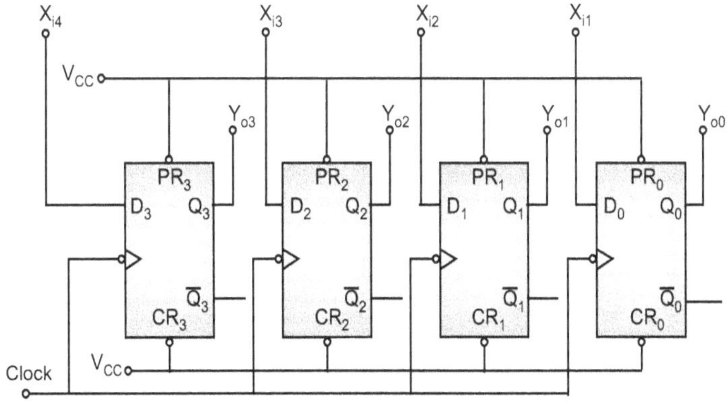

Fig. 3.44

## 3.20.5 Bi-Directional Shift Register

- In bi-directional shift register, the data is shifted to left as well as to right direction. The direction is controlled by the control input $R/\overline{L}$. The four-bit bi-directional shift register is shown in Fig. 3.45

- When R/$\overline{L}$ control signal is high, the gates $G_1$, $G_4$, $G_5$ and $G_7$ are enabled. The output of flip-flop A is input for flip-flop B, the output of flip-flop B is input for flip-flop C, the output of flip-flop C is input for flip-flop D and $X_{iR}$ is input for flip-flop. Data is shifted right with clock pulse.

- When R/$\overline{L}$ control signal is low, the gates $G_2$, $G_4$, $G_6$ and $G_8$ are enabled. The output of the flip-flop D is input for flip-flop C, the output of the flip-flop C is input for flip-flop B, the output of the flip-flop B is input for flip-flop A and $X_{iL}$ is input for flip-flop D. Data is shifted left with clock pulse.

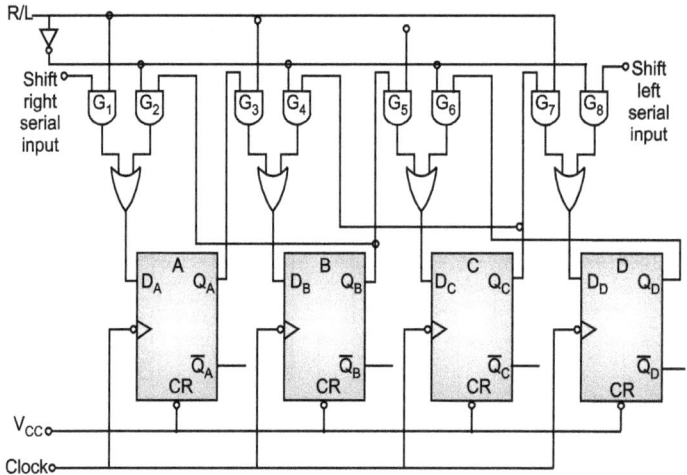

**Fig. 3.45**

### Application of Bi-Directional Shift Register :

- The bi-directional shift register is used to multiply or divide the number by $2^n$, provided that '1' is not shifted out of register. For the multiplication of number by $2^n$, the data is shifted in left side by the amount of n bits with $X_{iL} = 0$.

- For example : Consider the number is loaded in shift register 0001 and we have to multiply number by $4 = 2^2$.

$$0001$$
$$0001 \times 2 = 0010 \text{ shifted left by 1 bit with } X_{iL} = 0$$
$$0001 \times 2^2 = 0100 \text{ shifted left by 2 bits with } X_{iL} = 0$$

- In this process the most significant bit is lost.

- For the division of number by $2^n$, the data is shifted in right by the amount of n bits with $X_{iR} = 0$. For example, consider the number is loaded in shift register 1000 and we have to divide the number by $2^2$.

$$1000$$
$$1000/2 = 0100 \qquad \text{shifted right by 1 bit with } X_{iR} = 0$$
$$1000/2^2 = 0010 \qquad \text{shifted right by 2 bits with } X_{iR} = 0$$

In this process the least significant bit is lost.

### 3.20.6 Universal Register

- The universal shift register operates in all possible four modes (SISO, SIPO, PISO, PIPO) and also as bi-directional shift registers. Logic diagram of four-bit shift register operates in all four modes as shown in Fig. 3.46.

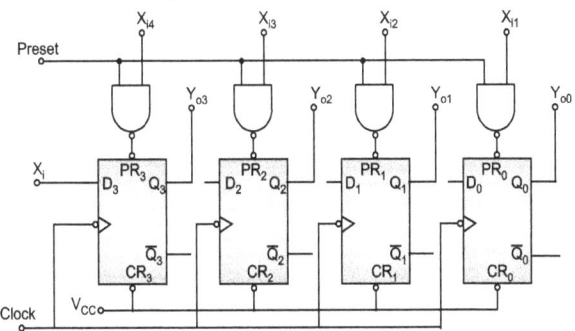

**Fig. 3.46**

where, $X_i$ is serial input of shift register

$X_{i4}, X_{i2}, X_{i1}, X_{i0}$ are four parallel inputs of shift register

$Y_O$ is serial output of shift register

$Y_{O4}, Y_{O2}, Y_{O1}, Y_{O0}$ are four parallel outputs of shift register.

### 3.20.7 4-bit Bidirectional Universal Shift Register (74HC194)

- The 74HC194 is a universal Bidirectional Universal Shift Register it has both serial and parallel input and output capability.

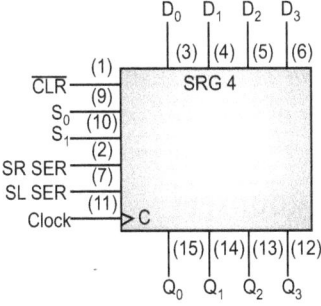

**Fig. 3.47 : The 74HC194 4-bit directional universal register**

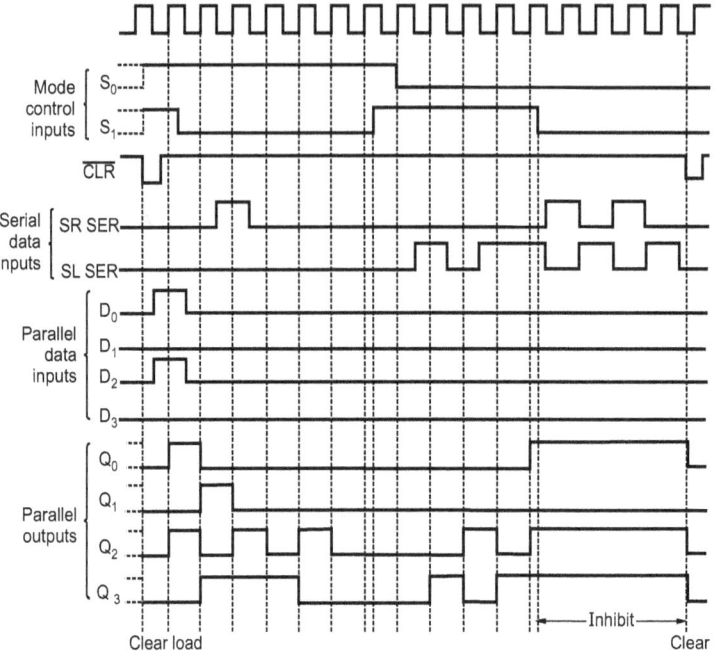

Fig. 3.48 : The timing diagram of 74HC194

## 3.21 COUNTERS

- Counter are used for counting the number of events occurred.
- A circuit that counts electrical pulses, applied as input to it is known as counter.
- In practice these circuits are used as event counters i.e. to count number of event occurred. Electrical pulses are generated corresponding to the occurrence of an event and these pulses are given as input to the counters.
- Flip-flops are used for the construction of counters an N-bit counter consists of N flip-flops.
- A counter with n flip-flops has $2^n$ possible states. Therefore a 4 bit up counter can count from 0 to 7 while 4-bit down counter can count from 15 down to 0.
- Number of distinct states in the operation of counter is known as modulus of that counter and that counter is called mod $2^n$ counter.

  e.g. 4-bit counter, the number of states is $2^4 = 8$. Thus modulus of three bit counter is 8 and it is also called as modulo $2^4$ i.e. mod 8 counter.

### 3.21.1 Classification of Counters

- Basically counters are divided into types
- **(a) Synchronous Counter :** In synchronous counters all the flip-flops receive the external clock pulse simultaneously e.g. ring and Johnson counter.

**(b) Asynchronous Counter :** For asynchronous counters the external clock signal is applied to one flip-flop and then the output of preceding flip-flop is connected to the clock of next flip-flop.

- Based upon output sequence the counters are also classified into three categories.

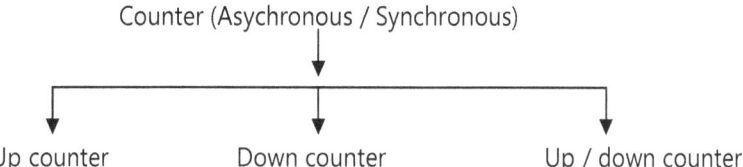

- **Up Counter-** If the decimal equivalent of the counter output increases with successive clock pulses, it is called as up counter. For example in a three bit up counter output goes from 0 to 7.
- **Down Counter-** If the decimal equivalent of the counter output decreases with successive clock pulses, it is called as down counter. For example in a four bit down counter output goes from 15 down to 0.
- **Up/Down Counter-** A counter which can count in any direction i.e. up or down, depending upon direction control input is called as up/down counter.

## 3.22 ASYNCHRONOUS (RIPPLE) COUNTERS

- A two-bit asynchronous counter is shown in Fig. 3.49 (a). The external clock is connected to the clock input of the first flip-flop ($FF_0$) only. So, $FF_0$ changes state at the falling edge of each clock pulse, but $FF_1$ changes only when triggered by the falling edge of the Q output of $FF_0$.
- Because of the inherent propagation delay through a flip-flop, the transition of the input clock pulse and a transition of the Q output of FF0 can never occur at exactly the same time. Therefore, the flip-flops cannot be triggered simultaneously, producing an asynchronous operation.

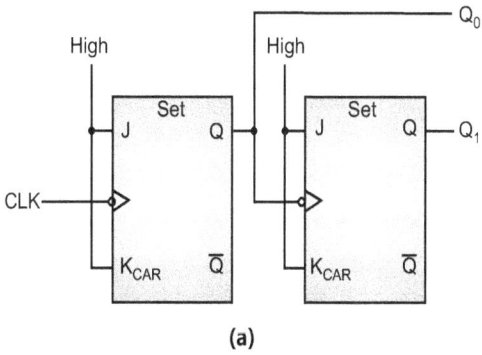

(a)

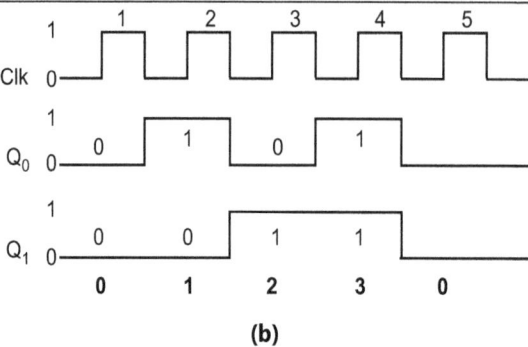

(b)

Fig. 3.49

- Note that for simplicity, the transitions of $Q_0$, $Q_1$ and CLK in the timing diagram above are shown as simultaneous even though this is an asynchronous counter. Actually, there is some small delay between the CLK, $Q_0$ and $Q_1$ transitions.

- Usually, all the CLEAR inputs are connected together, so that a single pulse can clear all the flip-flops before counting starts. The clock pulse fed into $FF_0$ is rippled through the other counters after propagation delays, like a ripple on water, hence the name Ripple Counter.

- The 2-bit ripple counter circuit above has four different states, each one corresponding to a count value. Similarly, a counter with n flip-flops can have 2 to the power n states. The number of states in a counter is known as its mod (modulo) number. Thus a 2-bit counter is a mod-4 counter.

- A mod-n counter may also described as a divide-by-n counter. This is because the most significant flip-flop (the furthest flip-flop from the original clock pulse) produces one pulse for every n pulses at the clock input of the least significant flip-flop (the one triggers by the clock pulse).

## 3.22.1 3-Bit Asynchronous Up (Ripple) Counter

- For the implementation of 4-bit counter, three flip flops are required.
- The number of distinct states in the operation of this counter is $2^3$ = 8. Therefore, it is also called as mod-8 counter.
- In case of 4-bit up counter, the output goes from 0 to 7.
- Let $Q_2$, $Q_1$ and $Q_0$ be the outputs of the three flip flops used for the design. The count sequence is as shown in the table 3.23.

Table 3.23 : Count sequence of 4-bit up counter

| $Q_2$ | $Q_1$ | $Q_0$ | State of the counter |
|---|---|---|---|
| 0 | 0 | 0 | 0 |
| 0 | 0 | 1 | 1 |
| 0 | 1 | 0 | 2 |
| 0 | 1 | 1 | 4 |
| 1 | 0 | 0 | 4 |
| 1 | 0 | 1 | 5 |
| 1 | 1 | 0 | 6 |
| 1 | 1 | 1 | 7 |

- From the table 3.23 it is clear that the output $Q_0$ of the least significant flip flop changes for every clock pulse applied to it. So it can be implemented using a T type flip flop with $T_0 = 1$.

- Also, the output $Q_1$ changes from 0 to 1 or 1 to 0, only when in the corresponding states $Q_0$ changes from 0 to 1. So it can be implemented using a T-type flip flop with $T_1 = 1$ and $Q_0$ is connected as its clock input.

- Similarly the output $Q_2$ changes only when $Q_1$ changes from 0 to 1. So it can be implemented using a T-type flip flop with $T_2 = 1$ and $Q_1$ is connected as its clock input. This completes the design and the resulting circuit is as shown as Fig. 3.50(a).

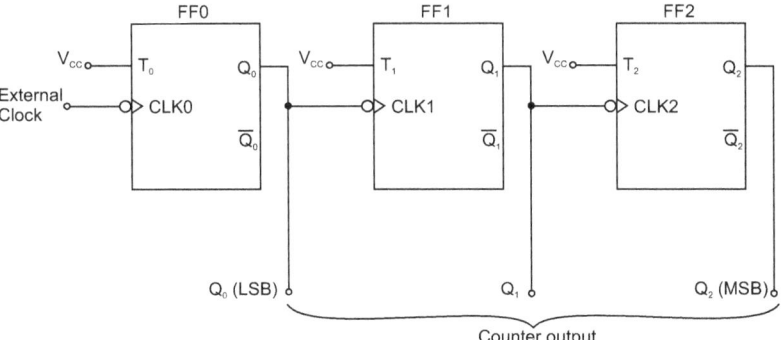

Fig. 3.50 (a) : 3-bit ripple up counter

- The waveforms of the outputs are shown in Fig. 3.50(b).

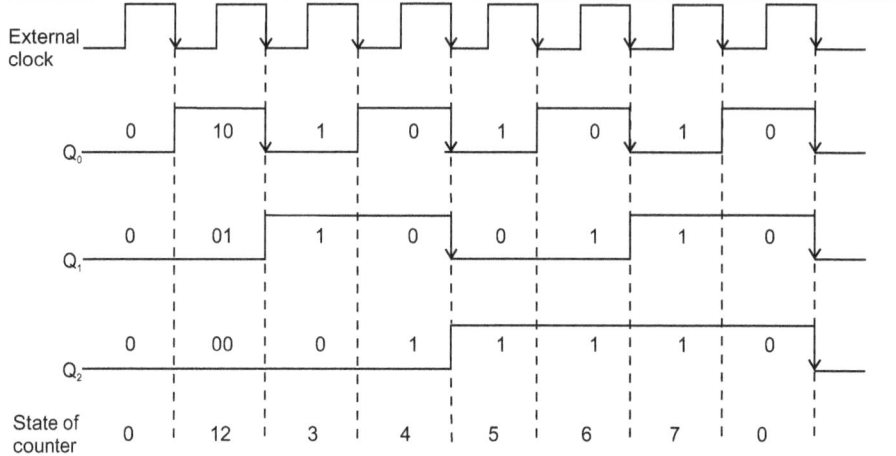

Fig. 3.50 (b) : Waveforms/Timing diagram of 4 bit ripple up counter

- From the waveform of external clock and $Q_0$, it is clear that two clock periods are required for the completion of one cycle of $Q_0$. Therefore, clock frequency is twice to that of $Q_0$ output. In other words the $Q_0$ is the divide by 2 ($\div$ 2) output with respect to clock frequency. Similarly $Q_1$ is the divide by 4 ($\div$ 4) output and $Q_2$ is divide by 8 ($\div$ 8) output with respect to clock frequency.
- Therefore this mod - 8 counter is also known as divide by 8 ($\div$ 8) counter.

## 3.22.2 4-Bit Asynchronous Up Counter

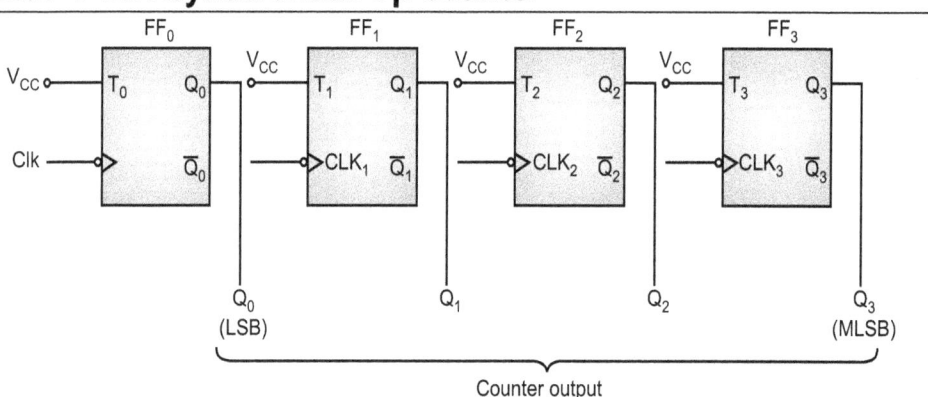

Fig. 3.51 : 4-bit (asynchronous ripple) counter

Fig. 3.51 shows the circuit diagram of 4-bit asynchronous counter using the T flip-flops.

- Since it is 4 bit asynchronous up counter, we need to use four flip-flops number of distinct states in the operation of this counter is $2^4 = 16$.
  Therefore, it is called as mod-16 counter.
- Let $Q_0$, $Q_1$, $Q_2$ and $Q_4$ be the outputs of the three flip-flops used for the design. The count sequence is as shown in the table.
- Table 3.24 count sequence of 4-bit up counter.

Table 3.24

| Q₄ | Q₂ | Q₁ | Q₀ | State of the counter |
|---|---|---|---|---|
| 0 | 0 | 0 | 0 | 0 |
| 0 | 0 | 0 | 1 | 1 |
| 0 | 0 | 1 | 0 | 2 |
| 0 | 0 | 1 | 1 | 4 |
| 0 | 1 | 0 | 0 | 4 |
| 0 | 1 | 0 | 1 | 5 |
| 0 | 1 | 1 | 0 | 6 |
| 0 | 1 | 1 | 1 | 7 |
| 1 | 0 | 0 | 0 | 8 |
| 1 | 0 | 0 | 1 | 9 |
| 1 | 0 | 1 | 0 | 10 |
| 1 | 0 | 1 | 1 | 11 |
| 1 | 1 | 0 | 0 | 12 |
| 1 | 1 | 0 | 1 | 14 |
| 1 | 1 | 1 | 0 | 14 |
| 1 | 1 | 1 | 1 | 15 |

- From the table it is clear that the output $Q_0$ of the least significant flip-flop changes for every clock pulse applied to it. So it can be implemented using at type flip-flop with $T_0 = 1$. Also the output $Q_1$ changes from 0 to 1 or 1 to 0, only when in the corresponding states $Q_0$ changes from 0 to 1. So it can be implemented using a T-type flip flop with $T_1 = 1$ and $Q_0$ is connected as its clock input. Similarly the output $Q_2$ changes only when $Q_1$ changes from 0 to 1 so it can be implemented using a T-type flip-flop with $T_2 = 1$ and $Q_1$ is connected as its clock input.
- Similarly the output $Q_4$ changes only when $Q_2$ changes from 0 to 1 so it can be complemented using at type flip-flop with $T_4 = 1$ and $Q_2$ is connected as its clock input. Waveform of output shown below for 4 bit asynchronous (ripple) counter.

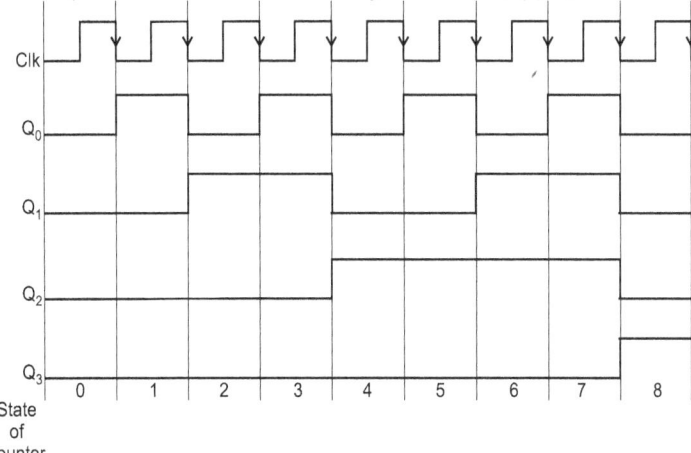

Fig. 3.52

## 3.22.3 3-bit Asynchronous Down Counter

**Example 3.3 :** Design 4 bit down ripple counter. Draw waveforms.

**Solution :**

- 4 bit ripple down counter requires three flip flops. The counter output goes from 7 down to 0. The count sequence is as shown in table 3.25.

**Table 3.25 : Count sequence of 4-bit down counter**

| $Q_2$ | $Q_1$ | $Q_0$ | State of the counter |
|---|---|---|---|
| 1 | 1 | 1 | 7 |
| 1 | 1 | 0 | 6 |
| 1 | 0 | 1 | 5 |
| 1 | 0 | 0 | 4 |
| 0 | 1 | 1 | 4 |
| 0 | 1 | 0 | 2 |
| 0 | 0 | 1 | 1 |
| 0 | 0 | 0 | 0 |

- As like previous example, the least significant stage can be implemented using T flip flop with $T_0 = 1$.
- Output $Q_1$ changes whenever there is 0 to 1 transition of $Q_0$, in the corresponding states. So we can realize it with a flip flop which is positive edge triggered. The $Q_0$ output needs to be connected to the clock input and $T_1 = 1$.
- When $Q_0$ makes transition from 0 to 1, $\bar{Q}_0$ changes from 1 to 0. So we can realize the second stage by using a negative edge triggered flip flop as shown in Fig. 3.53 with $T_1 = 1$. $\bar{Q}_0$ output needs to be connected as clock input.
- Similarly, the most significant stage can be realized with a negative edge triggered T flip flop with $T_2 = 1$ and $\bar{Q}_1$ connected as its clock input. This completes the design and the resulting circuit is as shown in Fig. 3.53. Also the waveforms of the outputs are shown in Fig. 3.54.

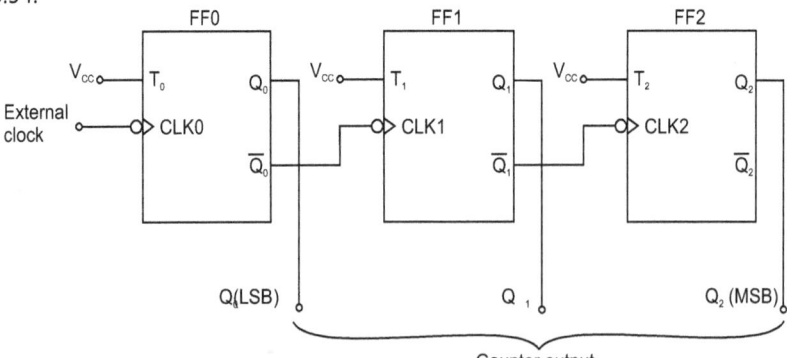

**Fig. 3.53 : 3 bit ripple down counter**

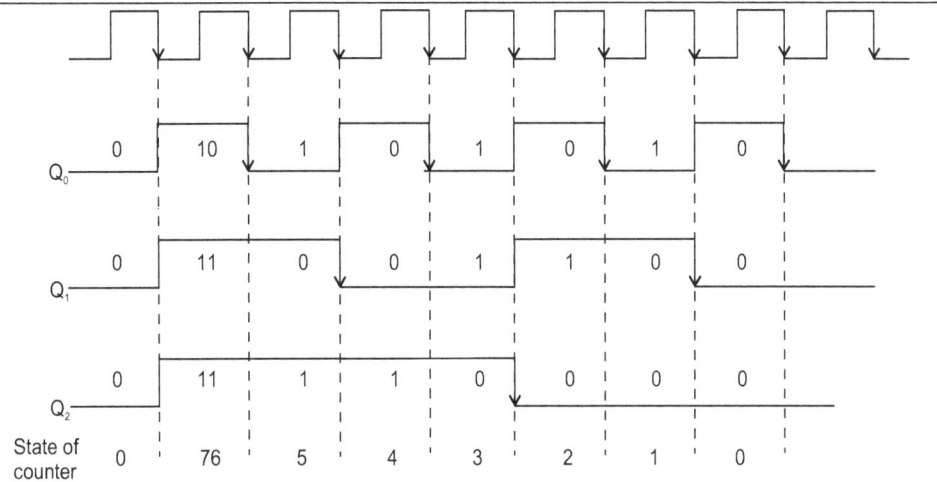

Fig. 3.54 : Waveforms/Timing diagram of 4 bit ripple down counter

## 3.22.4 4-bit Up / Down Ripple Counter

**Example 3.4 :** Design a 4-bit binary Up/Down ripple counter with a control for Up/Down counting. Also draw timing diagram.

**Solution :**

- A ripple up counter Q output of the preceding stages are to be connected to the clock inputs of next stages.

- Similarly from example we know that for a ripple down counter $\bar{Q}$ outputs of preceeding stages are to be connected to the clock input of next stages.

- Therefore to design a Up/Down counter, AND-OR gates are used between flip flops as shown in Fig. 3.55.

- The upper AND gates are enabled when UP/Down input is at logic 1 which connect Q outputs to the inputs. While the lower AND gates are enabled when UP/Down input is 0 which connect $\bar{Q}$ outputs to the clock inputs. For 4-bit counter, 4 four flip flops are required.

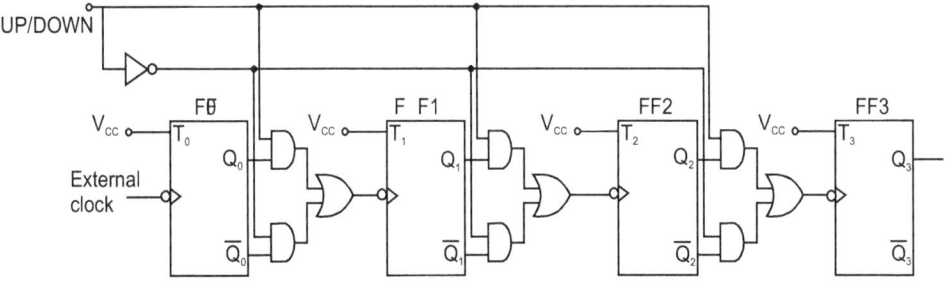

Fig. 3.55 : 4-bit ripple Up/Down counter

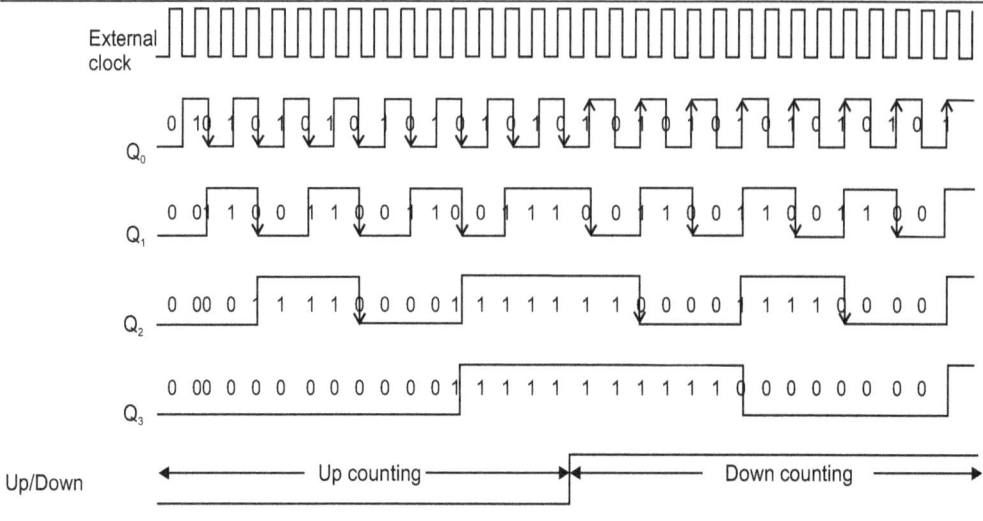

Fig. 3.56 : Timing diagram of 4-bit Up/Down counter

## 3.22.5 MOD-N Counter (Modulus of the Counter)

- N bit ripple counter is called as modulus N counter.
- Modulus of counter = $2^n$
- From the modulus we can conclude the number of states of counter.

Table 3.26

| Sr. No. | Counter type | Modulus |
|---|---|---|
| 1 | 2 bit | MOD – 4 |
| 2 | 4 bit | MOD – 8 |
| 4 | 4 bit | MOD - 16 |

**Example 3.5 :** Design mod 5 ripple up counter.

**Solution :**

- It is given that modulus of counter is 5. So number of distinct states in the operation of the counter are 5. The number of flip flops required can be obtained using the following ineqality.

$$2^N \geq \text{Modulus of counter} \quad \ldots(3.9)$$

Where N = number of flip flops.

For N = 1 & N = 2 the inequality is not satisfied.

Putting N = 4, we get,

$$2^3 \geq 5$$
$$\Rightarrow 8 \geq 5$$

- The inequality is satisfied. Therefore for the implementation of mod 5 counter three flip flops are required.

- As ripple up counter is to be designed, we have to use three T flip flops with the T inputs connected to $V_{CC}$. Also $Q_0$ and $Q_1$ outputs are to be connected as the clock input of the respective next stages.
- The count sequence is shown in table 3.27.

Table 3.27 : count sequence of mod 5 ripple up counter

| $Q_2$ | $Q_1$ | $Q_0$ | State of the counter |
|---|---|---|---|
| 0 | 0 | 0 | 0 |
| 0 | 0 | 1 | 1 |
| 0 | 1 | 0 | 2 |
| 0 | 1 | 1 | 4 |
| 1 | 0 | 0 | 4 |
| 0 | 0 | 0 | 0 |

- The counter output goes from 0 to 4. Therefore, it is a truncated counter. So we need to design 'reset logic'.
- From the table it is clear that after the state 4 the counter should be resetted i.e. The state 5 should not occur.

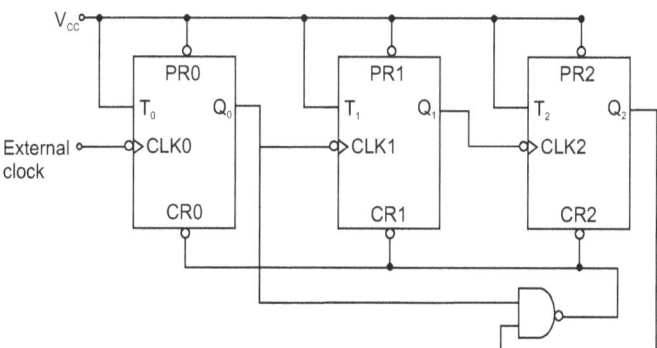

Fig. 3.57: Mod-5 ripple up counter

- For state 5, $Q_2 Q_1 Q_0 = 101$. Therefore whenever both $Q_2$ & $Q_0$ become 1, at that instant the counter should be resetted. It can be achived with a simple 2 input NAND gate. The output of the NAND gate must be connected to the clear input of all flip flops, so that the counter gets resetted after the state 4. The resulting circuit diagram is as shown in Fig. 3.57.

## 3.22.6 Frequency Division

- The feature of the D-type flip-flop is as a binary divider, for frequency division or as a "divide-by-2" counter. Here the inverted output terminal Q (NOT-Q) is connected directly back to the Data input terminal D giving the device "feedback" as shown below.

- **Divide-by-2 Counter**

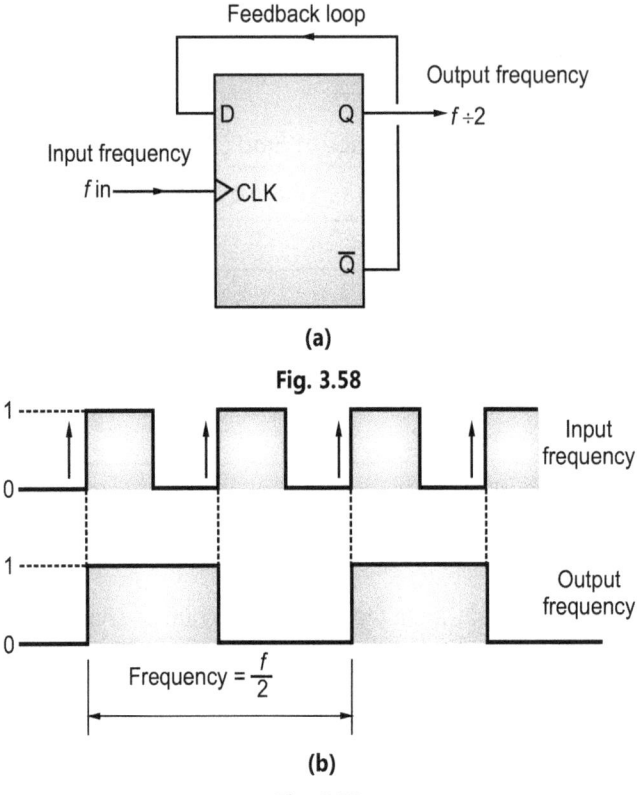

(a)
Fig. 3.58

(b)
Fig. 3.58

- It can be seen from the frequency waveforms above, that by "feeding back" the output from Q to the input terminal D, the output pulses at Q have a frequency that are exactly one half (f ÷ 2) that of the input clock frequency. In other words the circuit produces frequency division as it now divides the input frequency by a factor of two (an octave).
- This then produces a type of counter called a "ripple counter" and in ripple counters, the clock pulse triggers the first flip-flop whose output triggers the second flip-flop, which in turn triggers the third flip-flop and so on through the chain producing a ripple effect (hence their name) of the timing signal as it passes through the chain.

**Frequency Division using Toggle Flip-flops**

- This type of counter circuit used for frequency division is commonly known as an Asynchronous 4-bit Binary Counter as the output on QA to QC, which is 4 bits wide, is a binary count from 0 to 7 for each clock pulse. In an asynchronous counter, the clock is applied only to the first stage with the output of one flip-flop stage providing the clocking signal for the next flip-flop stage and subsequent stages derive the clock from the previous stage with the clock pulse being halved by each stage.

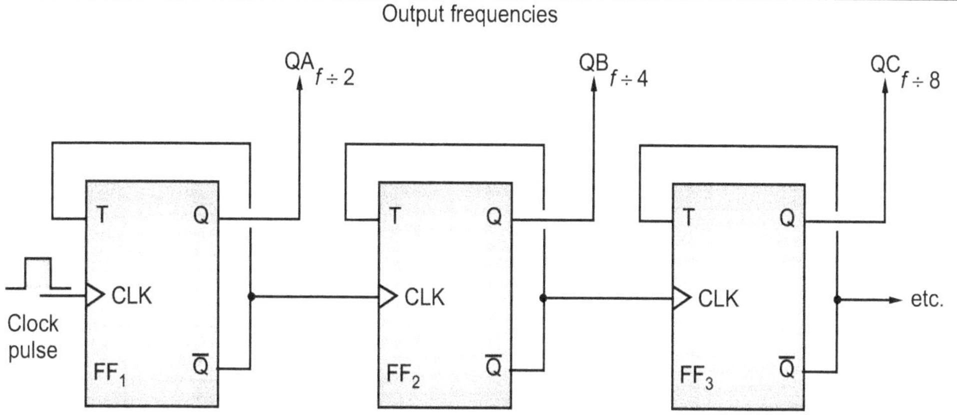

Output frequencies

**Fig. 3.59**

**Example 3.6 :** A certain counter is being pulsed by a 256 kHz clock signal. The output frequency from the last flip flop is 2 kHz : (i) Determine the mod of counter (ii) Determine the counting range.

**Solution :**

- Input clock frequency is 256 kHz & the output frequency from last flip flop is 2 kHz.
- Therefore it is divide by (256/2=128) counter (÷ 128).
- As it is a divide by 128 counters, the modulus of counter is also 128. Therefore it is a mod-128 counter.
- The counting range in case of up counter will be from 0 to 127 i.e. the binary output will go from 0000000 to 1111111.
- Similarly, the counting range in case of down counter will be from 127 down to 0 ie. the binary output will go from 1111111 to 0000000.

## 3.22.7 4 bit Asynchronous BCD Ripple Counter

**Example 3.7 :** Design BCD ripple counter.

**Solution :**

- We know that, binary coded decimal (BCD) is in the range from 0 to 9. Therefore modulus of counter is 10.
- For N = 1, N = 2 & N = 4 the inequality 2.9 is not satisfied.
- Putting N=4 in the inequality we get,

$$2^4 \geq 10$$
$$\Rightarrow 16 \geq 10$$

- The inequality is satisfied. Therefore for the implementation of BCD counter four flip flops are required.
- Here we shall design a up counter, for which we require four T flip flops with the T inputs connected to $V_{CC}$. Also $Q_0$, $Q_1$ & $Q_2$ outputs are connected as the clock inputs of the respective next stages.

- In BCD counter the state $Q_4 Q_2 Q_1 Q_0 = 1010$ should not occur i.e. when $Q_4$ & $Q_1$ both become 1, at the same instant the counter should be resetted. Therefore we require a 2 input NAND gate as reset logic for BCD counter. The resulting circuit diagram is shown in Fig. 3.60.

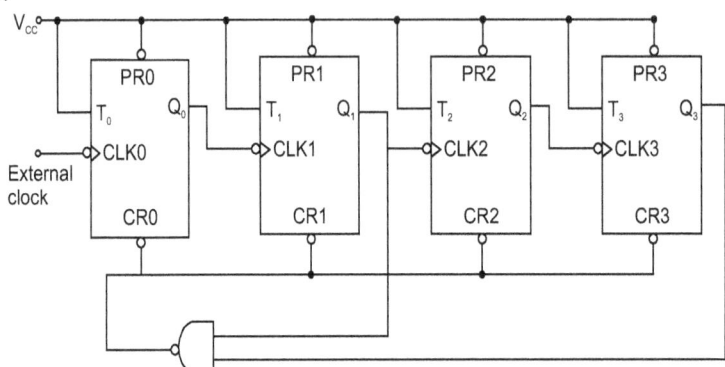

**Fig. 3.60 : BCD ripple up counter**

## 3.22.8 Drawbacks of Ripple Counter

- Observe the timing diagram of 4 bit ripple up counter shown in Fig. 3.49.
- Upon application of clock pulse, the count sequence proceeds from 7 to 0. That is the output changes from $Q_2 Q_1 Q_0 = 111$ to $Q_2 Q_1 Q_0 = 000$.
- This change from 111 to 000 does not take place simultaneously. As shown in Fig. 3.49 external clock applied to FF0 will change the output $Q_0$ from 1 to 0 first. Further the 1 to 0 change in $Q_0$ acts as trigger for FF1 and its output also change from 1 to 0. Now this 1 to 0 transition in $Q_1$ triggers FF2 to change its output from 1 to 0. In this manner the next state 000 is obtained from the present state 111.
- As explained above, the carry ripples through the circuit, like the ripple in water. Therefore asynchronous counters are known as ripple counters.
- Let us assume that each flip flop shown in Fig. 3.49 has propogation delay of 50 nS duration, the output $Q_0$ will change from 1 to 0. After another 50 nS duration $Q_1$ will change from 1 to 0, i.e. after 50 + 50 = 100 nS duration since the clock pulse is applied to FF0. Similarly FF2 will take separate 50 ns duration for the change from 1 to 0. So $Q_2$ will change after 50+50+50=150 nS duration since the clock pulse is applied to FF0.
- This time period will increase as the numbers of flip flops are increased. This limits the frequency of operation of ripple counters.
- In short, 4 bit ripple up counter requires 150 nS duration to change from state 111 to 000 while in case of synchronous counter shown in Fig. 3.46 as all the flip flops are clocked simultaneously, it takes 50 nS duration for the same change. Also this duration is constant for any number of flip flops.
- Thus asynchronous counters are slower than synchronous counters.

- Another drawback of asynchronous counters is that they can generate straight binary sequences in up or down direction while synchronous counters can be designed for any count sequence.
- Also we have to use JK or T flip flops only in the design of asynchronous counters.

## 3.23 STUDY of IC 7490

- IC 74C90 is also known as decade counter IC or MOD-10 counter IC as number of distinct states in its operation are ten.
- It consists of two separate asynchronous counters such as MOD-2 and MOD-5.
- MOD-2 counter is build with a single flip flop known as FF A.
- It can accept clock signal externally at input A and has the output.
- MOD-5 counter is built internally with three flip flops - FF B, FF C and FF D. It also can accept clock signal externally at input B and has the outputs $Q_B$, $Q_C$, $Q_D$.
- Thus, there are four flip flops in the IC 74C90, which are negative edge triggered.
- When MOD-2 and MOD-5 counters are cascaded, it acts as a MOD (2 × 5) = MOD 10 counter.
- The IC has two reset inputs $R_1$, $R_2$ and two set inputs $S_1$, $S_2$ which are active high inputs. When $R_1$, $R_2$ both are connected to all flip flops are cleared i.e. $Q_D$ $Q_C$ $Q_B$ $Q_A$ = 0000. When $S_1$, $S_2$ both are connected to logic 1 the counter output is = 1001. The internal structure of IC 74C90 is as shown in Fig. 3.61.

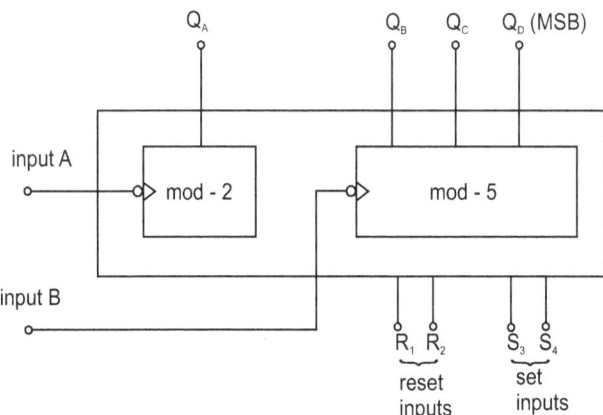

**Fig. 3.61 : Internal structure of IC74C90**

- As shown in Fig. 3.61 MOD - 2 and MOD - 5 counters can work separately with respect to clock signal applied at input A and input B respective.
- If we connect the output of MOD-2 counter as to input B i.e. as clock signal of MOD-5 counter then it becomes a MOD-10 counter. The count sequence is given in table 3.28.

Table 3.28

| Flip-flop Outputs | | | | State of the counter |
|---|---|---|---|---|
| $Q_D$ | $Q_C$ | $Q_B$ | $Q_A$ | |
| 0 | 0 | 0 | 0 | 0 |
| 0 | 0 | 0 | 1↘ | 1 |
| 0 | 0 | 1 | 0↙ | 2 |
| 0 | 0 | 1 | 1↘ | 4 |
| 0 | 1 | 0 | 0↙ | 4 |
| 0 | 1 | 0 | 1↘ | 5 |
| 0 | 1 | 1 | 0↙ | 6 |
| 0 | 1 | 1 | 1↘ | 7 |
| 1 | 0 | 0 | 0↙ | 8 |
| 1 | 0 | 0 | 1 | 9 |

- As the external clock signal is applied at input A, output of MOD 2 counter changes at the negative edge of every clock pulse.
- Further MOD-5 counter changes from 0 to 4 ($Q_D$ $Q_C$ $Q_B$ = 000 to $Q_D$ $Q_C$ $Q_B$ = 100) only when the $Q_A$ output changes from 1 to 0 as shown in table 3.28.
- MOD-10 counter using IC 74C90 is as shown in Fig. 3.62.

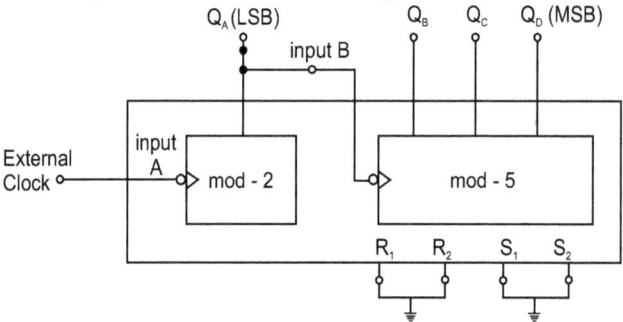

Fig. 3.62 : MOD-10 counter using 74C90

- As shown in Fig. 3.62, for normal operation the set and reset inputs are disabled by connected them to ground.

**Example 3.8 :** Design MOD-8 counter using 74C90

**Solution :**

- For MOD-8 counter, we first connect the IC 74C90 as MOD-10 counter as shown in Fig. 3.63.

- In MOD-8 counter, there are 8 distinct states and output varies from 0000 to 0111 i.e. when the state 1000 is required the counter must be resetted.
- For the state 1000, output $Q_D = 1$ Study of IC 7490. Therefore, $Q_D$ is to be connected to the reset inputs $R_1$ & $R_2$ and
- As soon as the circuit reaches to state 1000, $Q_D$ becomes 1 and immediately the counter is reset to 0000. Fig. 3.63 shows the MOD-8 counter.

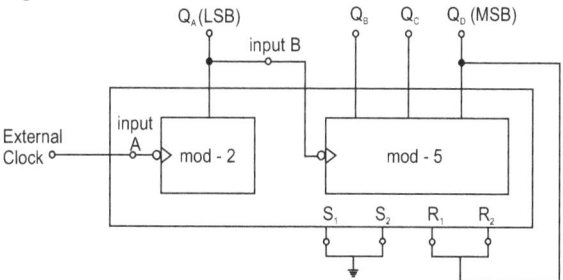

Fig. 3.63 : MOD - 8 counter using IC 74C90

**Example 3.9 :** Design divide by 94 counter using IC 74C90.

**Solution :**

- For divide by 94 or MOD-94 counter we first correct the two ICs 74C90 as MOD -100 counter as shown in Fig. 3.64.
- In MOD 94 counter 9 is the ten's digit & 4 is the one's digit. There are 94 distinct states and output varies from 0000 to 0010 ie. when the state 1001 0011 is reached the counter must be resetted.
- For the state 1001 0011, the outputs $Q_D$, $Q_A$ of ten's digit IC and the outputs $Q_B$, $Q_A$ of one's digit IC are 1.Therefore the respective outputs need to be AND ed together and connect them to the reset inputs of both ICs. It is shown in Fig. 3.64.

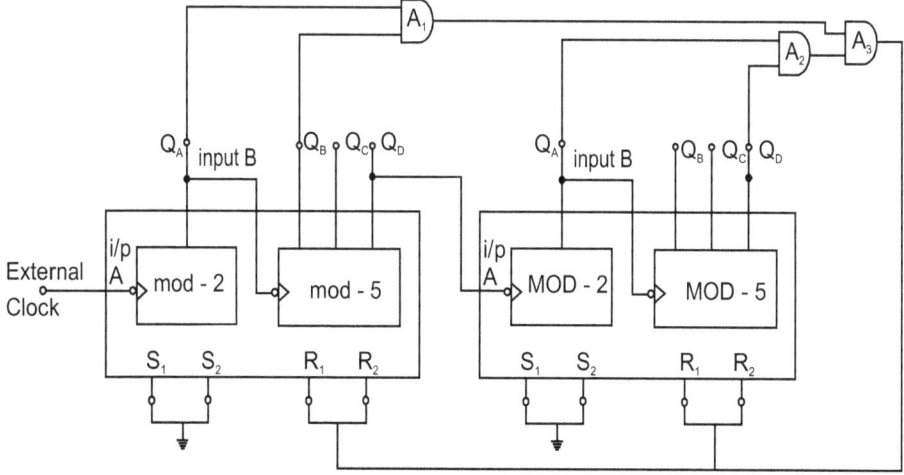

Fig. 3.64 : MOD 94 counter

- As shown in Fig. 3.64, when the circuit reaches to state 1001 00011, the outputs of all AND gates $A_1$, $A_2$, $A_4$ become 1 and as outputs of $A_4$ is connected to reset inputs of both ICs, immediately the counter is reset to 0000 0000.

**Example 3.10 :** In 7490, if Q output is connected to input A & pulses are applied at input B, find counter sequence.

**Solution :**

- The circuit is as shown in Fig. 3.65.
- When the clock pulses are applied at input B, the output of the MOD-5 counter changes from 0 to 4 ( from Q Q Q =000 to Q Q Q =100) with the application of successive pulses.
- As Q output is connected to input A, the output QA will make transition when Q changes from 1 to 0. The count sequence is as shown in table 3.29.

**Table 3.29**

| Flip-flop Outputs | | | | State of the counter |
|---|---|---|---|---|
| $Q_D$ | $Q_C$ | $Q_B$ | $Q_A$ | |
| 0 | 0 | 0 | 0 | 0 |
| 0 | 0 | 1 | 0 | 2 |
| 0 | 1 | 0 | 0 | 4 |
| 0 | 1 | 1 | 0 | 6 |
| 1 | 0 | 0 | 0 | 8 |
| 0 | 0 | 0 | 1 | 1 |
| 0 | 0 | 1 | 1 | 4 |
| 0 | 1 | 0 | 1 | 5 |
| 0 | 1 | 1 | 1 | 7 |
| 1 | 0 | 0 | 1 | 9 |
| 0 | 0 | 0 | 0 | 0 |

- Though the states of counter are not in straight binary form, the number of distinct states are ten, therefore it is also a MOD-10 counter.

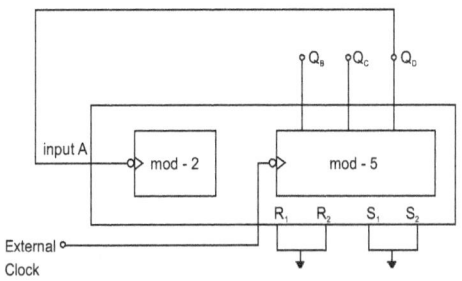

**Fig. 3.65**

## 3.24 SYNCHRONOUS COUNTER

- The Synchronous Counter, the external clock signal is connected to the clock input of every individual flip-flop within the counter so that all of the flip-flops are clocked together simultaneously (in parallel) at the same time giving a fixed time relationship.
- In the synchronous counter the individual output bits changing state at exactly the same time in response to the common clock signal with no ripple effect and therefore, no propagation delay.
- Synchronous Counters use edge-triggered flip-flops that change states on either the "positive-edge" (rising edge) or the "negative-edge" (falling edge) of the clock pulse on the control input resulting in one single count when the clock input changes state.
- Synchronous counters count on the rising-edge which is the low to high transition of the clock signal and asynchronous ripple counters count on the falling-edge which is the high to low transition of the clock signal.

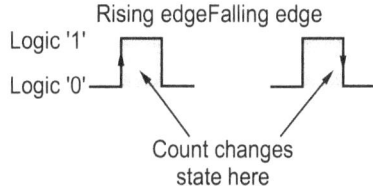

Fig. 3.66

- It may seem unusual that ripple counters use the falling-edge of the clock cycle to change state, but this makes it easier to link counters together because the most significant bit (MSB) of one counter can drive the clock input of the next.
- This works because the next bit must change state when the previous bit changes from high to low – the point at which a carry must occur to the next bit. Synchronous counters usually have a carry-out and a carry-in pin for linking counters together without introducing any propagation delays.

**Design Steps of Synchronous Counter**

- In synchronous counter all the flip flops are clocked simultaneously. Therefore it is faster in operation.
- It can be designed for any count sequence which need not be always straight binary.
- For the design of synchronous counter, first find out the number of flip flops required.
- Then prepare a table consisting of present state, next state and determine the flip flop inputs which must be present to obtain the next state using the excitation table of the flip flop.
- Prepare k-map for each flip flop input and obtain the simplified expressions from which complete the circuit diagram.

## 3.24.1 3-bit Synchronous Counter

**Example 3.11:** Design 4-bit synchronous counter using JK flip flop and explain.

**Solution:**
- We know that for 4 bit counter three flip flops are required.
- The table consisting of present state, next state and the required inputs of flip flop is as shown in table 3.30. Here $Q_2$, $Q_1$ and $Q_0$ represent the present state variables with $Q'_2$ $Q'_1$ and $Q'_0$ represent the next state variables.

**Table 3.30**

| Present state | | | Next state | | | Flip flip inputs | | | | | |
|---|---|---|---|---|---|---|---|---|---|---|---|
| $Q_2$ | $Q_1$ | $Q_0$ | $Q'_2$ | $Q'_1$ | $Q'_0$ | $J_2$ | $K_2$ | $J_1$ | $K_1$ | $J_0$ | $K_0$ |
| 0 | 0 | 0 | 0 | 0 | 1 | 0 | X | 0 | X | 1 | X |
| 0 | 0 | 1 | 0 | 1 | 0 | 0 | X | 1 | X | X | 1 |
| 0 | 1 | 0 | 0 | 1 | 1 | 0 | X | X | 0 | 1 | X |
| 0 | 1 | 1 | 1 | 0 | 0 | 1 | X | X | 1 | X | 1 |
| 1 | 0 | 0 | 1 | 0 | 1 | X | 0 | 0 | X | 1 | X |
| 1 | 0 | 1 | 1 | 1 | 0 | X | 0 | 1 | X | X | 1 |
| 1 | 1 | 0 | 1 | 1 | 1 | X | 0 | X | 0 | 1 | X |
| 1 | 1 | 1 | 0 | 0 | 0 | X | 1 | X | 1 | X | 1 |

- Observe the first row of the table 3.41. Present state is $Q_2$ $Q_1$ $Q_0$ = 0 0 0 and next state $Q'_2$ $Q'_1$ $Q'_0$ = 0 0 1. For flip flop 2, $Q_2 = Q'_2 = 0$. Therefore, from first row of excitation table of JK flip flop we get the $J_2$ $K_2$ input combination as 0 X.
- Similarly for flip flop 1 as $Q_1 = Q'_1 = 0$, the $J_1$ $K_1$ input combination is 0 X.
- For flip flop 0, present state = $Q_0$ = 0 while the next state = $Q'_0$ =1. Therefore from the second row of excitation table of JK flip flop we get $J_0$ $K_0$ input combination as 1 X.
- This completes the first row of the table 3.30. Proceeding in a similar manner, the remaining rows of the table are completed.
- Now we represent each individual input in a k map and obtain the simplified expressions.

K-map for $J_2$ ⇒

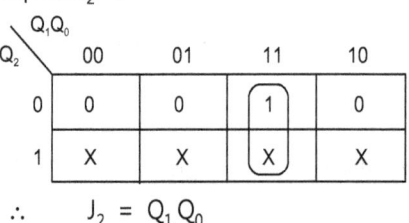

$$\therefore J_2 = Q_1 Q_0$$

K-map for $K_2$ ⇒

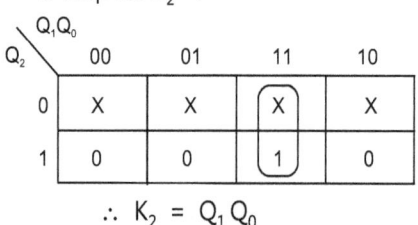

$$\therefore K_2 = Q_1 Q_0$$

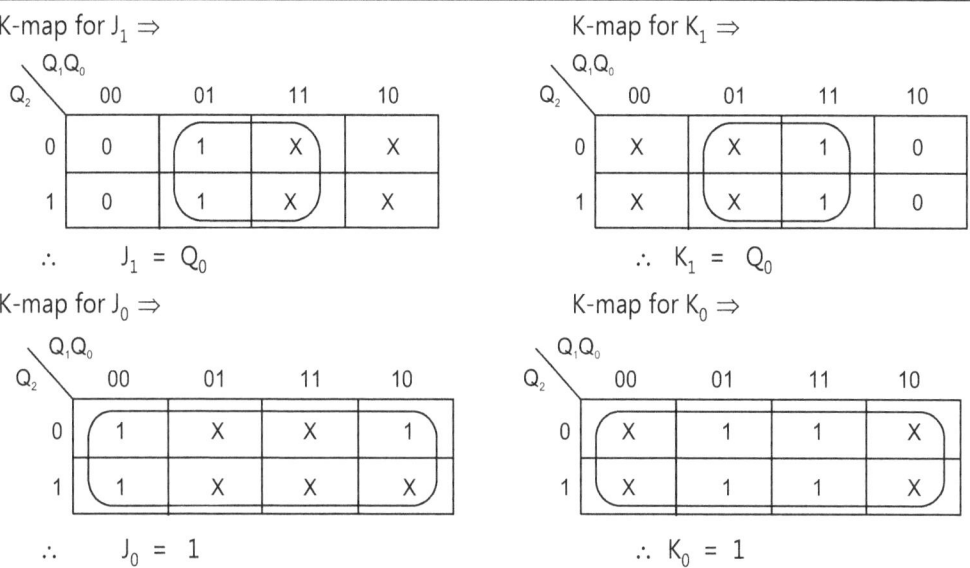

$$\therefore J_1 = Q_0$$
$$\therefore K_1 = Q_0$$
$$\therefore J_0 = 1$$
$$\therefore K_0 = 1$$

- Based on above expressions, the resulting circuit diagram is drawn in Fig. 3.67.

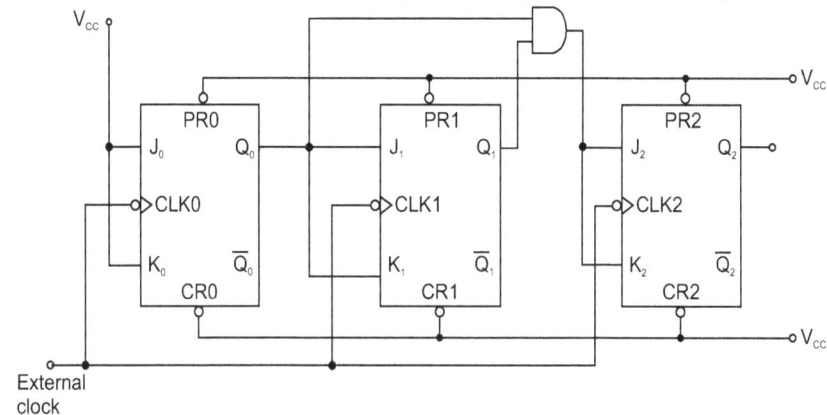

**Fig. 3.67 : 3-bit synchronous up counter**

## 3.24.2 4-bit Synchronous Counter

It can be seen that the external clock pulses (pulses to be counted) are fed directly to each J-K flip-flop in the counter chain and that both the J and K inputs are all tied together in toggle mode, but only in the first flip-flop, flip-flop A (LSB) are they connected HIGH, logic "1" allowing the flip-flop to toggle on every clock pulse. Then the synchronous counter follows a predetermined sequence of states in response to the common clock signal, advancing one state for each pulse.

The J and K inputs of flip-flop B are connected to the output "Q" of flip-flop A, but the J and K inputs of flip-flops C and D are driven from AND gates which are also supplied with signals from the input and output of the previous stage.

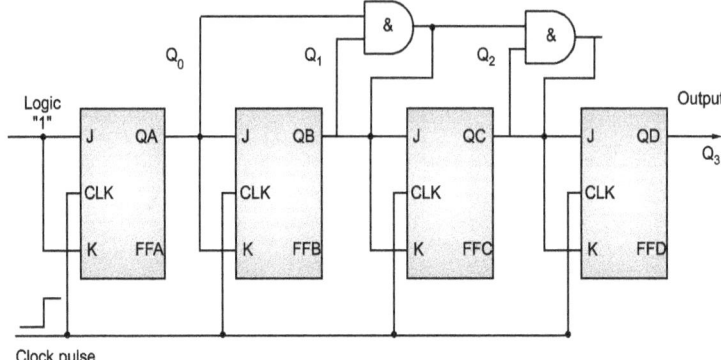

**Fig. 3.68**

- If we enable each J-K flip-flop to toggle based on whether or not all preceding flip-flop outputs (Q) are "HIGH" we can obtain the same counting sequence as with the asynchronous circuit but without the ripple effect, since each flip-flop in this circuit will be clocked at exactly the same time.

Then as there is no inherent propagation delay in synchronous counters, because all the counter stages are triggered in parallel at the same time, the maximum operating frequency of this type of frequency counter is much higher than that for a similar asynchronous counter circuit.

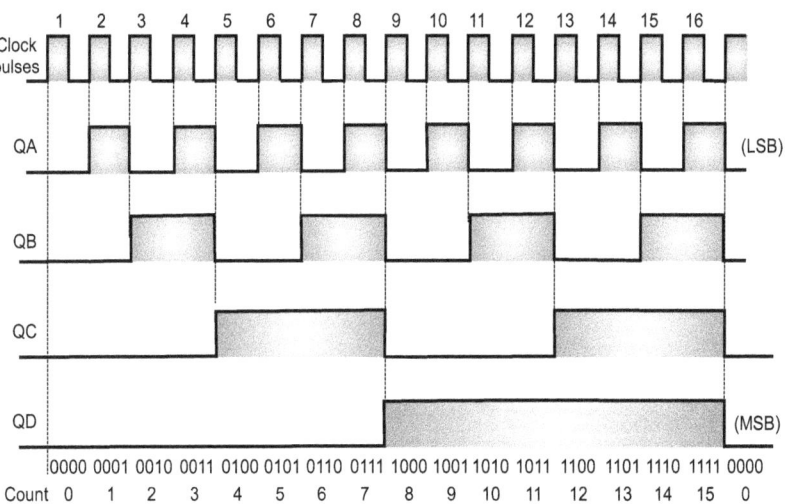

**Fig. 3.69 : 4-bit synchronous counter waveform timing diagram**

Because this 4-bit synchronous counter counts sequentially on every clock pulse the resulting outputs count upwards from 0 ( "0000" ) to 15 ( "1111" ). Therefore, this type of counter is also known as a 4-bit Synchronous Up Counter.

- As synchronous counters are formed by connecting flip-flops together and any number of flip-flops can be connected or "cascaded" together to form a "divide-by-n" binary counter, the modulo's or "MOD" number still applies as it does for asynchronous counters so a Decade counter or BCD counter with counts from 0 to 2n-1 can be built along with truncated sequences.

# 3.24.3 4-bit Up/Down Synchronous Counter

- We know that for 4 bit counter four flip-flop are required.
- The table consisting of present state, next state and the required inputs of flip-flop is as shown in table. Here $Q_2$, $Q_1$ and $Q_0$ are present state variable and $Q_2'$, $Q_1'$ and $Q_0'$ represents the next state variables.

**Table 3.31**

| Mode control M | Present state | | | Next state | | | Flip-flop inputs | | |
|---|---|---|---|---|---|---|---|---|---|
| | $Q_2$ | $Q_1$ | $Q_0$ | $Q_2'$ | $Q_1'$ | $Q_0'$ | $T_2$ | $T_1$ | $T_0$ |
| 0 | 0 | 0 | 0 | 0 | 0 | 1 | 0 | 0 | 1 |
| 0 | 0 | 0 | 1 | 0 | 1 | 0 | 0 | 1 | 1 |
| 0 | 0 | 1 | 0 | 0 | 1 | 1 | 0 | 0 | 1 |
| 0 | 0 | 1 | 1 | 1 | 0 | 0 | 1 | 1 | 1 |
| 0 | 1 | 0 | 0 | 1 | 0 | 1 | 0 | 0 | 1 |
| 0 | 1 | 0 | 1 | 1 | 1 | 0 | 0 | 1 | 1 |
| 0 | 1 | 1 | 0 | 1 | 1 | 1 | 0 | 0 | 1 |
| 0 | 1 | 1 | 1 | 0 | 0 | 0 | 1 | 1 | 1 |

**Table 3.32 : For down counting**

| Mode control M | Present state | | | Next state | | | Flip-flop inputs | | |
|---|---|---|---|---|---|---|---|---|---|
| | $Q_2$ | $Q_1$ | $Q_0$ | $Q_2'$ | $Q_1'$ | $Q_0'$ | $T_2$ | $T_1$ | $T_0$ |
| 1 | 0 | 0 | 0 | 1 | 1 | 1 | 1 | 1 | 1 |
| 1 | 0 | 0 | 1 | 0 | 0 | 0 | 0 | 0 | 1 |
| 1 | 0 | 1 | 0 | 0 | 0 | 1 | 0 | 1 | 1 |
| 1 | 0 | 1 | 1 | 0 | 1 | 0 | 0 | 0 | 1 |
| 1 | 1 | 0 | 0 | 0 | 1 | 1 | 1 | 1 | 1 |
| 1 | 1 | 0 | 1 | 1 | 0 | 0 | 0 | 0 | 1 |
| 1 | 1 | 1 | 0 | 1 | 0 | 1 | 0 | 1 | 1 |
| 1 | 1 | 1 | 1 | 1 | 1 | 0 | 0 | 0 | 1 |

- Now we represent each individual input in a Kmap and obtain the simplified expression.

$$T_2 = \overline{M}Q_1Q_0 + M\overline{Q_1}\overline{Q_0}$$

$$T_1 = \overline{M}Q_0 + M\overline{Q_0}$$

$$T_1 = 1$$

- So logic diagram for 4-bit synchronous up down counter is given below :

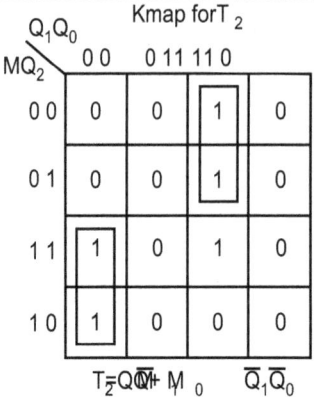
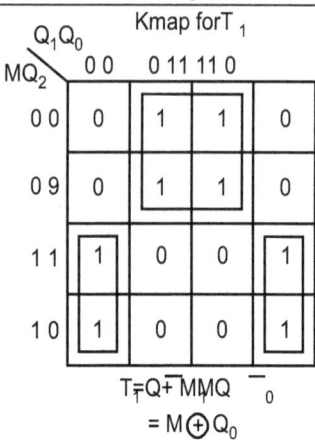
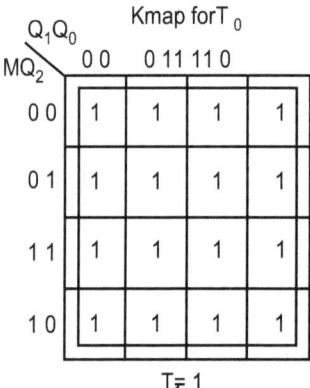

Fig. 3.70 : K-map for 4-bit synchronous up / down counter

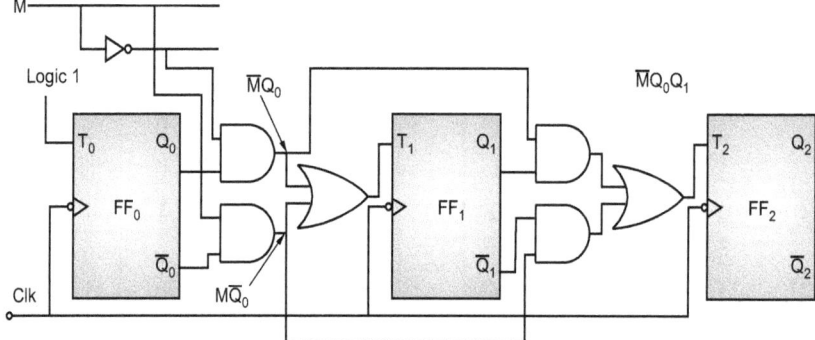

Fig. 3.71 : 4-bit synchronous up / down counter

## 3.24.4 Modulo N Synchronous Counter

### Decade 4-bit Synchronous Counter
- A 4-bit decade synchronous counter can also be built using synchronous binary counters to produce a count sequence from 0 to 9.
- A standard binary counter can be converted to a decade (decimal 10) counter with the aid of some additional logic to implement the desired state sequence.

- After reaching the count of "1001", the counter recycles back to "0000". We now have a decade or Modulo-10 counter.

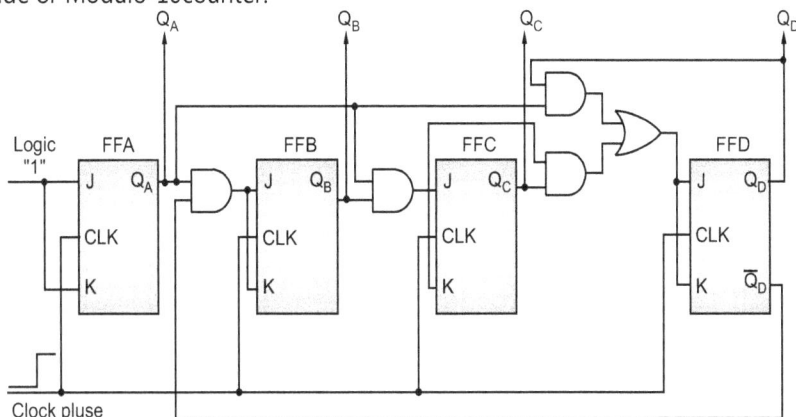

Fig. 3.72 : decade 4-bit synchronous counter

- The additional AND gates detect when the counting sequence reaches "1001", (Binary 10) and causes flip-flop FF4 to toggle on the next clock pulse. Flip-flop FF0 toggles on every clock pulse. Thus, the count is reset and starts over again at "0000" producing a synchronous decade counter.
- We could quite easily re-arrange the additional AND gates in the above counter circuit to produce other count numbers such as a Mod-12 counter which counts 12 states from "0000" to "1011" (0 to 11) and then repeats making them suitable for clocks, etc.

**Example 3.12 :** Design mod-12 synchronous counter using D flip flop.

**Solution :**
- For the implementation of MOD-12 counter four D flip flops are required.
- It is also a truncated counter. 0 to 11 are used states while 12 to 15 are unused states.
- Next state of unused state is unknown. Let it be don't care. Therefore the corresponding flip flop input is also don't care.
- The table 3.33 consist of present state, next state & the required input of flip flop.

Table 3.33

| Present state | | | | Next state | | | | Flip flop input | | | |
|---|---|---|---|---|---|---|---|---|---|---|---|
| $Q_4$ | $Q_2$ | $Q_1$ | $Q_0$ | $Q'_4$ | $Q'_2$ | $Q'_1$ | $Q'_0$ | $D_4$ | $D_2$ | $D_1$ | $D_0$ |
| 0 | 0 | 0 | 0 | 0 | 0 | 0 | 1 | 0 | 0 | 0 | 1 |
| 0 | 0 | 0 | 1 | 0 | 0 | 1 | 0 | 0 | 0 | 1 | 0 |
| 0 | 0 | 1 | 0 | 0 | 0 | 1 | 1 | 0 | 0 | 1 | 1 |
| 0 | 0 | 1 | 1 | 0 | 1 | 0 | 0 | 0 | 1 | 0 | 0 |
| 0 | 1 | 0 | 0 | 0 | 1 | 0 | 1 | 0 | 1 | 0 | 1 |
| 0 | 1 | 0 | 1 | 0 | 1 | 1 | 0 | 0 | 1 | 1 | 0 |
| 0 | 1 | 1 | 0 | 0 | 1 | 1 | 1 | 0 | 1 | 1 | 1 |
| 0 | 1 | 1 | 1 | 1 | 0 | 0 | 0 | 1 | 0 | 0 | 0 |
| 1 | 0 | 0 | 0 | 1 | 0 | 0 | 1 | 1 | 0 | 0 | 1 |

| 1 | 0 | 0 | 1 | 1 | 0 | 1 | 0 | 1 | 0 | 1 | 0 |
| 1 | 0 | 1 | 0 | 1 | 0 | 1 | 1 | 1 | 0 | 1 | 1 |
| 1 | 0 | 1 | 1 | 0 | 0 | 0 | 0 | 0 | 0 | 0 | 0 |

- Now we represent each individual input in a K-map & obtain the simplified expressions.

K-map for $D_4 \Rightarrow$

| $Q_3Q_2 \backslash Q_1Q_0$ | 00 | 01 | 11 | 10 |
|---|---|---|---|---|
| 00 | 0 | 0 | 0 | 0 |
| 01 | 0 | 0 | 1 | 0 |
| 11 | X | X | X | X |
| 10 | 1 | 1 | 0 | 1 |

$D_4 = Q_4 \bar{Q}_1 + Q_4 \bar{Q}_0 + Q_2 Q_1 Q_0$

K-map for $D_2 \Rightarrow$

| $Q_3Q_2 \backslash Q_1Q_0$ | 00 | 01 | 11 | 10 |
|---|---|---|---|---|
| 00 | 0 | 1 | 0 | 1 |
| 01 | 0 | 1 | 0 | 1 |
| 11 | X | X | X | X |
| 10 | 0 | 1 | 0 | 1 |

$D_1 = \bar{Q}_1 Q_0 + Q_1 \bar{Q}_0 = Q_1 \oplus Q_0$

K-map for $D_2 \Rightarrow$

| $Q_3Q_2 \backslash Q_1Q_0$ | 00 | 01 | 11 | 10 |
|---|---|---|---|---|
| 00 | 0 | 0 | 1 | 0 |
| 01 | 1 | 1 | 0 | 1 |
| 11 | X | X | X | X |
| 10 | 0 | 0 | 0 | 0 |

$D_2 = Q_2 \bar{Q}_1 + Q_2 \bar{Q}_0 + \bar{Q}_4 \bar{Q}_2 Q_1 Q_0$

K-map for $D_0 \Rightarrow$

| $Q_3Q_2 \backslash Q_1Q_0$ | 00 | 01 | 11 | 10 |
|---|---|---|---|---|
| 00 | 1 | 0 | 0 | 1 |
| 01 | 1 | 0 | 0 | 1 |
| 11 | X | X | X | X |
| 10 | 1 | 0 | 0 | 1 |

$D_0 = \bar{Q}_0$

- Based on above expressions the resulting circuit diagram is shown in Fig. 3.73.

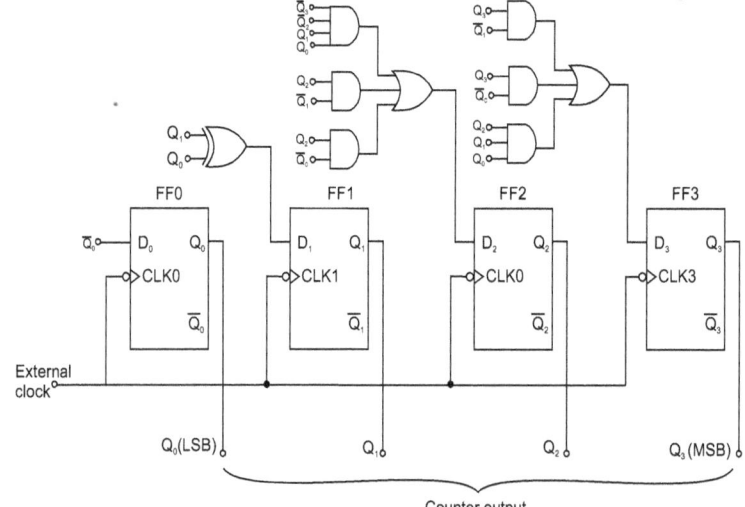

Fig. 3.73

### 3.24.5 BCD Synchronous Counter

**Example 3.13 :** Design and implement synchronous BCD counter using T flip flops.
**Solution :** From example, we know that a BCD counter requires four flip flops.
- BCD counter is a truncated counter. In BCD up counter 0 to 9 are used states while 11 to 15 are unused states. Next state of unused state is unknown. Let it be don't care. Therefore the corresponding flip flop input is also don't care. The table 3.34 consist of present state, next state & the required input of flip flop.

**Table 3.34**

| Present state | | | | Next state | | | | Flip flip input | | | |
|---|---|---|---|---|---|---|---|---|---|---|---|
| $Q_4$ | $Q_2$ | $Q_1$ | $Q_0$ | $Q'_4$ | $Q'_2$ | $Q'_1$ | $Q'_0$ | $T_4$ | $T_2$ | $T_1$ | $T_0$ |
| 0 | 0 | 0 | 0 | 0 | 0 | 0 | 1 | 0 | 0 | 0 | 1 |
| 0 | 0 | 0 | 1 | 0 | 0 | 1 | 0 | 0 | 0 | 1 | 1 |
| 0 | 0 | 1 | 0 | 0 | 0 | 1 | 1 | 0 | 0 | 0 | 1 |
| 0 | 0 | 1 | 1 | 0 | 1 | 0 | 0 | 0 | 1 | 1 | 1 |
| 0 | 1 | 0 | 0 | 0 | 1 | 0 | 1 | 0 | 0 | 0 | 1 |
| 0 | 1 | 0 | 1 | 0 | 1 | 1 | 0 | 0 | 0 | 1 | 1 |
| 0 | 1 | 1 | 0 | 0 | 1 | 1 | 1 | 0 | 0 | 0 | 1 |
| 0 | 1 | 1 | 1 | 1 | 0 | 0 | 0 | 1 | 1 | 1 | 1 |
| 1 | 0 | 0 | 0 | 1 | 0 | 0 | 1 | 0 | 0 | 0 | 1 |
| 1 | 0 | 0 | 1 | 0 | 0 | 0 | 0 | 1 | 0 | 0 | 1 |

- Now we represent each individual input in a K-map and obtain the simplified expressions.

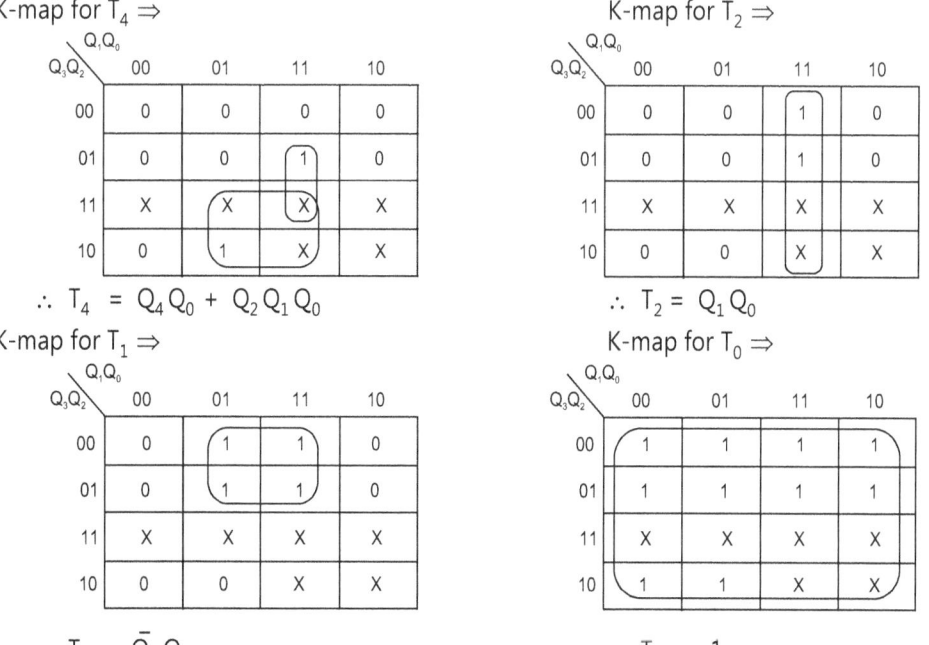

K-map for $T_4 \Rightarrow$

$\therefore T_4 = Q_4 Q_0 + Q_2 Q_1 Q_0$

K-map for $T_2 \Rightarrow$

$\therefore T_2 = Q_1 Q_0$

K-map for $T_1 \Rightarrow$

$\therefore T_1 = \overline{Q_4} Q_0$

K-map for $T_0 \Rightarrow$

$\therefore T_0 = 1$

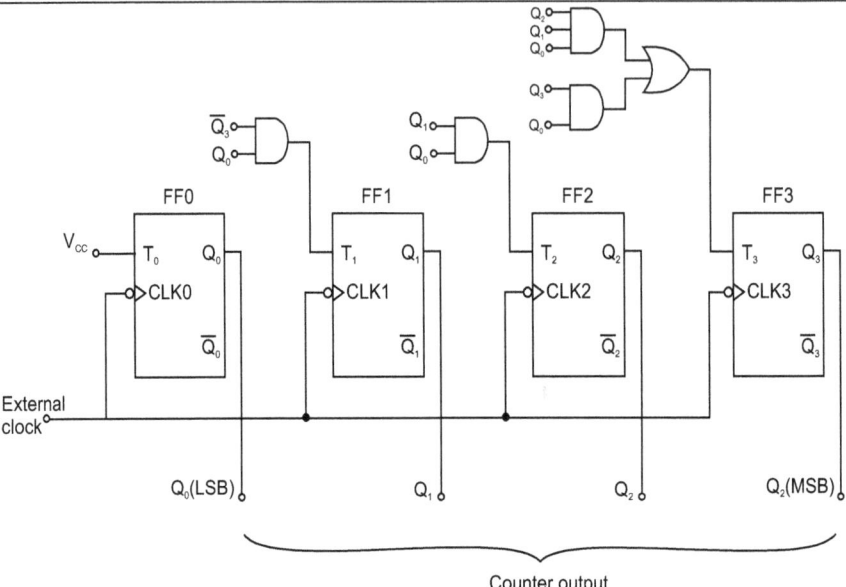

**Fig. 3.74**

Based on the above expressions the resulting circuit diagram is shown in Fig. 3.74

## 3.24.6 Ring Counter

- The shift register acts as ring counter, if the serial output is connected back to the serial input as shown in Fig. 3.75.

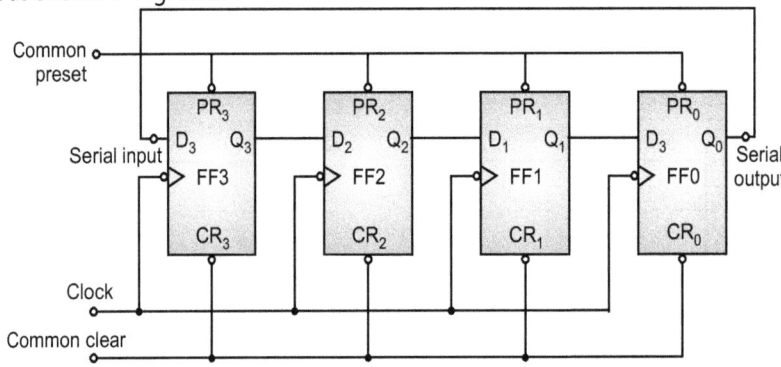

**Fig. 3.75 : Ring counter**

- Let us consider the initial state of the circuit as $Q_4 Q_2 Q_1 Q_0 = 1000$.
- The output of each flip flop after every clock pulse will be as shown in the table 3.35.

**Table 3.35**

| Clock pulse Number | $Q_4$ | $Q_2$ | $Q_1$ | $Q_0$ |
|---|---|---|---|---|
| Initially | 1 | 0 | 0 | 0 |
| 1 | 0 | 1 | 0 | 0 |
| 2 | 0 | 0 | 1 | 0 |
| 4 | 0 | 0 | 0 | 1 |
| 4 | 1 | 0 | 0 | 0 |

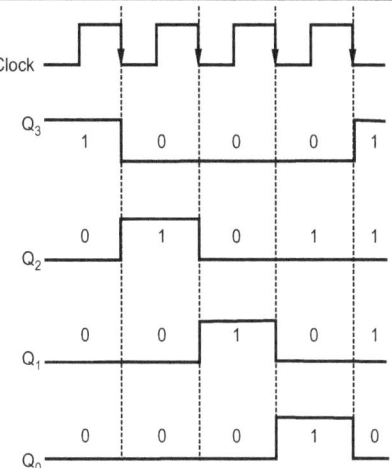

**Fig. 3.76 : Waveforms of ring counter**

- The n-bit ring counter counts n clock pulses, therefore the circuit shown in Fig. 3.76 counts four clock pulses.
- From table 3.35 it is clear that the number of distinct states in the operation of this counter is four. Therefore, it is a mod – 4 counter. In general n-bit ring counter is mod- n counter. The waveforms are as shown in Fig. 3.76.
- From the waveforms it is clear that, frequency of pulses obtained at any output is equal to frequency of clock pulses divided by four. Therefore this counter is a divide by four (÷ 4) counter.
- In general n-bit ring counter is a divide by n (÷ n) counter.
- The outputs $Q_4$, $Q_2$, $Q_1$ & $Q_0$ are sequential non-overlapping pulses which can be used to excite the stepper motor.

**Example 3.14 :** Explain ring counter design having initial state 01011.

- There are 5 bits in the given initial state, so we have to use 5 flip flops as shown in Fig. 3.36. When apply clear (CLR) pulse then flip flop will preset to 1 output and 4 and 2 are reset to 0 output.

$$Q_4\ Q_4\ Q_2\ Q_1 = 01011$$

Fig. 3.77 shows the arrangement of 5 bit ring counter.

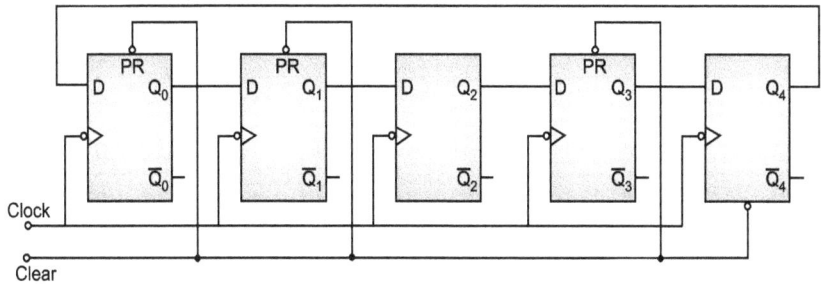

**Fig. 3.77**

### Table 3.36 : 5-bit ring counter table

| CLR | CLK | Q₀ | Q₁ | Q₂ | Q₄ | Q₄ |
|---|---|---|---|---|---|---|
| 0 | 1 | 1 | 1 | 0 | 1 | 0 |
| 1 | 1 | 0 | 1 | 1 | 0 | 1 |
| 1 | 1 | 1 | 0 | 1 | 1 | 0 |
| 1 | 1 | 0 | 1 | 0 | 1 | 1 |
| 1 | 1 | 1 | 0 | 1 | 0 | 1 |
| 1 | 1 | 1 | 1 | 0 | 1 | 0 |

## 3.24.7 Johnson Counter

- It is also known as twisted ring counter or moebius counter.

- The shift register acts as a Johnson counter if the $\bar{Q}_0$ output is connected to the serial input as shown in Fig. 3.78.

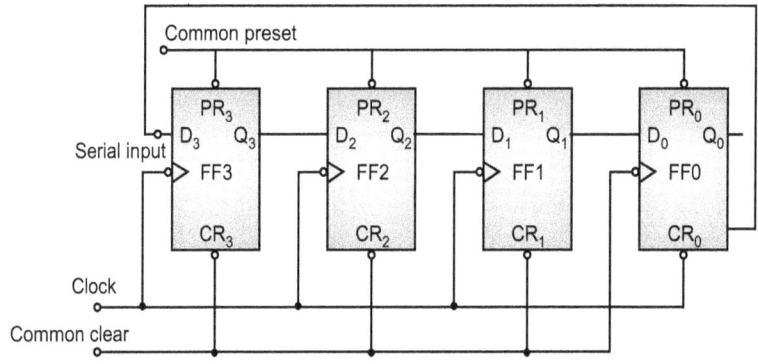

**Fig. 3.78 : Johnson counter**

- Initially all the flip flops are cleared using the common clear input ie. the initial state of the circuit is $Q_4 Q_2 Q_1 Q_0 = 0000$.
- The output of each flip flop after clock pulse will be as shown in the table 3.37.

### Table 3.37

| Clock pulse Number | Q₄ | Q₂ | Q₁ | Q₀ |
|---|---|---|---|---|
| Initially | 0 | 0 | 0 | 0 |
| 1 | 1 | 0 | 0 | 0 |
| 2 | 1 | 1 | 0 | 0 |
| 4 | 1 | 1 | 1 | 0 |
| 4 | 1 | 1 | 1 | 1 |

| 5 | 0 | 1 | 1 | 1 |
| 6 | 0 | 0 | 1 | 1 |
| 7 | 0 | 0 | 0 | 1 |
| 8 | 0 | 0 | 0 | 0 |

- From table 3.37 it is clear that the number of distinct states in the operation of this counter is eight. Therefore it is a mod 8 counter. In general, every n-bit Johnson counter is a mod 2n counter. The waveforms are as shown in Fig. 3.79.

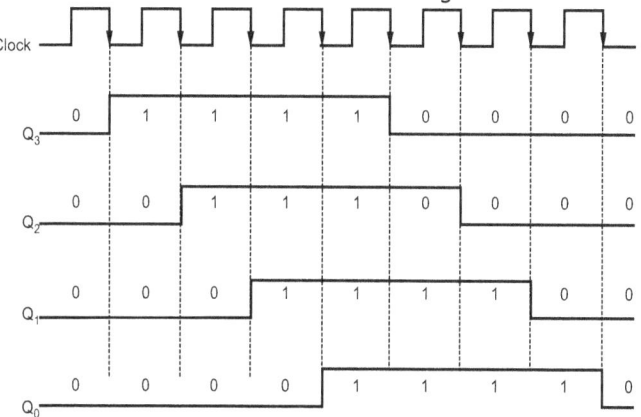

Fig. 3.79 : Waveforms of Johnson counter

- As shown in Fig. 3.79 square waveforms are obtained at each flip flop output.
- Also for completion of one cycle, each output requires eight clock pulses therefore it is a divide by 8 ($\div 8$) counter.
- In general, n-bit Johnson counter is a divide by 2n ($\div 2n$) counter.

**Example 3.15 :** Design Johnson counter using 2-bit shift register. Draw waveforms.

**Solution :**

- A 2-bit Johnson counter can be designed using two flip flops. When the output of FF0 is connected to the $D_1$ input of FF1 as shown in Fig. 3.80 we get the 2 bit Johnson counter.

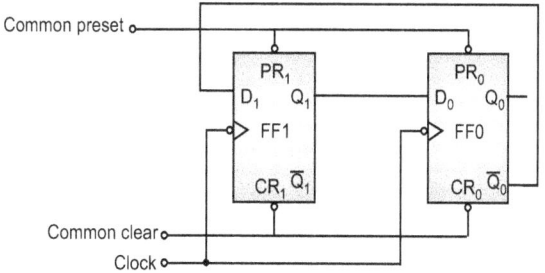

Fig. 3.80 : 2-bit Johnson counter

- The waveforms are shown in Fig. 3.81.

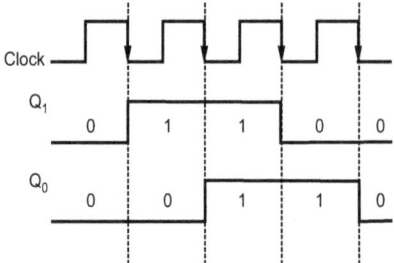

Fig. 3.81 : Waveforms of 2-bit Johnson counter

## 3.24.8 Unused States and Lock Out Condition

**Unused States :**

- In example 3.20, 1, 4, 4 and 7 states are known as unused states, while 0, 2, 5 & 6 states are known as used states. Upon application of successive clock pulses the counter output goes from 0 to 2, 2 to 5, 5 to 6, 6 to 0 and then the cycle repeats. Therefore these are known as used states.
- Counter output never goes to 1, 4, 4 and 7 states, therefore they are known as un used states.

**Lock Out Condition :**

- If the counter output goes to unused state and the next state of it is also another unused state & it repeats again & again so that counter never goes to used state, then that counter is said to be in lock out condition.
- In example 3.20 suppose the counter goes to unused state 1 & upon application of successive clock pulses it goes through a series of unused states as shown below.

$$1 \rightarrow 4 \rightarrow 4 \rightarrow 7$$
$$\uparrow _____|$$

Then it is said that the counter is in lock out condition.

- If the counter goes into lock out condition, then it becomes useless as it can not generate correct output.
- Lock out condition can be avoided by assigning next state as used state, for every unused state. So whenever counter finds itself in one of the unused state then upon application of clock pulse automatically it will come to the used state & will produce the correct output.

**Example 3.16 :** Using JK flip flops design a synchronous counter that has the following sequence.

$$\text{---------- } 0 \rightarrow 2 \rightarrow 5 \rightarrow 6 \rightarrow 0 \text{ --------}$$

Unused states 1, 4, 4, 7 must always go to 0 on the next clock pulse.

**Solution :**

- From the given sequence it is clear that number of states are 8. Therefore three JK flip flops are required to design the counter.

- The table consist of present state, next state and the required inputs of the flip.

Table 3.38

| Present state | | | Next state | | | Flip flop inputs | | | | | |
|---|---|---|---|---|---|---|---|---|---|---|---|
| $Q_2$ | $Q_1$ | $Q_0$ | $Q'_2$ | $Q'_1$ | $Q'_0$ | $J_2$ | $K_2$ | $J_1$ | $K_1$ | $J_0$ | $K_0$ |
| 0 | 0 | 0 | 0 | 1 | 0 | 0 | X | 1 | X | 0 | X |
| 0 | 0 | 1 | 0 | 0 | 0 | 0 | X | 0 | X | X | 1 |
| 0 | 1 | 0 | 1 | 0 | 1 | 1 | X | X | 1 | 1 | X |
| 0 | 1 | 1 | 0 | 0 | 0 | 0 | X | X | 1 | X | 1 |
| 1 | 0 | 0 | 0 | 0 | 0 | X | 1 | 0 | X | 0 | X |
| 1 | 0 | 1 | 1 | 1 | 0 | X | 0 | 1 | X | X | 1 |
| 1 | 1 | 0 | 0 | 0 | 0 | X | 1 | X | 1 | 0 | X |
| 1 | 1 | 1 | 0 | 0 | 0 | X | 1 | X | 1 | X | 1 |

- Now we represent each individual input in a k-map & obtain the simplified expressions.

K-map for $J_2 \Rightarrow$

| $Q_2$ \ $Q_1Q_0$ | 00 | 01 | 11 | 10 |
|---|---|---|---|---|
| 0 | 0 | 0 | 0 | 1 |
| 1 | X | X | X | X |

$\therefore J_2 = Q_1 \bar{Q_0}$

K-map for $J_1 \Rightarrow$

| $Q_2$ \ $Q_1Q_0$ | 00 | 01 | 11 | 10 |
|---|---|---|---|---|
| 0 | 1 | 0 | X | X |
| 1 | 0 | 1 | X | X |

$\therefore J_1 = \bar{Q_2}\bar{Q_0} + Q_2 Q_0 = \overline{Q_2 \oplus Q_0}$

K-map for $J_0 \Rightarrow$

| $Q_2$ \ $Q_1Q_0$ | 00 | 01 | 11 | 10 |
|---|---|---|---|---|
| 0 | 0 | X | X | 1 |
| 1 | 0 | X | X | X |

$\therefore J_0 = \bar{Q_2} Q_1$

K-map for $K_2 \Rightarrow$

| $Q_2$ \ $Q_1Q_0$ | 00 | 01 | 11 | 10 |
|---|---|---|---|---|
| 0 | X | X | X | X |
| 1 | 1 | 0 | 1 | 1 |

$\therefore K_2 = Q_1 + \bar{Q_0}$

K-map for $K_1 \Rightarrow$

| $Q_2$ \ $Q_1Q_0$ | 00 | 01 | 11 | 10 |
|---|---|---|---|---|
| 0 | X | X | 1 | 1 |
| 1 | X | X | 1 | 1 |

$\therefore K_1 = 1$

K-map for $K_0 \Rightarrow$

| $Q_2$ \ $Q_1Q_0$ | 00 | 01 | 11 | 10 |
|---|---|---|---|---|
| 0 | X | 1 | 1 | X |
| 1 | X | 1 | 1 | X |

$\therefore K_0 = 1$

Based on above expressions the resulting circuit diagram is shown in Fig. 3.82.

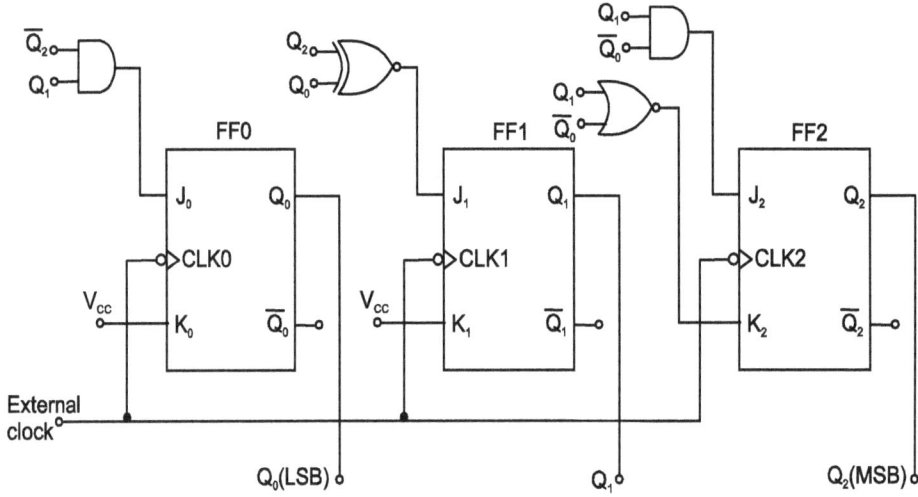

Fig. 3.82

## 3.25 DIFFERENCE BETWEEN SYNCHRONOUS AND ASYNCHRONOUS COUNTERS

| Sr. No. | Asynchronous counters | Synchronous counters |
|---|---|---|
| 1. | In this type of counter flip-flops are connected in such a way that output of first flip-flop drives the clock for the next flip-flop. | In this type there is no connection between output of first flip-flop and clock input of the next flip-flip. |
| 2. | Main drawback of these counters is their low speed as the clock is propagated through number of flip-flips before it reaches last flip-flop. | As clock is simultaneously given to all flip-flop there is no problem of propagation delay. Hence they are high speed counters and are preferred when number of flip-flop increase in the given design. |
| 4. | Logic circuit is very simple even for more number of states. | Design involves complex logic circuit as number of state increases. |
| 4. | As the flip-flops are not clocked simultaneously. | All the flip-flops are clocked simultaneously. |

## QUESTIONS

1. Explain sequential circuit?
2. Explain difference between combinational and sequential circuit.
3. Explain difference between Latch and Flip flop.
4. Explain different type of level triggered and edge triggered?
5. Explain what is meant by latch?
6. Explain SR latch using NAND gate?
7. Explain SR latch using NOR gate?
8. What is D latch?
9. Explain clocked SR flip flop?
10. Explain SR flip flop with preset and clear inputs?
11. What is race around condition? Explain with the help of timing diagram how it is removed in basic flip-flop circuit.
12. Compare race and race around condition. How will you avoid race around condition? Explain?
13. Draw neat diagram of JK flip-flop using SR flip-flop. Write the truth table and explain what happens if both the inputs are 1 ( J = K = 1).
14. How the race around condition is avoided?
15. What is the advantage of MS JK flip-flop ? Also explain working of MS JK flip-flop.
16. What do you mean by master slave JK flip-flop. Explain the advantages of this flip-flop draw suitable circuit diagram and timing diagram.
17. Explain D flip flop with preset and clear input?
18. Explain D flip flop with preset and clear input?
19. What is excitation table of flip flop?
20. Convert SR flip-flop (SR FF) into D FF.
21. Convert JK flip-flop into TFF. Show the truth table.
22. How will you convert JK flip-flop into T-flip-flop. Explain application of T flip-flop in sequential circuit.
23. Convert SR flip-flop into T-flip-flop.
24. Convert SR FF into JK FF.
25. Convert JK FF into D FF
26. Draw and explain 4-bit asynchronous up-counter. Also draw the necessary timing diagram.
27. What is Mod N counter

28. What is frequency division
29. What are drawbacks of ripple counter
30. Which IC is useful for Mod 10 counter
31. What are synchronous counters?
32. Design and implement 4-bit up/down synchronous counter using MS-JK flip-flop with its truth table. Also draw timing diagram.
33. Draw 4-bit asynchronous counter. Explain with timing diagram.
34. Draw and explain 4-bit binary up counting with this concept. Also draw the necessary timing diagram. Is there any frequency division concept in it? Comment on frequency generated at the output of each flip-flop.

# Unit - IV

# 8085 MICROPROCESSOR ARCHITECTURE AND MEMORY INTERFACING

## 4.1 INTRODUCTION

The Intel 8085 is an 8-bit microprocessor introduced by Intel in 1977. It was backward binary compatible with the more-famous Intel 8080 required less supporting hardware, thus allowing simpler and less expensive microcomputer systems to be built.

The "5" in the model number came from the fact that the 8085 requires only a +5-Volt (V) power supply by using depletion mode transistors, rather than requiring the +5 V, −5 V and +12 V supplies the 8080 needed. These processors were sometimes used in computers running the CP/M operating system.

The Intel 8085 required at least an external ROM and RAM and an 8 bit address latch (both latches combined in the Intel 8755 2K × 8 EPROM / 2 × 8 I/O, Intel 8155 256-byte RAM and 22 I/O and 14 bit programmable Timer/Counter) so cannot technically be called a microcontroller.

Both designs (8080/8085) were eclipsed for desktop computers by the compatible Zilog Z80, which took over most of the CP/M computer market as well as taking a share of the booming home computer market in the early-to-mid-1980s.

The 8085 had a long life as a controller. Once designed into such products as the DEC tape controller and the VT100 video terminal in the late 1970s, it served for new production throughout the life span of those products (generally longer than the product life of desktop computers).

Microprocessing unit is synonymous to central processing unit, CPU used in traditional computer. Microprocessor (MPU) acts as a device or a group of devices which do the following tasks.

- Communicate with peripherals devices
- Provide timing signal
- Direct data flow
- Perform computer tasks as specified by the instructions in memory

## 4.2 ARCHITECTURE OF 8085 MICROPROCESSOR

The 8085 microprocessor is an 8-bit general purpose microprocessor which is capable to address 64kB of memory. This processor has forty pins, requires +5 V single power supply and a 3MHz single phase clock.

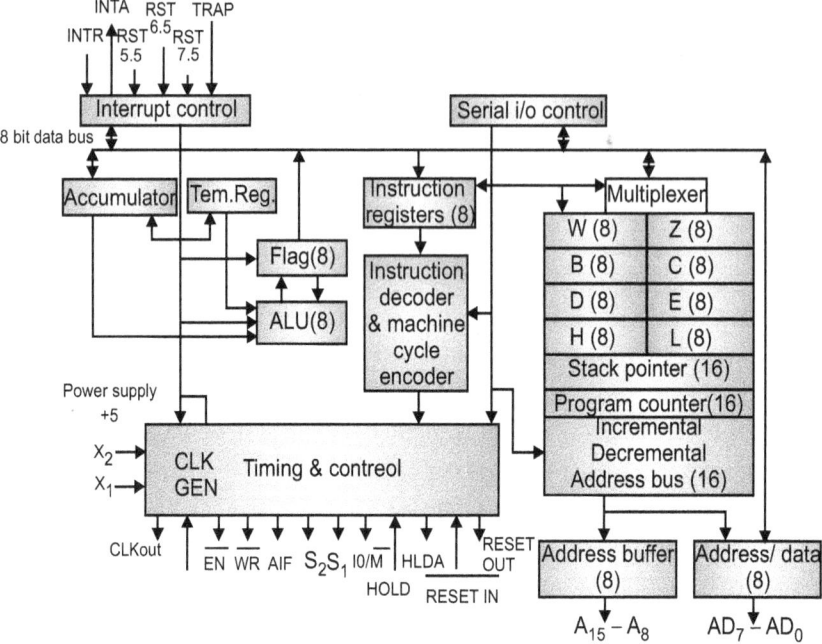

Fig. 4.1 : Architecture of 8085

## 4.2.1 ALU

The ALU perform the computing function of microprocessor. It includes the accumulator, temporary register, arithmetic & logic circuit & and five flags. Result is stored in accumulator & flags.

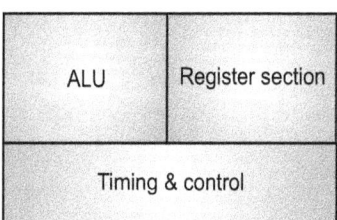

Fig. 4.2 : Arithmatic and logic unit

## 4.2.2 Accumulator

It is an 8-bit register that is part of ALU. This register is used to store 8-bit data & in performing arithmetic & logic operation. The result of operation is stored in accumulator.

## 4.2.3 Flags

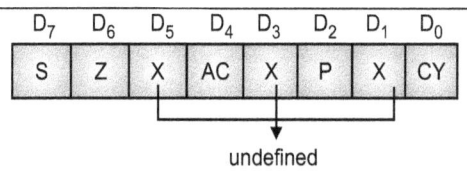

Fig. 4.3

The register are programmable. It can be used to store and transfer the data from the registers by using instruction. The ALU includes five flip-flops that are set & reset acc. to data condition in accumulator and other registers.

- **S (Sign) Flag** : After the execution of an arithmetic operation, if bit $D_7$ of the result is 1, the sign flag is set. It is used to signed number. In a given byte, if $D_7$ is 1 means negative number. If it is zero means it is a positive number.
- **Z (Zero) Flag** : The zero flag is set if ALU operation result is 0.
- **AC (Auxiliary Carry) Flag** : In arithmetic operation, when carry is generated by digit D3 and passed on to digit $D_4$, the AC flag is set. This flag is used only internally BCD operation.
- **P (Parity) Flag** : After arithmetic or logic operation, if result has even no. of 1s, the flag is set. If it has odd no. of 1s, flag is reset.
- **C (Carry) Flag** : If arithmetic operation result in a carry, the carry flag is set, otherwise it is reset.

## 4.2.4 Register Section

It is a basically storage device & transfer data from registers by using instruction.

- **Stack Pointer (SP)** : The stack pointer is also a 16-bit register which is used as a memory pointer. It points to a memory location in Read/Write memory known as stack. In between execution of program, some time data to be stored in stack. The beginning of the stack is defined by loading a 16-bit address in the stack pointer.
- **Program Counter (PC)** : This 16-bit register deals with fourth operation to sequence the execution of instruction. This register is also a memory pointer. Memory location have 16-bit address. It is used to store the execution address. The function of the program counter is to point to memory address from which next bytes is to be fetched.
- **Storage Registers** : These registers store 8-bit data during a program execution. These register are identified as B,C,D,E,H,L. They can be combined as register pair BC, DE and HL to perform some 16 bit operations.

## 4.2.5 Timing and Control Section

This unit is responsible to synchronize Microprocessor operation as per the clock pulse and to generate the control signals which are necessary for smooth communication between Microprocessor and peripherals devices. The RD bar and WR bar signal are syncronous pulses which indicates whether data is available on the data bus or not. The control unit is responsible to control the flow of data between microprocessor, memory and peripheral devices.

## 4.3 PIN DIAGRAM OF 8085 MICROPROCESSOR

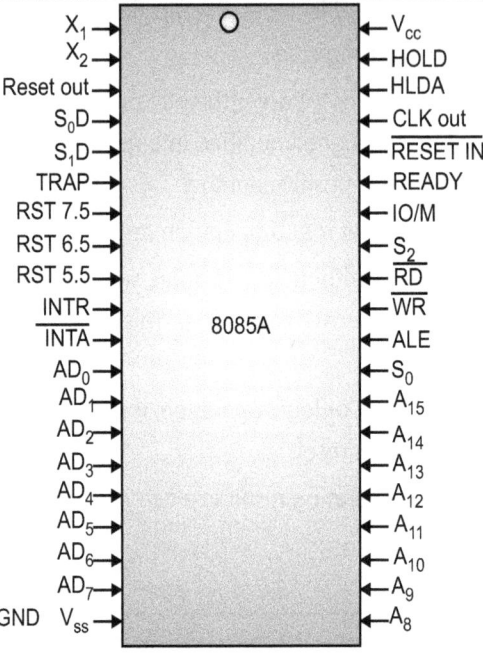

Fig. 4.4 : Pin diagram

All the signal can be classified into six groups

Table 4.1

| S.N. | Group | Description |
|---|---|---|
| 1 | Address bus | • The 8085 microprocessor has 8 signal line, $A_{15}$ - $A_8$ which are unidirectional & used as a high order address bus. |
| 2 | Data bus | • The signal line AD7 - AD0 are bidirectional for dual purpose. They are used as low order address bus as well as data bus. |
| 3 | Control signal and Status signal | Control Signal<br>• **RD Bar :** It is a read control signal (active low). It is active then memory read the data.<br>• **WR Bar :** It is write control signal (active low). It is active when written into selected memory.<br>Status signal<br>• **ALU (Address Latch Enable) :** When ALU is high. 8085 microprocessor is use address bus. When ALU is low. 8085 microprocessor is use data bus.<br>• **IO/M Bar :** This is a status signal used to differentiate between i/o and memory operation. When it is high, it |

| | | |
|---|---|---|
| | | indicate an i/o operation and low, it indicate memory operation.<br>• **$S_1$ and $S_0$:** These status signal, similar to i/o and memory bar, can identify various operation, but they are rarely used in small system. |
| 4 | Power supply and frequency signal | • **$V_{cc}$ :** +5v power supply.<br>• **$V_{ss}$ :** ground reference.<br>• **X, X :** A crystal is connected at these two pins. The frequency is internally divided by two operate system at 3-MHz, the crystal should have a frequency of 6-MHz.<br>• **CLK Out :** This signal can be used as the system clock for other devices. |
| 5 | Externally initiated signal | • **INTR(i/p) :** Interrupt request.<br>• **INTA Bar (o/p) :** It is used as acknowledge interrupt.<br>• **TRAP(i/p) :** This is non maskable interrupt and has highest priority.<br>• **HOLD(i/p) :** It is used to hold the executing program.<br>• **HLDA(o/p) :** Hold acknowledge.<br>• **READY(i/p) :** This signal is used to delay the microprocessor read or write cycle until a slow responding peripheral is ready to accept or send data.<br>• **RESET IN Bar :** When the signal on this pin goes low, the program counter is set to zero, the bus are tri-stated, & MPU is reset.<br>• **RESET OUT :** This signal indicate that MPU is being reset. The signal can be used to reset other devices.<br>• **RST 7.5, RST 6.5, RST 5.5 (Request Interrupt) :** It is used to transfer the program control to specific memory location. They have higher priority than INTR interrupt. |
| 6 | Serial I/O ports | • The 8085 microprocessor has two signals to implement the serial transmission serial input data and serial output data. |

## 4.4 MICROPROCESSOR COMMUNICATION AND BUS TIMING

There are three buses in Microprocessor:
1. Address Bus
2. Data Bus
3. Control Bus

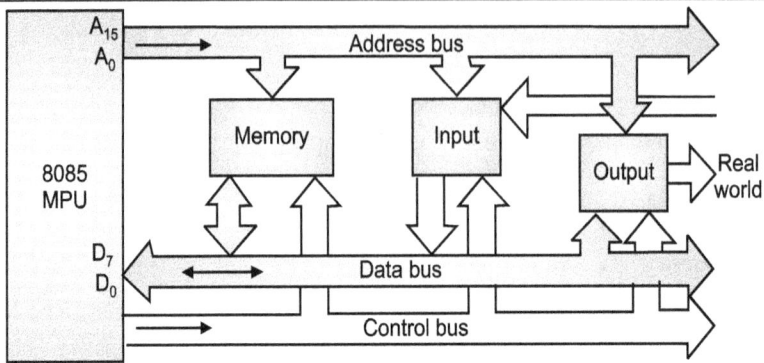

Fig. 4.5

**1. Address Bus :** Microprocessor has 16 bit address bus. The bus over which the CPU sends out the address of the memory location is known as Address bus. The address bus carries the address of memory location to be written or to be read from.

The address bus is unidirectional. It means bits flowing occurs only in one direction, only from microprocessor to peripheral devices.

We can find that how much memory location it can using the formula 2^N. where N is the number of bits used for address lines.

here, $2^{16}$ = 65536bytes or 64Kb

So we can say that it can access upto 64 Kb memory location.

**Example 4.1 :** If a processor has 4 GB memory then how many address lines are required to access this memory?

**Solution :**
$$4GB = 4 \times 1GB$$
$$4 = 2^2$$
$$1GB = 2^{30}$$
$$4GB = 2^2 \times 2^{30} = 2^{32}$$

So 32 address lines are required to access the 4 GB memory.

**2. Data Bus :** 8085 Microprocessor has 8 bit data bus. So it can be used to carry the 8 bit data starting from 00000000H(00H) to 11111111H(FFH). Here 'H' tells the Hexadecimal Number. It is bidirectional. These lines are used for data flowing in both direction means data can be transferred or can be received through these lines. The data bus also connects the I/O ports and CPU. The largest number that can appear on the data bus is 11111111.

It has 8 parallel lines of data bus. So it can access upto $2^8$ = 256 data bus lines.

**3. Control Bus :** The control bus is used for sending control signals to the memory and I/O devices. The CPU sends control signal on the control bus to enable the outputs of addressed memory devices or I/O port devices.

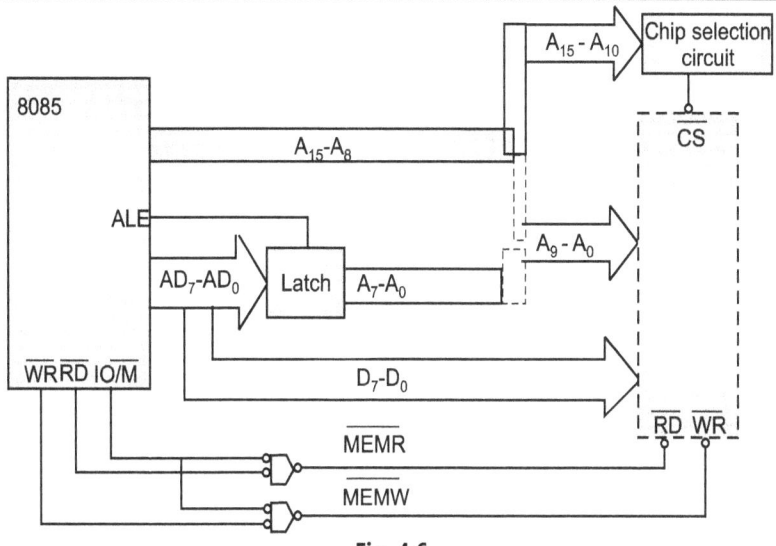

**Fig. 4.6**

The Intel 8085 is an 8-bit microprocessor. Its data bus is 8-bit wide and hence, 8 bits of data can be transmitted in parallel from or to the microprocessor. The Intel 8085 requires a 16-bits. The 8 most significant bits of the address are transmitted by the address bus, ($A_8$ to $A_{15}$). The 8 least significant bits of the address are transmitted by address/data bus, ($AD_0$ to $AD_7$). The address/data bus transmits data and address at different moments. At a particular moment it transmits either data or address. Thus the Address bus operates in time shared mode. This technique is known as multiplexing. First of all 16-bit memory address is transmitted by the microprocessor the 8 MSBs of the address on the A-bus and the 8 LSBs of the address on Address bus. Thus the effective width of the address is latched so that the complete 16-bit address remains available for further operation. The 8-bit AD-bus now becomes free, and it is available for data transmission $2^{16}$ (i.e. 64K, where 1K = 1024 bytes) memory location can be addressed directly by Intel 8085. Each memory location contains 1 byte of data.

## 4.5 DIFFERENCE BETWEEN 8085 AND 8086

**Size :** 8085 is 8 bit microprocessor whereas 8086 is 16 bit microprocessor.

**Address Bus :** 8085 has 16 bit address bus and 8086 has 20 bit addres bus.

**Memory :** 8085 can access upto 216 = 64 Kb of memory whereas 8086 can access upto 220 = 1 MB of memory.

**Instruction Queue :** 8085 doesn't have an instruction queue whereas 8086 has instruction queue.

**Pipelining:** 8085 does not support pipelined architechture whereas 8086 supports pipelined architechture.

**Multiprocessing Support :** 8085 does not support multiprocessing support whereas 8086 supports.

**Input /Output :** 8085 can address 28 = 256 I/O's and 8086 can access 216 = 65,536 Input /Output devices.

**Airthmetic Support:** 8085 only supports integer and decimal whereas 8086 supports integer, decimal and ASCII arithmetic.

**Multiplication and Division :** 8085 doesn't support whereas 8086 supports.

**Operating Modes:** 8085 supports only single operating mode whereas 8086 operates in two modes.

**External Hardware :** 8085 requires less external hardware whereas 8086 requires more external hardware.

**Cost :** The cost of 8085 is low and 8086 is high.

**Memory Segmentation :** In 8085, memory space is not segmented but in 8086, memory space is segmented.

## 4.6 TIMING DIAGRAM

Timing diagram is the display of initiation of read/write and transfer of data operations under the control of 3-status signals IO / M , S1, and S0. As the heartbeat is required for the survival of the human being, the CLK is required for the proper operation of different sections of the microprocessors. All actions in the microprocessor is controlled by either leading or trailing edge of the clock. If I ask a man to bring 6-bags of wheat, each weighing 100 kg, he may take 6-times to perform this task in going and bringing it. A stronger man might perform the same task in 3- times only. Thus, it depends on the strength of the man to finish the job quickly or slowly. Here, we can assume both weaker and strong men as machine. The weaker man has taken 6-machine cycle(6-times going and coming with one bag each time) to execute the job where as the stronger man has taken only 3-machine cycle for the same job. Similarly, a machine may execute one instruction in as many as 3-machine cycles while the other machine can take only one machine cycle to execute the same instruction. Thus, the machine that has taken only one machine cycle is efficient than the one taking 3-machine cycle. Each machine cycle is composed of many clock cycle. Since, the data and instructions, both are stored in the memory, the µP performs fetch operation to read the instruction or data and then execute the instruction. The µP in doing so may take several cycles to perform fetch and execute operation. The 3-status signals : IO / M , S1, and S0 are generated at the beginning of each machine cycle. The unique combination of these 3-statussignals identify read or write operation and remain valid for the duration of the cycle. Table shows details of the unique combination of these status signals to identify different machine cycles. Thus, time taken by any µP to execute one instruction is calculated in terms of the clock period.

The execution of instruction always requires read and writes operations to transfer data to or from the µP and memory or I/O devices. Each read/ write operation constitutes one machine cycle (MC1) as indicated in Fig. 4.7 (a). Each machine cycle consists of many clock periods/

cycles, called T-states. The heartbeat of the microprocessor is the clock period. Each and every operation inside the microprocessor is under the control of the clock cycle. The clock signal determines the time taken by the microprocessor to execute any instruction. The clock cycle shown in Fig. 4.7 (b) has two edges. State is defined as the time interval between 2-trailing or leading edges of the clock. Machine cycle is the time required to transfer data to or from memory or I/O devices.

**Table 4.2 : Machine cycle status and control signals**

| Machine cycle | Status | | | Controls | | |
|---|---|---|---|---|---|---|
| | $\overline{IO/M}$ | $S_1$ | $S_0$ | $\overline{RD}$ | $\overline{WR}$ | $\overline{INTA}$ |
| Opcode Fetch (OF) | 0 | 1 | 1 | 0 | 1 | 1 |
| Memory Read | 0 | 1 | 0 | 0 | 1 | 1 |
| Memory Write | 0 | 0 | 1 | 1 | 0 | 1 |
| I/O Read (I/OR) | 1 | 1 | 0 | 0 | 1 | 1 |
| I/O Write (I/OW) | 1 | 0 | 1 | 1 | 0 | 1 |
| Acknowledge of INTR (INTA) | 1 | 1 | 1 | 1 | 1 | 0 |
| BUS Idle (BI) : DAD | 0 | 1 | 0 | 1 | 1 | 1 |
| ACK of RST, TRAP | 1 | 1 | 1 | 1 | 1 | 1 |
| HALT | Z | 0 | 0 | Z | Z | 1 |
| HOLD | Z | X | X | Z | Z | 1 |

X Unspecified, and Z High impedance state

## 4.6.1 Op-Code Fetch Machine Cycle / Fetch Operation

In fetch operation the microprocessor gets the 1st byte of the instruction, which is operation code (opcode), from the memory. The program counter keeps the track of address of the next instruction to be executed. In the beginning of the fetch cycle the content of the program counter is sent to the memory. This takes one clock cycle. The memory first reads the opcode. This operation also takes one clock cycle. Then the memory sends the opcode to the microprocessor, which takes one clock period. The total time for fetch operation is the time required for fetching an opcode from the memory. This time is called fetch cycle. Having received the address from the microprocessor the memory takes two clock cycles to respond memory is slow, it may take more time. In that case the microprocessor has to wait for some time till it receives the opcode from the memory. The time for which the microprocessor waits is called wait cycle. Most of the microprocessor have provision for wait cycles to cope with slow memory.

The 8085 microprocessor is designed to execute 74 different instruction types. Each instruction has two parts: operation code, an operand. The op-code is a command such as add and the operand is the object to be operated on, such as a byte or the content of register. Some instruction is 1-bytes instruction and some are multi bytes instruction.

Each instruction of the processor has one byte opcode.

The opcodes are stored in memory. So, the processor executes the opcode fetch machine cycle to fetch the opcode from memory.

Hence, every instruction starts with opcode fetch machine cycle.

The time taken by the processor to execute the opcode fetch cycle is 4T.

In this time, the first, 3 T-states are used for fetching the opcode from memory and the remaining T-states are used for internal operations by the processor.

To execute instruction, the 8085 needs to perform various operations such as memory read/write and I/O read/write. However there is no direct relationship between the number of the bytes of an instruction and the number of the operation s 8085 signals and to perform.

Basically the micro-processor have three major function

- Memory read and write
- I/O read and write
- Request acknowledge

These function are further divided to various operation

**Op-Code Fetch**

The first operation in any instruction is op-code fetch. The micro-processor needs to get this machine code from the memory register where it is stored before the micro-processor can begin execute the instruction

This op-code fetch cycle is called M1 cycle and has four t-state . this 8085 uses the first three states T1-T3 to fetch the code and T4 to decode and execute the op-code .in the 8085 the instruction set some instruction have six T-state .

## 4.6.2 Execute Operation

The opcode fetched from the memory goes to the data register, DR (data/address buffer in Intel 8085) and then to instruction register, IR. From the instruction register it goes to the decoder circuitry is within the microprocessor. After the instruction is decoded, execution begins. If the operand is in the general purpose registers, execution is immediately performed. The time taken in decoding and the address of the data, some read cycles are also necessary to receive the data from the memory. These read cycle are similar to opcode fetch cycle. The fetch quantities in these cycles are address or data. Fig. 4.7 (a) and Fig. 4.7 (b) shows an instruction and fetch cycle respectively.

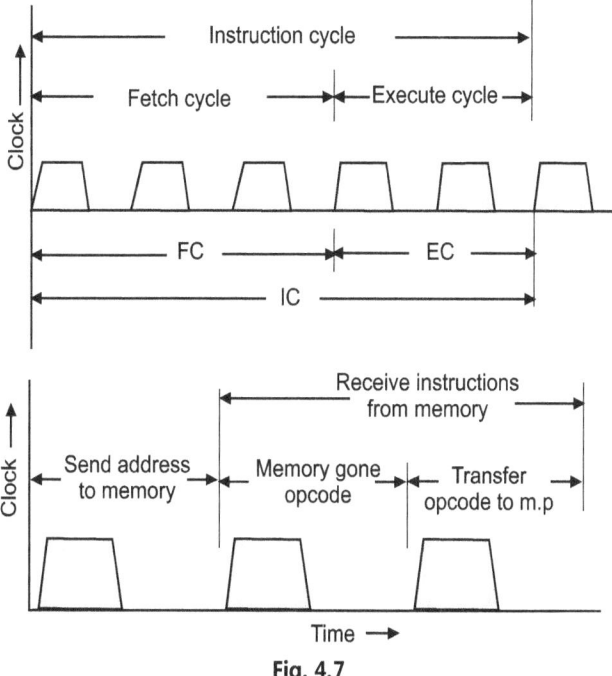

Fig. 4.7

## 4.6.3 Machine Cycle

An instruction cycle consists of one or more machine cycles as shown in Fig. 4.8. This figure is for MVI instruction. A machine cycle consists of a number of clock cycles. One clock cycle is known as state.

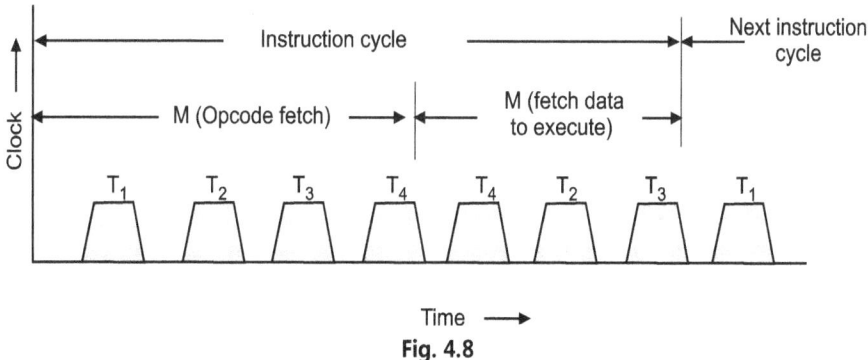

Fig. 4.8

## 4.6.4 Processor Cycle

The function of the microprocessor is divided into fetch and execute cycle of any instruction of a program. The program is nothing but number of instructions stored in the memory in sequence. In the normal process of operation, the microprocessor fetches (receives or reads) and executes one instruction at a time in the sequence until it executes the halt (HLT) instruction. Thus, an instruction cycle is defined as the time required to fetch and execute an instruction. For executing any program, basically 2-steps are followed sequentially with the help of clocks.

## Fetch and Execute :

The time taken by the µP in performing the fetch and execute operations are called fetch and execute cycle. Thus, sum of the fetch and execute cycle is called the instruction cycle.

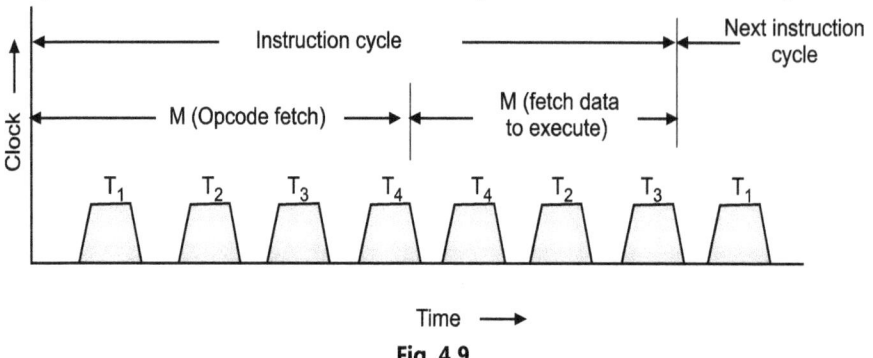

Fig. 4.9

**Instruction Cycle (IC) = Fetch Cycle (FC) + Execute Cycle (EC)**

Timing Diagram is a graphical representation. It represents the execution time taken by each instruction in a graphical format. The execution time is represented in T-states.

## Instruction Cycle:

The time required to execute an instruction is called instruction cycle.

## Machine Cycle:

The time required to access the memory or input/output devices is called machine cycle.

## T-State:

- The machine cycle and instruction cycle takes multiple clock periods.
- A portion of an operation carried out in one system clock period is called as T-state.

## 4.7 MACHINE CYCLES OF 8085

The 8085 microprocessor has 5 (seven) basic machine cycles. They are

1. Opcode fetch cycle (4 T)
2. Memory read cycle (3 T)
3. Memory write cycle (3 T)
4. I/O read cycle (3 T)
5. I/O write cycle (3 T)

Each instruction of the 8085 processor consists of one to five machine cycles, i.e., when the 8085 processor executes an instruction, it will execute some of the machine cycles in a specific order.

The processor takes a definite time to execute the machine cycles. The time taken by the processor to execute a machine cycle is expressed in T-states.

One T-state is equal to the time period of the internal clock signal of the processor.

The T-state starts at the falling edge of a clock.

The timing and control unit generates timing signals for the execution of instruction and control of peripheral devices. The organization of a microprocessor and types of registers differ from processor to processor. The timing used for the execution of instructions and control of peripherals are different for different microprocessors. The selection of a suitable microprocessor for a particular application is a tough task for an engineer. The knowledge of the organization and timing and control system helps an engineer in the selection of a microprocessor. The design and cost of a processor also depends on the timing structure and register organization.

## 4.7.1 Memory Read Machine Cycle

Memory Read Machine cycle Execution of byte is or 3 byte instruction because in a 1 byte instruction the machine code is an op code; therefor the operation is always op code fetch.

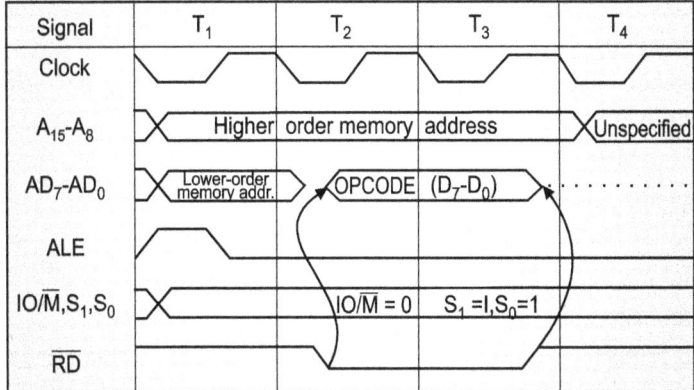

Fig. 4.10 : Memory Read Machine Cycle

The machine codes 0011 1110 (3EH) and 0011 0010 (32H) are stored in memory locations 2000H , respectively , as shown below.the first machine code 3 EH represent the op code to load a data byte in the accumulator and the second code 32H represent the data bytes to be loaded in the accumulator illustrate the bus timing as these machine codes are executed. Calculated the timer required to execute. Calculated the time require to execute the op code fetch and the memory read cycle and the entire instruction cycle if the clock frequency is 2MHz.

This instruction have two steps. First step is op code fetch second is data fetch. First step take 4 cycle and second take 3 cycle. Second cycle is memory read cycle.

- The first machine cycle M1 (opcode fetch) is identical in bus timing with the machine cycle. At T1 micro processor identifies that it is an op code fetch cycle by placing 011 on the status signals ( IO/M bar=0, S1=1, S0=1) it places the memory address 2000H from the program counter on the address bus 20H on A15 to A8 and 00H on AD7 to AD0 and increments the program counter to 2001H to point to the next machine code. The ALE signal goes high during T1 which is used to latch the low-order address 00H from the bus AD7 to AD0. At T2, the 8085 asserts the RD bar control signal, which enables the memory, and the memory places the byte 3EH from location 2000H on the data bus. Then the 8085 places the op code in the instruction register and disable the RD bar signal. The fetch cycle is completed in state T3. During T4 the 8085 decodes the op code and finds out that the second bytes needs to read. After the T3 state the contents of the bus A15 to A8 are unknown and the data bus AD7 to AD0 goes into high impedance.

- After completion of the op code fetch cycle the 8085 places the address 2001H on the address bus and increments the program counter to the next address 2002H. the second machine cycle M2 is identified as the Memory read cycle (IO/M bar=0, S1=1 and S2=0) and the ALE is asserted at T2 the RD bar signal become active and enable the memory chip.
- At the rising edge of T2 the 8085 activates the data bus as as input bus, memory places the data bytes 32H on the data bus and the 8085 reads and stores the byte in the accumulator during T3.

The execution times of the memory read machine cycle and the instruction cycle are calculated as follow.

clock frequency f -2 MHz

T-state = clock period (1/f) = 0.5 micro seconds

Execution time for op code fetch : ( 4 T) * 0.5 = 2 micro seconds

Execution time for memory read : ( 3 T ) * 0.5 = 1.5 micro seconds

Execution time for instruction. complete : ( 7 T) * 0.5= 3.5 micro seconds

The memory read machine cycle is executed by the processor to read a data byte from memory.

The processor takes (3T) states to execute this cycle.

The instructions which have more than one byte word size will use the machine cycle after the opcode fetch machine cycle.

## 4.7.2 Memory Write Machine Cycle / Operation

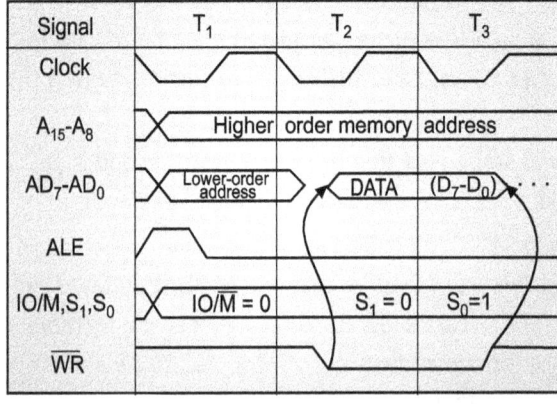

**Fig. 4.11 : Memory write Machine cycle**

## Write Cycle

Immediately after the termination of the low order address, at the beginning of the T2, data is asserted on the address/data bus by the processor. WR control is activated near the start of T2 and becomes inactive at the end of T3. The processor maintains valid data until after WR is terminated. This ensures that the memory or port has valid data while WR is active.

The data appears on the bus as a result of activating RD and for the WR bus cycle, the time the valid data is on the bus overlaps the time that the WR is active.

### 4.7.3 I/O Read Cycle / Operation of 8085

The I/O Read cycle is executed by the processor to read a data byte from I/O port or from the peripheral, which is I/O, mapped in the system.

The processor takes 3T states to execute this machine cycle.

The IN instruction uses this machine cycle during the execution.

They are similar to memory read and write signals but IO/(M bar) is high there to enable communication with input output device

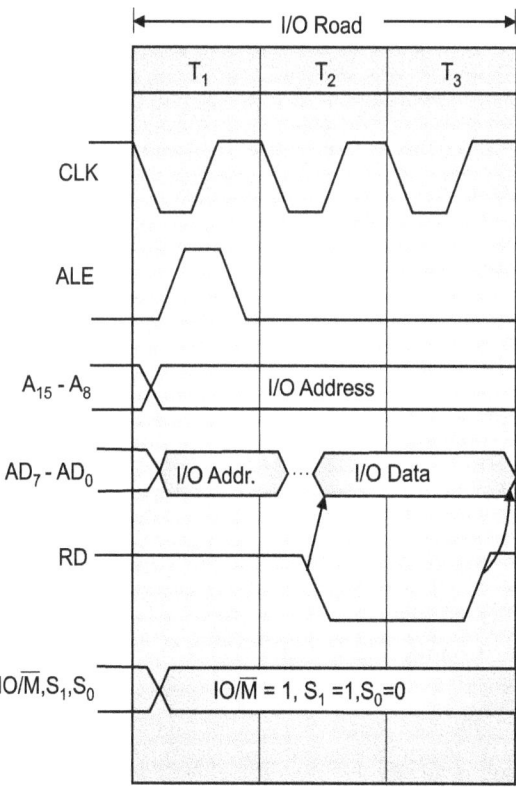

Fig. 4.12 : Timing Diagram for Memory Write Machine Cycle

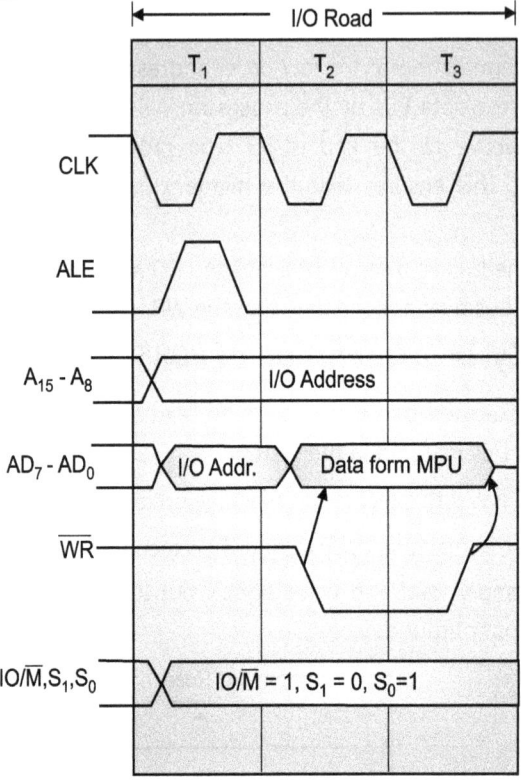

**Fig. 4.13 : Timing Diagram for I/O Read Machine Cycle**

The 8085 instructions consist of one to five machine cycles.

Actually the execution of an instruction is the execution of the machine cycles of that instruction in the predefined order.

The timing diagram of an instruction ate obtained by drawing the timing diagrams of the machine cycles of that instruction, one by one in the order of execution.

## 4.8 DE-MULTIPLEXING DEMULTIPLEXING OF ADDRESS AND DATA BUS IN INTEL 8085 MICROPROCESSOR

The address bus has 8 signal lines A8 to A15which are unidirectional.

The other 8 address bits are multiplexed(time shared) with the 8 data bits.

So, the bits AD0 to AD7are bi-directional and serve as A0 to A7and D0 to D7at the same time.

During the execution of the instruction, these lines carry the address bits during the early part, then during the late parts of the execution, they carry the 8 data bits. In order to separate the address from the data, we can use a latch to save the value before the function of the bits changes.

## Demultiplexing AD7 to AD0

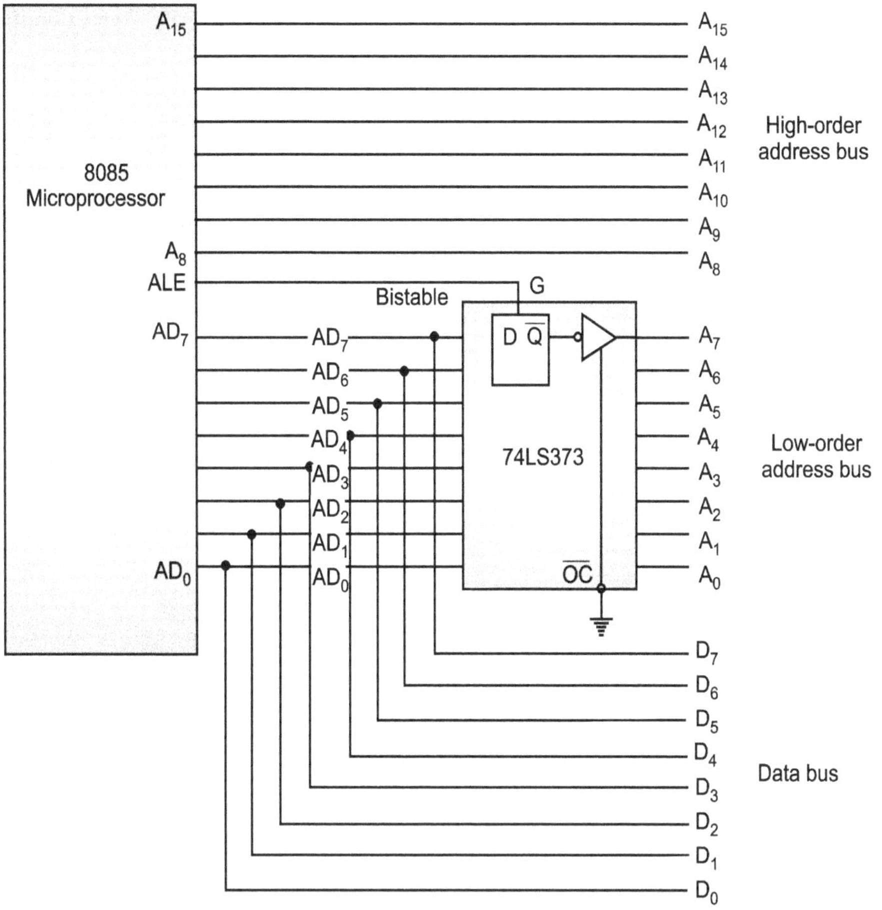

**Fig. 4.14**

From the above description, it becomes obvious that the AD7 to AD0lines are serving a dual purposeand that they need to be demultiplexed to get all the information.The high order bitsof the address remain on the bus for three clock periods. However, the low order bitsremain for only one clock period and they would be lost if they are not saved externally. Also, notice that the low order bitsof the address disappearwhen they are needed most. To make sure we have the entire address for the full three clock cycles, we will use an external latchto save the value of AD7 to AD0 when it is carrying the address bits. We use the ALE signal to enable this latch.

ALE operates as a pulse during T1, we will be able to latch the address. Then when ALE goes low, the address is saved and the AD7 to AD0 lines can be used for their purpose as the bi-directional data lines.

The high order address is placed on the address bus and hold for 3 clk periods, The low order address is lost after the first clk period, this address needs to be hold however we need to use latch.

The address AD7 to AD0 is connected as inputs to the latch 74LS373.

The ALE signal is connected to the enable (G) pin of the latch and the OC Output control of the latch is grounded which you can see in the given diagram.

## 4.9 GENERATING CONTROL SIGNALS

This group of signals includes two control signals (RD and WR), three status signals (IO/M, S1 and S0) to identify the nature of the operation. These signals are shown as following Fig. 4.15.

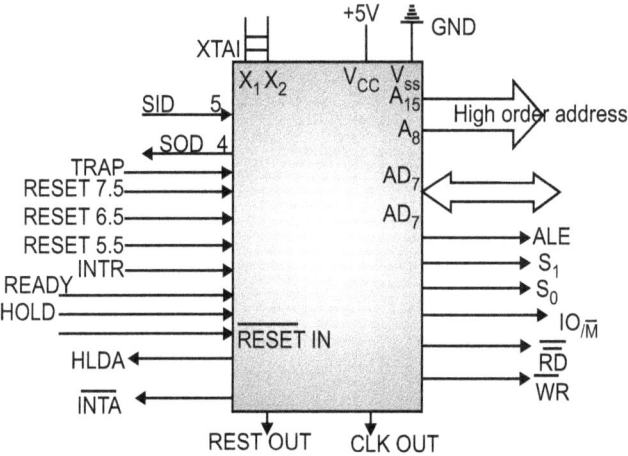

Fig. 4.15 : Data, address and control signal

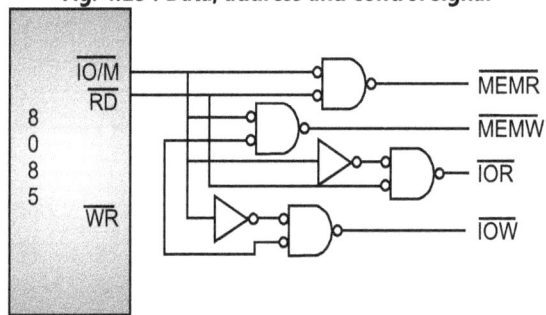

Fig. 4.16 : Signal generation

| IO/M (Active Low) | S1 | S2 | Data Bus Status (Output) |
|---|---|---|---|
| 0 | 0 | 0 | Halt |
| 0 | 0 | 1 | Memory WRITE |
| 0 | 1 | 0 | Memory READ |
| 1 | 0 | 1 | IO WRITE |
| 1 | 1 | 0 | IO READ |
| 0 | 1 | 1 | OPcode fetch |
| 1 | 1 | 1 | Interrupt acknowledge |

Fig. 4.17 : Status Signal

**ALE (Address Latch Enable):** This is a positive going pulse generated every time the 8085 begins an operation (machine cycle); it indicates that the bits on AD7 to AD0 are address bits. This signal is used primarily to latch the low-order address from the multiplexed bus and generate a separate set of eight address lines, A7 to A0.

**RD (Read):** This is a Read control signal (Active Low). This signal indicates that the selected I/O or memory device is to be read and data are available on the data bus.

**WR (Write):** This is a write control signal (Active Low). This signal indicates that the data on the data bus are to be written into a selected memory or I/O location.

**IO/M:** This is a status signal used to differentiate between I/O and memory operations. When it is high, it indicates an I/O operation: when it is low, it indicates a memory operation. This signal is combined with RD (read) and WR (Write) to generate I/O and memory control signals.

**S1 and S0:** These status signals, similar to IO/M, can be identify various operations, but they are rarely used in small systems.

## 4.10 MEMORY INTERFACING AND MEMORY STRUCTURE

- There needs to be a lot of interaction between the microprocessor and the memory for the exchange of information during program execution.

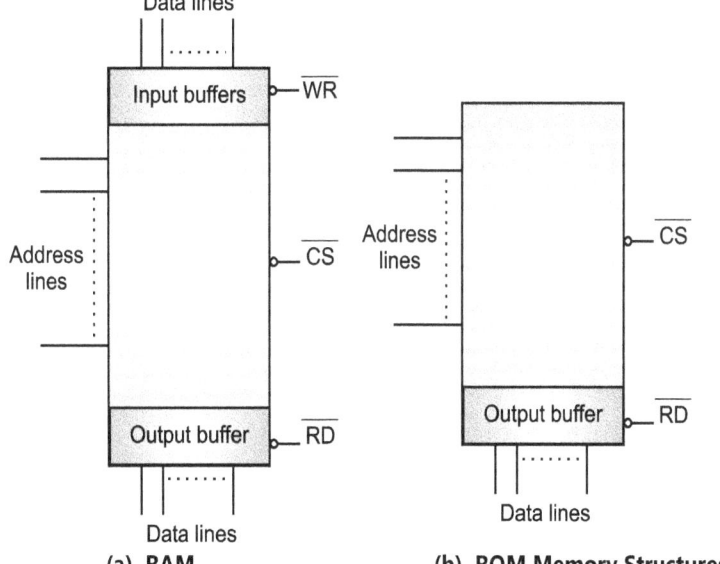

Fig. 4.18

- Memory has its requirements on control signals and their timing.
- The way of interfacing the above two chips to the microprocessor is the same.
- However, the ROM does not have a WR signal
- Accessing memory can be summarized into the following three steps:
- Select the chip.
- Identify the memory register.

- Enable the appropriate buffer.
- Translating this to microprocessor domain:
- The microprocessor places a 16-bit address on the address bus.
- Part of the address bus will select the chip and the other part will go through the address decoder to select the register.
- The signals IO/M and RD combined indicate that a memory read operation is in progress. The MEMR signal can be used to enable the RD line on the memory interfacing
- The result of 'address decoding' is the identification of a register for a given address.
- A large part of the address bus is usually connected directly to the address inputs of the memory chip.
- This portion is decoded internally within the chip.
- What concerns us is the other part that must be decoded externally to select the chip.
- This can be done either using logic gates or a decoder.

Any system which process digital data needs the facility for storing the data. Interfacing is a technique to be used for connecting the Microprocessor to Memory. Now a days Semiconductor memories are used for storing purpose. There are some of the advantages of the semiconductor memory.

- Small size
- High speed
- Better reliability
- Low cost

Generally, RAM or ROM is used for memory interfacing.

**Memory:** A memory is a digital IC which stores the data in binary form.

**Memory Size:** The number of location and number of bits per word will vary from memory to memory. For example, If a particular memory chip is capable of storing M words with each word having N-bits. Then the size of the memory will be M × N.

### Interfacing a ROM Memory of 4096*8 with 8085 Microprocessor:

Given      memory size = 4096 × 8

$$4096 = 2^{12}$$

So 12 lines will be used for interfacing. A0 to A11

In this system A0 to A11 lines of Microprocessor will be connected to the address lines of the memory. and D0 to D7 of the 8085 microprocessor will be connected to the data bus of the memory.

As we know that the it is EPROM, so only RD pin is connected to the microprocessor. There is not the facility for writing data.

In case if you are using RAM then you have to connect one more pin for writing operation. As you can see that there is a pin named CS. Generally this pin is used for Selction for the chip in case of two or more than memory chip.

Latch has been used to separate the data and address bus.

The memory locations that are directly addressed by the microprocessor is called physical memory space. For example a microprocessor like 8085 has 16 address lines, and it can access a physical memory space of 64K starting from 0000H to FFFFH. The process of interfacing memories to microprocessor and allocating address to each memory location is called memory mapping. The complete address space may be considered as a single memory block. But practically, when ICs are used as memory devices, instead of a single IC (Integrated Chip), few devices that fit into the address space will be used. This is due to the fact a microprocessor based system requires at least one ROM/EPROM and a RAM. For example instead of using a memory device of size 64KB (Kilo Bytes), we can use 8 memory devices with a capacity of 8KB each. This will reduce the chip replacement cost while servicing the microprocessor-based system. When memory blocks are used, to access all the locations in a block n address lines are needed.

So that $\quad 2^n = 8\,K$

$\qquad = 2^3\,K$

$\qquad = 2^3 \times 2^{10}$

$\qquad = 2^{13}$

Therefore, $\quad n = 13$

## 4.11 ADDRESS DECODING TECHNIQUES

- As we know, 8085 has 16 address lines using which allows addressing up to 64 KB of main memory.
- Most of the time we do not need complete 64 KB memory, so most of the address lines will remain free which can be used generate chip select and determine the range of the addresses the memory will occupy.
- There are two types of decoding technique depending on the number of lines used for the decoder.
- Full or absolute decoding
- Partial decoding
- In full decoding, all remaining address lines are used for the decoder to generate chip select signal for the memories as shown in Fig. 4.19

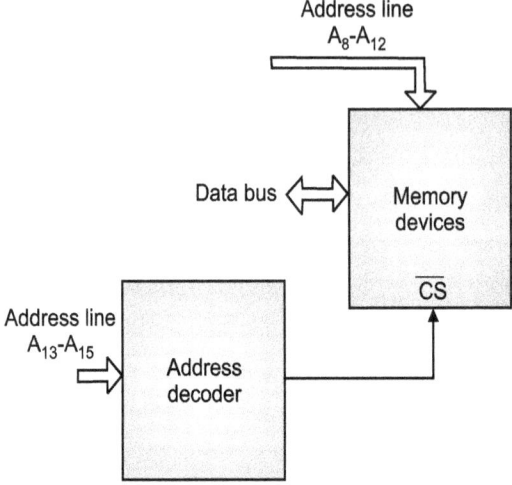

Fig. 4.19

- For example, suppose we want to interface 8k of memory, then thirteen address lines are required for the memory.
- Then remaining three address lines can be used for decoder, so more hardware is required for decoding the numbers of address bits.
- But in partial decoding, only one line out of remaining address lines is used to generate chip select signal as shown in Fig. 4.20.

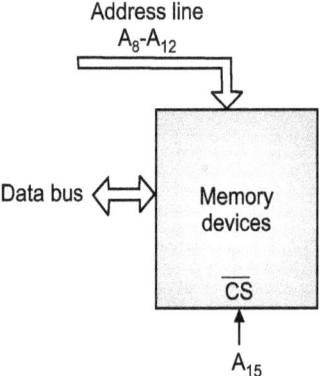

Fig. 4.20 : Partial Decading

For above example, out of remaining three address lines, we can use any one of them as chip select signal and rest of the address lines will remain open or unconnected, so less hardware is required for decoding.

## 4.11.1 Absolute Address Decoding

The 8085 microprocessor has 16 address lines. Therefore it can access 2$^{16}$ locations in the physical memory. If all these lines are connected to a single memory device, it will decode these 16 address lines internally and produces 216 different addresses from 0000H to FFFFH so that each location in the memory will have a unique address. This is called absolute address decoding.

Consider a system in which the available 64kb memory space is equally divided between EPROM and RAM. Interface the EPROM and RAM with 8085 processor.

- Implement 32kb memory capacity of EPROM using single IC 27256.
- 32kb RAM capacity is implemented using single IC 62256.
- The 32kb memory requires 15 address lines and so the address lines A0 - A14 of the processor are connected to 15 address pins of both EPROM and RAM.
- The unused address line A15 is used as to chip select. If A15 is 1, it select RAM and If A15 is 0, it select EPROM.
- Inverter is used for selecting the memory.
- The memory used is both Ram and EPROM, so the low RD and WR pins of processor are connected to low WE and OE pins of memory respectively.
- The address range of EPROM will be 0000H to 7FFFH and that of RAM will be 7FFFH to FFFFH.

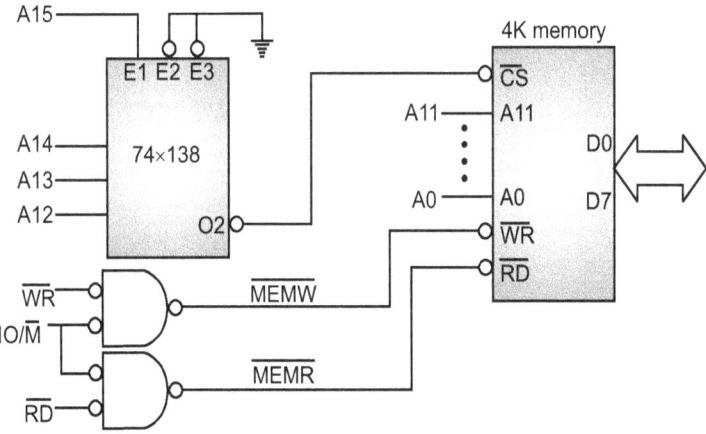

**Fig, 4,21 : 4KB Memory Intrface**

**Example 4.2 :** Consider a system in which the full memory space 64kb is utilized for EPROM memory. Interface the EPROM with 8085 processor.

- The memory capacity is 64 Kbytes. i.e
- $2^n = 64 \times 1000$ bytes where n = address lines.
- So, n = 16.

- In this system the entire 16 address lines of the processor are connected to address input pins of memory IC in order to address the internal locations of memory.
- The chip select (CS) pin of EPROM is permanently tied to logic low.
- Since the processor is connected to EPROM, the active low RD pin is connected to active low output enable pin of EPROM.
- The range of address for EPROM is 0000H to FFFFH.

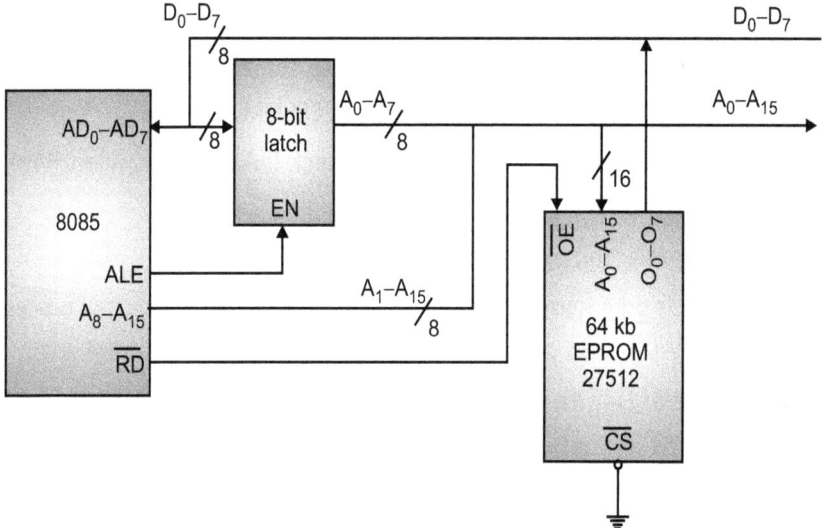

**Fig. 4.22 : Interfacing 64Kb EPROM with 8085**

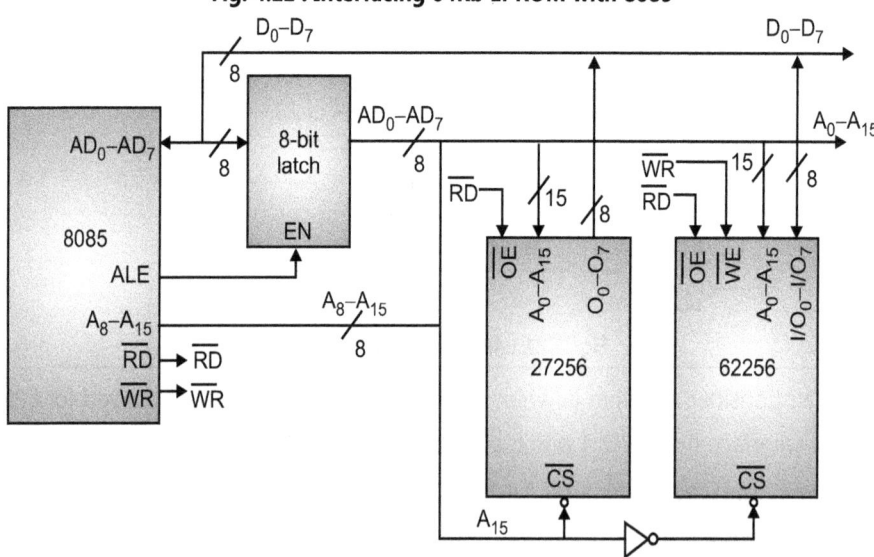

**Fig. 4.23 : Interfacing 32Kb EPROM and 32Kb RAM with 8085**

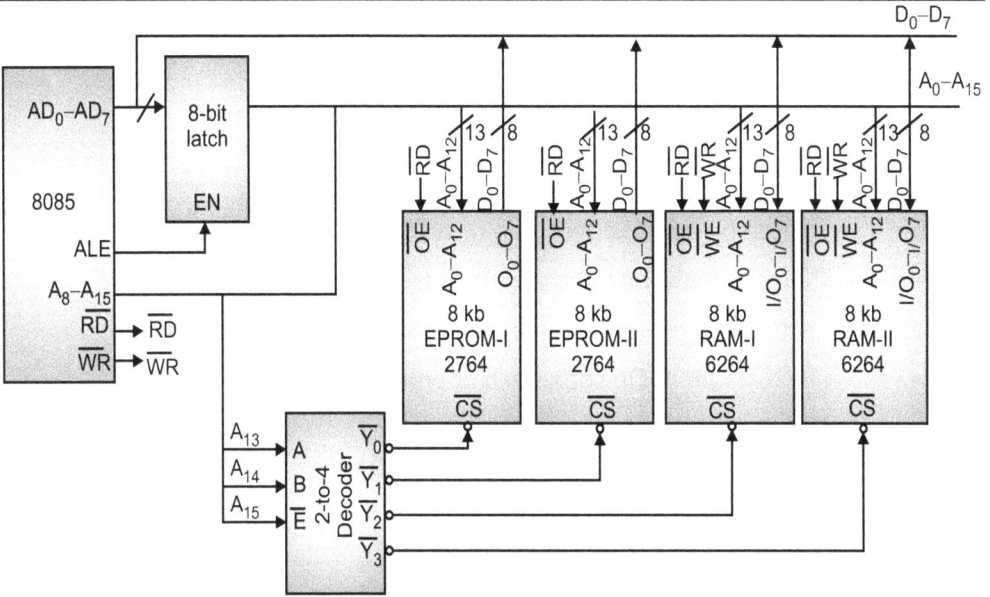

Fig. 4.24 : Interfacing with 16 KB of EPROM and 16 KB of RAM

## 4.11.2 Difference Between Full and Partial Decoding

| Sr. No. | Full Decoding | Partial Decoding |
|---|---|---|
| 1. | All address lines are used by memory chips and decoders. | All lines are not used. |
| 2. | Each memory location has only one unique address. | Each location has two or more address because the number of addresses per memory location is $2^n$ where n is number of unused address lines. |
| 3. | Address decoder hardware is complicated and expensive. | Address decoder is simple and less expensive. |
| 4. | The size of memory is not reduced. | The size of memory is reduced. |

## QUESTIONS

1. Draw the pin diagram of 8085 microprocessor and explain the various pins.
2. Explain the architecture of 8085 microprocessor with the help of the block diagram.
3. Explain with the help of a diagram various programmable registers of 8085.

4. With the help of a diagram, explain the format of the flag register.
5. Explain Program Counter and Stack Register.
6. Write a short note on 8085 system bus.
7. Explain de multiplexing of address bus of 8085.
8. Write a short note on address decoding techniques.
9. State the difference between full and partial decoding.
10. Explain de-multiplexing of address and data bus. State advantages.
11. Draw machine diagram of Op code fetch operation.
12. Draw machine diagram of Memory read operation.
13. Draw machine diagram of memory write operation.
14. Draw machine diagram of I/O read operation.
15. Draw machine diagram of I/O write operation.
16. Explain memory Interfacing with 8085.

# Unit - V
# 8085 PROGRAMMING TECHNIQUES

## 5.1 INSTRUCTION FORMAT

Each instruction is represented by a sequence of bits within the computer. The instruction is divided into group of bits called field. The way of instruction is expressed is known as instruction format. It is usually represented in the form of rectangular box. The instruction format may be of the following types.

### 5.1.1 Variable Instruction Formats

These are the instruction formats in which the instruction length varies on the basis of op-code & address specifiers. For Example, VAX instructions vary between 1 and 53 bytes while X86 instruction vary between 1 and 17 bytes.

**Format**

| Operation & no. of a operands | Address specifier 1 | Address field 2 | --- | Address specifier n | Address field n |

Fig. 5.1

**Advantage**
- These formats have good code density.

**Disadvantage**
- These instruction formats are very difficult to decode & pipeline.

### 5.1.2 Fixed Instruction Formats

In this type of instruction format, all instruction are same size. For Example, MIPS, Power PC, Alpha, ARM.

**Format**

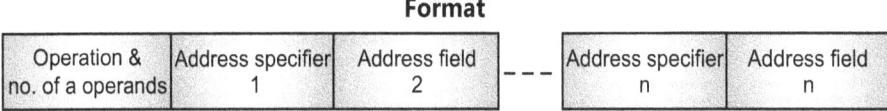

Fig. 5.2

**Advantage**
- They are easy to decode and pipeline.

**Disadvantage**
- They don't have as good code density.

## 5.1.3 Hybrid Instruction Formats

In this type of instruction formats, we have multiple format length specified by opcode. For example, IBM 360/70, MIPS 16, Thumb.

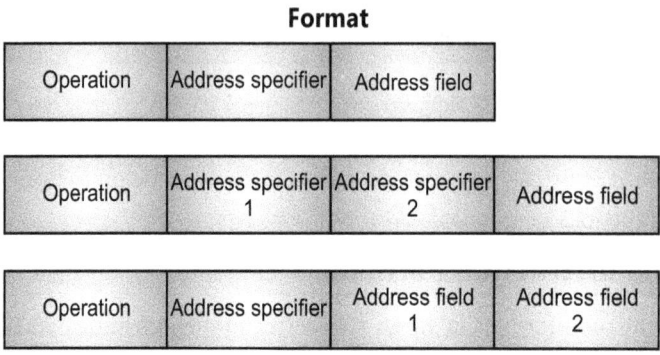

Fig. 5.3

**Advantage**

- These compromise between code density & instruction of these type are very easy to decode.

# 5.2 ADDRESSING MODES

Addressing mode provide different ways for access an address to given data to a processor. Operated data is stored in the memory location, each instruction required certain data on which it has operate. There are various techniques to specify address of data. These technique are called Addressing Modes.

**(1) Direct Addressing Mode :**

In the direct addressing mode, address of the operand is given in the instruction and data is available in the memory location which is provided in instruction. We will move this data in desired location. In direct addressing mode, the address of the data is specified in the instruction. The data will be in memory. In this addressing mode, the program instructions and data can be stored in different memory.

LDA 3000H (The content at the location 3000H is copied to the register A).

LDA 1050H (Load the data available in memory location 1050H in to accumulator);

SHLD 3000H

**(2) Indirect Addressing Mode  or Register Addressing :**

In the indirect addressing mode, the instruction specifies a register which contain the address of the operand. Both internal RAM and external RAM can be access via indirect addressing mode.

Data is copied from one register to another register. Many 8085 MPU instructions use register addressing Specify one of the registers A through E, H or L as well as the operation code. Use 1 byte or 2 byte instruction, The operand is retrieved from internal CPU Register

MOV B, A (the content of A is copied into the register B)

MOV A, C (the content of C is copied into the register A).

SUB L: Subtract L from A (Refer to the Figure below) First data : from Accumulator (Register A), Second data : contained in register L.

Others Instructions: ADD A, ADC B, ANA C, MOV A,L ,MOV A,L , MOV H,A , etc....

MOV A, M (data is transferred from the memory location pointed by the register to the accumulator).

In register addressing mode, the instruction specifies the name of the register in which the data is available.

MOV A, B - Move the content of B register to A register; SPHL; ADD C.

### (3) Immediate Addressing Mode :

In the immediate addressing mode, direct data is given in the operand which move the data in accumulator. It is very fast. Data immediately follow the op code in program memory.The operand comes from next byte in program memory. The immediate instructions indicate immediate data (add instruction is ADD add immediate instruction is ADI)  Use 2 bytes instruction.

In immediate addressing mode, the data is specified in the instruction itself. The data will be a part of the program instruction.

MVI A, 30H (30H is copied into the register A)

MVI B,40H(40H is copied into the register B).

MVI B, 3EH Move the data 3EH given in the instruction to B register; LXI SP, 2700H.

LXI SP Load SP with immediate data

Others Instructions: ADI , MVI A, MVI L , ORI

### (4) Register Indirect Addressing :

Relative addressing mode - In the relative address mode, the effective address is determined by the index mode by using the program counter instead of general purpose processor register.

This mode is called relative address mode. In register indirect addressing mode, the instruction specifies the name of the register in which the address of the data is available. Here the data will be in memory and the address will be in the register pair.

EX. MOV A, M - The memory data addressed by H L pair is moved to A register.

LDAX B.

## (5) Implied Addressing :

In the index address mode, the effective address of the operand is generated by adding a content value to the contents of the register. This mode is called index address mode. In implied addressing mode, the instruction itself specifies the data to be operated.

EX. CMA Complement the content of accumulator;

RAL, RAR.

## 5.3 INSTRUCTION SET OF 8085

An Instruction is a command given to the computer to perform a specified operation on given data. The instruction set of a microprocessor is the collection of the instructions that the microprocessor is designed to execute. The instructions described here are of Intel 8085. These instructions are of Intel Corporation. They cannot be used by other microprocessor manufactures. The programmer can write a program in assembly language using these instructions. These instructions have been classified into the following groups:

1. Data Transfer Group
2. Arithmetic Group
3. Logical Group
4. Branch Control Group
5. I/O and Machine Control Group

### (1) Data Transfer Group :

Instructions, which are used to transfer data from one register to another register, from memory to register or register to memory, come under this group. Examples are: MOV, MVI, LXI, LDA, STA etc. When an instruction of data transfer group is executed, data is transferred from the source to the destination without altering the contents of the source. For example, when MOV A, B is executed the content of the register B is copied into the register A, and the content of register B remains unaltered. Similarly, when LDA 2500 is executed the content of the memory location 2500 is loaded into the accumulator. But the content of the memory location 2500 remains unaltered.

**Data Transfer Group Instructions**

| Instruction | Description | Operation |
|---|---|---|
| MOV r1, r2 | (Move Data; Move the content of the one register to another) | [r1] ← [r2] |
| MOV r, m | (Move the content of memory register). | r ← [M] |
| MOV M, r | (Move the content of register to memory) | M ← [r] |
| MVI r, data | (Move immediate data to register). | [r] ← data |

| Instruction | Description | Operation |
|---|---|---|
| MVI M, data | (Move immediate data to memory) | M ← data |
| LXI rp, data 16 | (Load register pair immediate) | [rp] ← data 16 bits, [rh] ← 8 LSBs of data |
| LDA addr | (Load Accumulator direct) | [A] ← [addr]. |
| STA addr. | (Store accumulator direct) | [addr] ← [A] |
| LHLD addr. | (Load H-L pair direct) | [L] ← [addr], [H] ← [addr+1] |
| SHLD addr. | (Store H-L pair direct) | [addr] ← [L], [addr+1] ← [H] |
| LDAX rp. | (LOAD accumulator indirect) | [A] ← [[rp]] |
| STAX rp. | (Store accumulator indirect) | [[rp]] ← [A] |
| XCHG | (Exchange the contents of H-L with D-E pair) | [H-L] ↔ [D-E] |

**(2) Arithmetic Group :**

The instructions of this group perform arithmetic operations such as addition, subtraction; increment or decrement of the content of a register or memory. Examples are: ADD, SUB, INR, DAD etc.

**Arithmetic Group Instructions :**

| Instruction | Description | Operation |
|---|---|---|
| ADD r | (Add register to accumulator) | [A] ← [A] + [r] |
| MOV r, m | (Move the content of memory register). | r ← [M] |
| ADD M | (Add memory to accumulator) | [A] ← [A] + [[H-L]] |
| ADC r | (Add register with carry to accumulator) | [A] ← [A] + [r] + [CS] |
| ADC M | (Add memory with carry to accumulator) | [A] ← [A] + [[H-L]] [CS] |
| ADI data | (Add immediate data to accumulator) | [A] ← [A] + data |
| ACI data | (Add with carry immediate data to accumulator) | [A] ← [A] + data + [CS] |
| DAD rp | (Add register paid to H-L pair) | [H-L] ← [H-L] + [rp] |
| SUB r | (Subtract register from accumulator) | [A] ← [A] − [r] |
| SUB M | (Subtract memory from accumulator) | [A] ← [A] − [[H-L]] |

*(Contd.)*

| Instruction | Description | Operation |
|---|---|---|
| SBB r | (Subtract register from accumulator with borrow) | [A] ← [A] − [r] − [CS] |
| SBB M | (Subtract memory from accumulator with borrow) | [A] ← [A] − [[H − L]] − [CS] |
| SUI data | (Subtract immediate data from accumulator) | [A] ← [A] − data |
| SBI data | (Subtract immediate data from accumulator with borrow) | [A] ← [A] − data − [CS] |
| INR r | (Increment register content) | [r] ← [r] + 1 |
| INR M | (Increment memory content) | [[H-L]] ← [[H − L]] + 1 |
| DCR r | (Decrement register content) | [r] ← [r] − 1 |
| DCR M | (Decrement memory content) | [[H-L]] ← [[H − L]] − 1 |
| INX rp | (Increment register pair) | [rp] ← [rp] − 1 |
| DCX rp | (Decrement register pair) | [rp] ← [rp] − 1 |
| DAA | (Decimal adjust accumulator) | - |

The instruction DAA is used in the program after ADD, ADI, ACI, ADC, etc instructions. After the execution of ADD, ADC, etc instructions the result is in hexadecimal and it is placed in the accumulator. The DAA instruction operates on this result and gives the final result in the decimal system. It uses carry and auxiliary carry for decimal adjustment. 6 is added to 4 LSBs of the content of the accumulator if their value lies in between A and F or the AC flag is set to 1. Similarly, 6 is also added to 4 MSBs of the content of the accumulator if their value lies in between A and F or the CS flag is set to 1. All status flags are affected. When DAA is used data should be in decimal numbers.

### (3) Logical Group :

The Instructions under this group perform logical operation such as AND, OR, compare, rotate etc. Examples are: ANA, XRA, ORA, CMP, and RAL etc.

**Logical Group Instructions :**

| Instruction | Description | Operation |
|---|---|---|
| ANA r | (AND register with accumulator) | [A] ← [A] ∧ [r] |
| ANA M | (AND memory with accumulator) | [A] ← [A] ∧ [[H-L]] |
| ANI data | AND (immediate data with accumulator) | [A] ← [A] ∧ data |
| ORA r | (OR register with accumulator) | [A] ← [A] ∨ [r] |

*(Contd.)*

| Instruction | Description | Operation |
|---|---|---|
| ORA M | (OR memory with accumulator) | [A] ← [A] v [[H-L]] |
| ORI data | OR immediate data with accumulator | () [A] ← [A] v data |
| XRA r | (EXCLUSIVE-OR register with accumulator) | [A] ← [A] v [r] |
| XRA M | (EXCLUSIVE-OR memory with accumulator) | [A] ← [A] v [[H-L]] |
| XRI data | (EXCLUSIVE-OR immediate data with accumulator) | [A] ← [A] |
| CMA | (Complement the accumulator) | [A] ← [A] |
| CMC | (Complement the carry status) | [CS] ← [CS] |
| STC | (Set carry status) | [CS] ← 1 |
| CMP r | (Compare register with accumulator) | [A] – [r] |
| CMP M | (Compare memory with accumulator) | [A] – [[H-L]] |
| CPI data | (Compare immediate data with accumulator) | [A] – data |

The 2nd byte of the instruction is data, and it is subtracted from the content of the accumulator. The status flags are set according to the result of subtraction. But the result is discarded. The content of the accumulator remains unchanged.

- RLC (Rotate accumulator left) [An+1] ← [An], [A0] ← [A7],[CS] ← [A7].

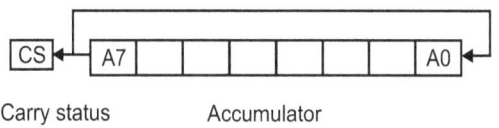

Carry status        Accumulator

**Fig. 5.4**

The content of the accumulator is rotated left by one bit. The seventh bit of the accumulator is moved to carry bit as well as to the zero bit of the accumulator. Only CS flag is affected.

- RRC (Rotate accumulator right) [A7] ← [A0], [CS] ← [A0], [An] ← [An+1].

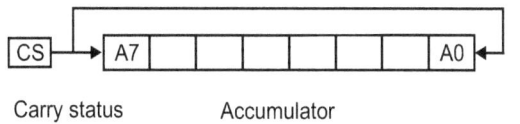

Carry status        Accumulator

**Fig. 5.5**

The content of the accumulator is rotated right by one bit. The zero bit of the accumulator is moved to the seventh bit as well as to carry bit. Only CS flag is affected.

- RAL. (Rotate accumulator left through carry) [An+1] ← [An], [CS] ← [A7], [A0] ← [CS].
- RAR. (Rotate accumulator right through carry) [An] ← [An + 1], [CS] ← [A0], [A7] ← [CS]

## (4) Branch Control Group

This group includes the instructions for conditional and unconditional jump, subroutine call and return, and restart. Examples are: JMP, JC, JZ, CALL, CZ, RST etc.

### Branch Group Instructions

- JMP addr (label). (Unconditional jump: jump to the instruction specified by the address). [PC] ← Label.
- Conditional Jump addr (label): After the execution of the conditional jump instruction the program jumps to the instruction specified by the address (label) if the specified condition is fulfilled. The program proceeds further in the normal sequence if the specified condition is not fulfilled. If the condition is true and program jumps to the specified label, the execution of a conditional jump takes 3 machine cycles: 10 states. If condition is not true, only 2 machine cycles; 7 states are required for the execution of the instruction.

| Instruction | Description |
|---|---|
| **JZ** addr (label). | (Jump if the result is zero) |
| **JNZ** addr (label). | (Jump if the result is not zero) |
| **JC** addr (label). | (Jump if there is a carry) |
| **JNC** addr (label). | (Jump if there is no carry) |
| **JP** addr (label). | (Jump if the result is plus) |
| **JM** addr (label). | (Jump if the result is minus) |
| **JPE** addr (label). | (Jump if even parity) |
| **JPO** addr (label). | (Jump if odd parity) |

- CALL addr (label) (Unconditional CALL: call the subroutine identified by the operand) CALL instruction is used to call a subroutine. Before the control is transferred to the subroutine, the address of the next instruction of the main program is saved in the stack. The content of the stack pointer is decremented by two to indicate the new stack top. Then the program jumps to subroutine starting at address specified by the label.
- RET (Return from subroutine)

- RST n (Restart) Restart is a one-word CALL instruction. The content of the program counter is saved in the stack. The program jumps to the instruction starting at restart location.

### (5) I/O and Machine Control Group

This group includes the instructions for input/output ports, stack and machine control. Examples are: IN, OUT, PUSH, POP, and HLT etc.

**Stack, I/O and Machine Control Group Instructions :**

| Instruction | Description | Operation |
|---|---|---|
| IN port-address. | (Input to accumulator from I/O port) | [A] ← [Port] |
| OUT port-address. | (Output from accumulator to I/O port) | [Port] ← [A] |
| PUSH rp. | (Push the content of register pair to stack) | |
| PUSH PSW. | (PUSH Processor Status Word) | |
| POP rp. | | |
| POP PSW. | (Pop Processor Status Word) | |
| HLT (Halt). | | |
| XTHL. | (Exchange stack-top with H-L) | |
| SPHL. | (Move the contents of H-L pair to stack pointer) | |
| EI. | (Enable Interrupts) | |
| DI. | (DISABLE♂ Interrupts) | |
| SIM. | (Set Interrupt Masks) | |
| RIM. | (Read Interrupt Masks) | |
| NOP. | (No Operation) | |

## 5.4 STACK OPERATIONS, INPUT/OUTPUT AND MACHINE CONTROL GROUP

Before going to study 'the instruction from this group it is necessary understand what is a stack ? The stack is a part of Read/Write memory that is used for temporary storage of binary information during the execution of a program. The binary information is basically the intermediate results and the return address in case of subroutine programs.

- For the application the, internal memory of the microprocessor (registers) is not programs sufficient to store the intermediate results. These intermediate results can be stored temporarily on the stack and can be referred back when required.
- A subroutine is a group of instructions, performs particular subtask which is executed number of times. It is written separately. The microprocessor executes this subroutine by transferring program control to the subroutine program. After completion of subroutine program execution, the program control is returned back to the main program. The use of subroutines is a very important technique in designing software for microprocessor systems because it eliminates more efficiently. For implementation of subroutine technique, it is necessary to define stack. In the. stack, the address of instruction in the main program which follows the subroutine call is stored.
- The stack is a portion of Read/Write memory set aside by the user for the purpose of storing information temporarily. When the information is written on the stack, the operation is called PUSH. When the information read -from stack, the operation is called a POP.
- The microprocessor stores the information, much like stacking plates. Using this analogy of stacking plates it is easy to illustrate the stack operation.

**Fig. 5.6 : Stacked plates**

Fig. 5.6 shows the stacked plates. Here, we realize that if it is desired to take out the first stacked plate we will have to remove all plates above the first plate in thee-reverse order. This means that to remove first plate we will have to remove the third plate, then the second plate :and finally the first plate. This means that, the first information pushed on the stack is the last information poped from the stack. This type of operation is known as a first in, last out (FILO). This stack is implemented with the help of special memory pointer register. The special pointer register is called the stack pointer. During PUSH and POP operation stack pointer register gives the address of memory where the information is to be stored or to be read. The stack pointer's contents are automatically manipulated to point to stack. The memory location currently pointed by stack pointer is called as top of stack.

The stack pointer SP, is a 16-bit register in the 8085A which is manipulated by the microprocessor's control section, during stack related instructions.

Stack Operations : This group consists of the following set of instructions
- LXI SP, data and SPHL
- PUSH and POP instructions

- CALL and RETURN instructions
- RESTART instructions
- XTHL
- SPHL

**LXI SP, Data and SPHL : Initializes Stack Pointer.**

Before execution of any stack related instruction, stack pointer must be initialized with the a valid memory address. The stack pointer can be initialized by two way.

- **Direct way ; LXI SP, data (16)**  ; Loads 16-bit data into SP
- **Indirect way ; C LXI H. data (16)** ; Load the bit data into HL
  SPHL                        ; Loads the contents of HL into SP

Normally, the stack pointer is -initialized by the direct way. When a programmer wishes to set the stack pointer to a value that has been computed by the program, indirect way is used. The computed value is placed in H and L and the contents of HL register pair then moved into the stack pointer.,

| | |
|---|---|
| **SPHL** | : Move data from HL to stack pointer. |
| **Peration** | : SP E ← HL |
| **Description** | : This-instruction copies the contents of HL register pair into the stack pointer. The contents of H register are copied to higher order byte of stack pointer and contents of L register are copied to the lower byte of stack pointer. |
| **No. of bytes** | : 1 byte. |
| | Opcode of SPHL. |
| **Addressing Mode** | : Register addressing. |
| **Flags** | : Flags are not affected. |
| **Example** | |
| | : SP = 2700H |
| | : HL = 2500H |
| **SPHL** | ; This instruction will copy 2500H into stack pointer. So after ; execution of instruction stack pointer contents will be 2500H. |

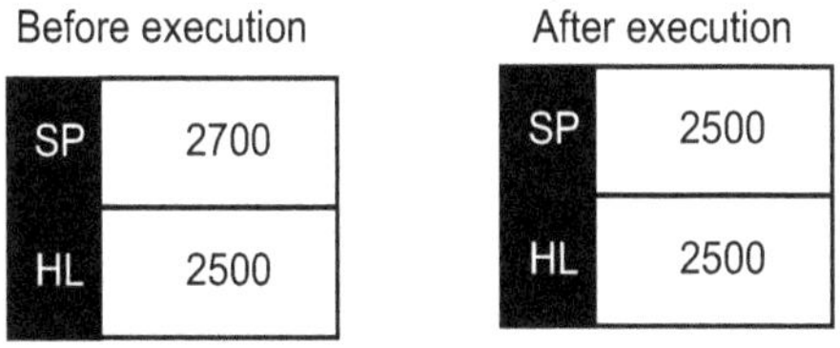

Before execution      After execution

| SP | 2700 |
|---|---|
| HL | 2500 |

| SP | 2500 |
|---|---|
| HL | 2500 |

**Fig. 5.7**

**Note :**
- The stack pointer can be initialized anywhere in the Read/Write memory map.. -However, as'a general practice, the stack pointer is initialized at the highest Read/Write memory location so that it will be less likely to interfere with a program.
- Since the 8085A's stack pointer is decremented before data. is written to the stack, the stack pointer con actually be initialized to a value one higher than the highest Read/Write memory location available.

## 5.4.1 PUSH and POP Instructions

Temporary Stores the Contents of Register Pair and Program Internal Status Word

When programmer realizes the shortage of, the registers he, stores the present contents of the registers in the stack with the help of PUSH instruction and then uses the registers for other function. After completion of other function programmer loads the previous contents of the register from the stack with the help of POP instruction.

### PUSH Operation

In PUSH operation, 16-bit data is stored in the. stack. This 16-bit data is stored in two operations. In the first then stack-pointer is decremented by one and byte of the 16-bit data is stored at the memory location pointed by stack pointer. In the second operation, stack pointer is again decremented by one, and then the lower byte of the 16-bit data is stored at the memory location pointed by stack pointer.

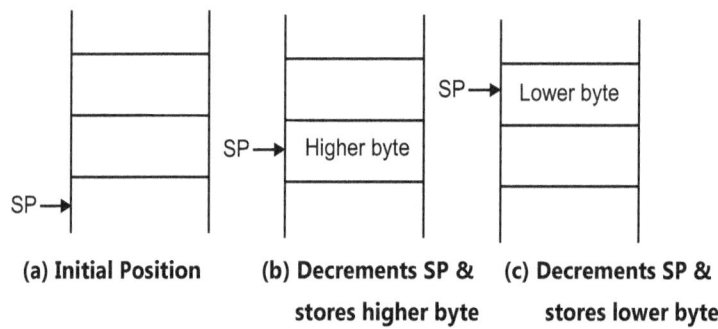

(a) Initial Position  (b) Decrements SP & stores higher byte  (c) Decrements SP & stores lower byte

**Fig. 5.8 Steps involved in PUSH Operation**

### PUSH Instructions

1. **PUSH rp** : Push specified register pair on the stack.
   **Operation** : SP ← SP – 1, (SP) ← rpH, SP ← SP – 1, (SP) <– rpL. Description
   This instruction decrements stack pointer by one and copies the higher byte of the register pair into the memory location pointed by stack pointer. It then decrements the stack pointer again by one and copies the lower byte of the register pair into the memory location

pointer by stack pointer. The rp is 16-bit register pair such as BC, DE, HL, Only higher order register is to be specified within the instruction.

**No. of Bytes** : 1 byte.
Opcode of PUSH rp.

**Addressing Mode** : Register indirect addressing.

**Flags** : Flags are not affected.

**Example** : SP = 2000H, DE = 1050H.

**PUSH D** : This instruction will decrement the stack pointer (2000H) by one (SP = 1FFFH) and copies the contents of D register (10H) into the memory location 1FFFH. It then decrements the stack pointer again by one (SP = 1FFEH) and copies the contents of E register (50H) into the memory location 1FFEH.

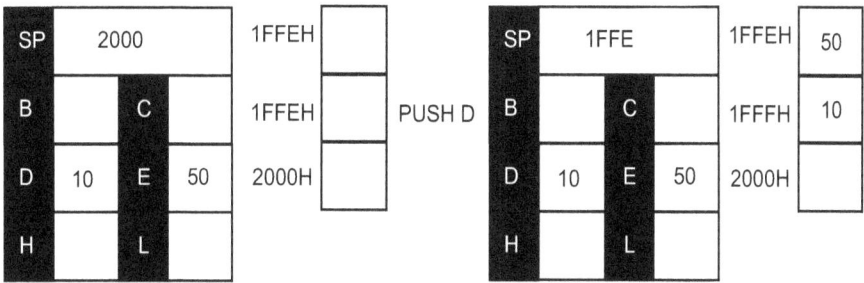

Fig. 5.9

2. **PUSH PSW** : Push program status word on the stack.

**Operation** : SP ← SP – 1
(SP) ← A
SP ← SP = 1
(SP) ← Flag register

**Description** : This instruction decrements stack pointer by one and copies the accumulator contents into- the memory location pointed by stack pointer. It then decrements the stack pointer again by one and copies the flag register into the memory location pointed by the stack pointer.

**No. of Bytes** : 1 byte.
Opcode of PUSH PSW.

**Addressing Mode** : Register indirect addressing.

**Flag** : Flags are not affected.

**Example** : SP = 2000H, A = 20H, Flag register 80H

**PUSH PSW** : This instruction decrements the stack pointer (SP 2000H) by one (SP = 1FFFH) and copies the contents of the accumulator (20H) into the memory location 1FFFH. Jt then decrements the stack pointer again by one (SP = 1FFEH) and copies the contents of the flag register (80H) into the memory location 1FFEH.

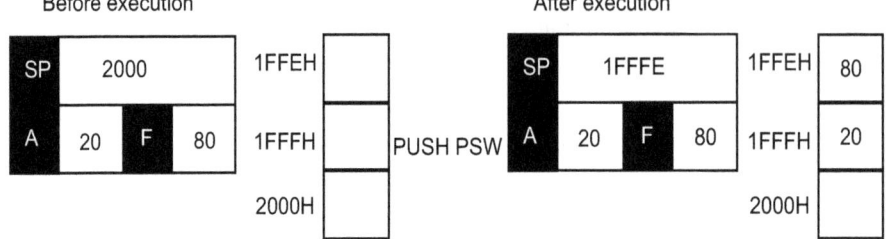

Fig. 5.10

## POP Operation :

In POP operation, 16-bit data is read from the stack. This 16-bit data is read in two operations. In the first operation, the contents from the memory location pointed by stack pointer are loaded into lower byte of register pair and then the stack pointer is incremented by one. In the second operation, the contents from the memory location pointed by stack pointer are loaded into, higher byte of register pair and then the stack pointer is incremented by one.

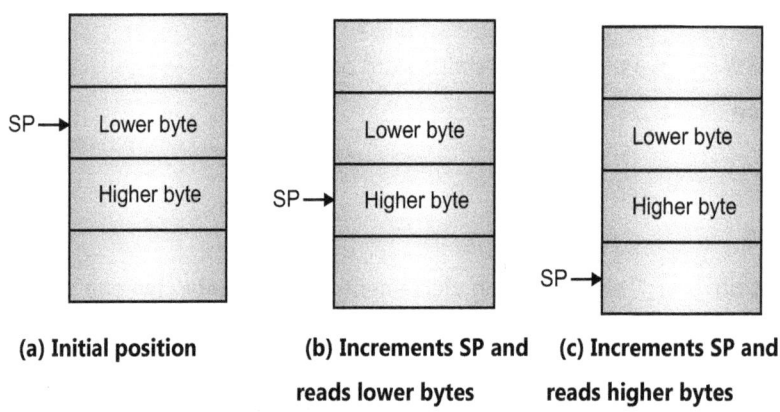

(a) Initial position   (b) Increments SP and reads lower bytes   (c) Increments SP and reads higher bytes

Fig. 5.11 : Stop Involved in POP Operation

**POP Instructions :**

1. **POP rp** : POP specified register pair of the stack.
   **Operation** : rpL ← (SP)
   SP ← SP + I
   rpH ← (SP), SP ← SP + 1

**Description** : This instruction copies the contents of memory location pointed by the stack pointer into the lower byte of the specified register pair and increments the stack pointer by one. It then copies the contents of memory location pointed by stack pointer into the higher byte of the specified register pair and increments the stack pointer again by one. The rp is 16-bit register pair such-as BC, DE, HL. Only higher order register is to be specified within the instruction.

**No. of Bytes** : 1 byte.
Opcode of POP rp.

**Addressing Mode** : Register indirect Addressing.

**Flags** : Flags are not affected.

**Example** : SP = 2000H, (2000H) = 30H, (2001H) = 50H

**POP B** : This instruction will copy the contents of memory location pointed by stack pointer, 2000H (i.e. data 30H) into the C register. It will then increment the stack pointer by one, 2001H and will copy the contents of memory location pointed by stack pointer, 2001H (i.e. data 50H) into B register, and increment the stack pointer again by one.

Before execution

| SP | 2000 |
|---|---|

| B | C |
|---|---|

| 2000H | 30 |
|---|---|
| 2001H | 50 |
| 2002H | |

POP B

After execution

| SP | 2002 |
|---|---|

| B | 50 | C | 30 |
|---|---|---|---|

| 2000H | 30 |
|---|---|
| 2001H | 50 |
| 2002H | |

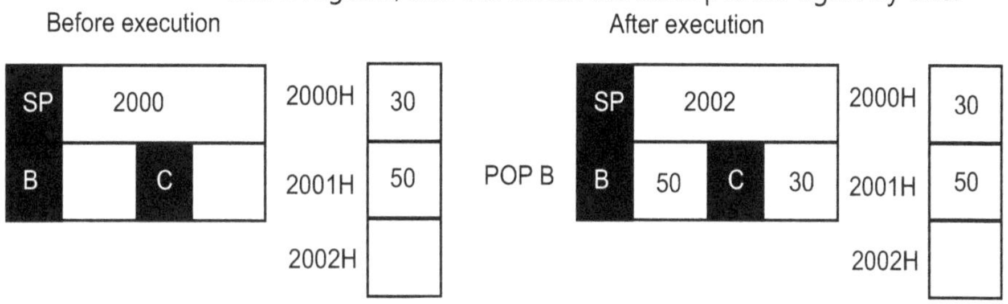

**Fig. 5.12**

2. **POP PSW** : POP program status word of the stack.

   **Operation** : Flag register ← (SP)
   SP ← SP + 1
   A ← (SP)
   SP ← SP + 1

   **Description** : This instruction copies the contents of memory location pointed by the stack pointer into the flag register and increments the stack pointer by one. It then copies the contents of memory location pointed by stack pointer into the accumulator and increments the stack pointer again by one.

   **No. of Bytes** : 1 byte.
   Opcode of PORPSW.

**Addressing Mode :** Register indirect addressing.
**Flags** : Flags are not affected.
**Example** : SP = 2000H, (2000H) = 30H, (2001H) 50H
**POP PSW** : This instruction will copy the contents of memory location pointed by the stack pointer, 2000H (i.e. data 30H).into the flag register. It will then increment the stack pointer by one, 2001H and will copy the contents of memory location pointed by stack pointer into the accumulator and increment the stack pointer again by one.

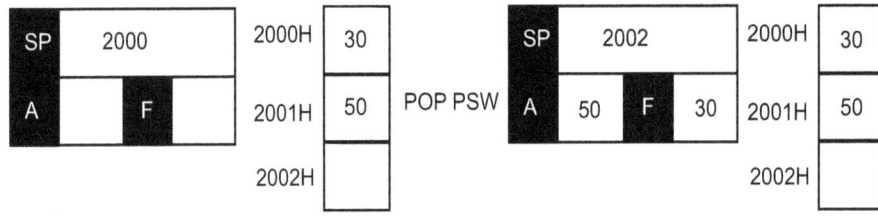

Fig. 5.13

## 5.4.2 CALL Address and RET : Implements Subroutines

Whenever we need to use a group of instructions several times throughout a program there are two ways to avoid rewriting of the group of instructions. One way is to write the group of instructions as a separate subroutine. We can then just CALL the subroutine whenever we need to execute that group of instructions. For calling the subroutine we have to store the return address onto the stack.

**Subroutines**

From the previous discussions, we know that the subroutine is a group of instructions ructions stored as a separate program in the memory and it is called from the main program whenever required. The 8085A microprocessor has two instructions to implement subroutines: CALL and RET. CALL instruction is used to call a subroutine in the main program and RET instruction is the last instruction in the subroutine to return it back to the main program. The CALL instruction saves the address of the instruction following it and then transfers the program control to the first instruction in the subroutine. When subroutine execution is completed the RET instruction reads s the return address from the stack and transfers control back to the instruction following the CALL.

| Main Program | | DELAY Subroutine |
|---|---|---|
| 6000H | LXI SP, 3000H | 6500H DELAY : MVI C, FFH |
| 6003H | - | 6502 BACK : DCR C |
|  | - | 6503 H   JNZ BACK |
|  | - | 6503 H   RET |
| 6010H | CALL DELAY (6500H) | |
| 6013H | | |

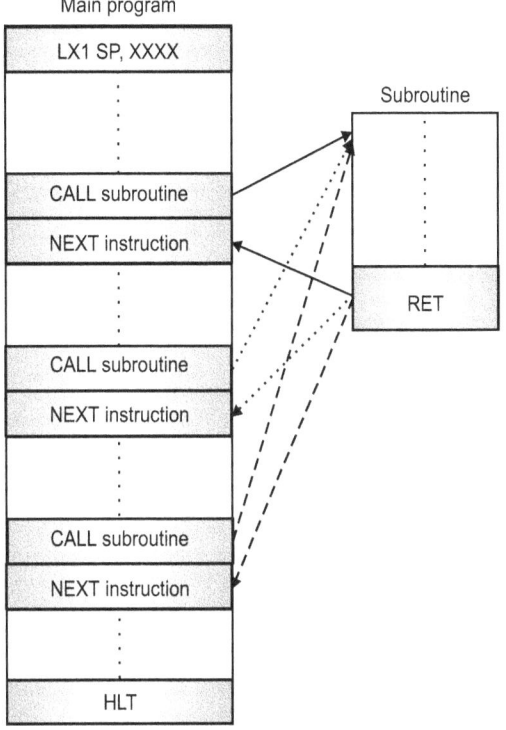

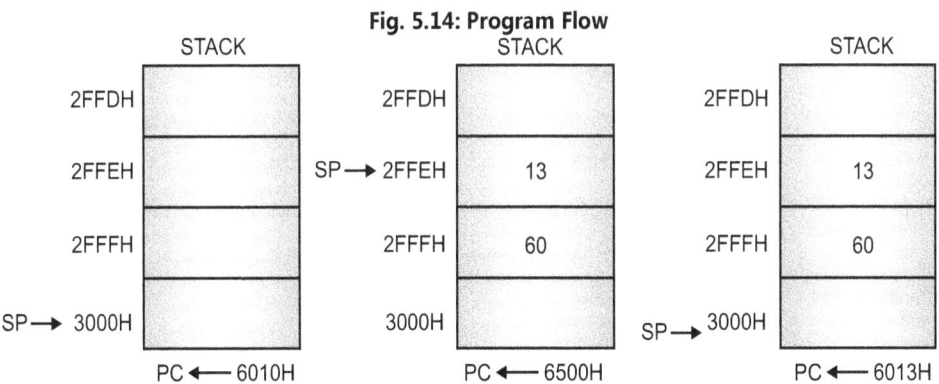

**Fig. 5.15 : Details in the Execution of CALL and RETURN Instructions**

Here, the main program initializes, stack pointer at 3000H memory location and executes instructions in sequence till the execution of CALL instruction. After execution of CALL instruction program control is transferred to the delay subroutine stored at memory address 6500H. Before transfer of control to the subroutine program, the address of the ,instruction (6013H) which is after the CALL instruction, is stored in the stack. At the end of delay subroutine RET instruction is executed, ted, which reads the return address (6013H) from-the stack and transfers the program control to the instruction which is after CALL instruction.

## CALL

This is group consists of the following set of instructions.
1. CALL addr
2. C condition addr

**1. CALL addr** : CALL unconditionally a subroutine whose starting address is given within the instruction.

**Operation** : $(SP - 1) \leftarrow PC_H$
$(SP - 1) \leftarrow PC_L$
$(SP \leftarrow SP - 2)$
$PC \leftarrow addr$

**Description** : The CALL instruction is used to transfer program control to a subprogram or subroutine. This instruction pushes the current PC contents onto the stack and loads the given address into the PC. Thus the program control is transferred to the address given in the instruction. Stack pointer is decremented by two.

When the subroutine is called, the program control is transferred from calling program to the. subroutine. After execution of subroutine it is necessary to transfer program control back to the calling program. To do this processor must remember- the address of the instruction next to the CALL instruction. Processor saves this address on the stack when the CALL instruction is executed.

**Note** : The stack is a part of read/write memory set aside for storing intermediate results and addresses.

**No. of Bytes** : 3 bytes.
First byte : Opcode of CALL.
Second byte : Low order, byte of the address.
Third byte High order byte of the address.

**Addressing Mode** : Immediate register indirect addressing.

**Flags** : Flags are not affected.

**Example** : Stack pointer = 3000H.

**6000H CALL 2000H :** This instruction will store the address of instruction next to

**6003H** : CALL (i.e. 6003H) onto stack and load PC with 2000H.

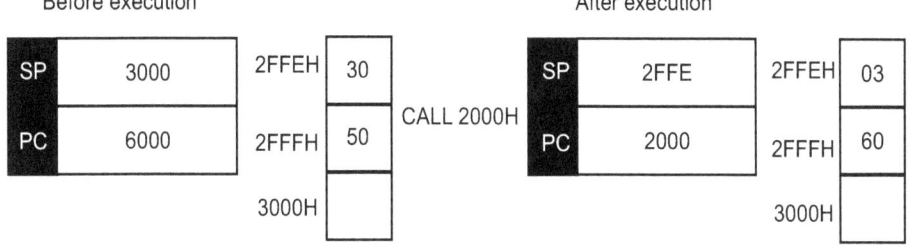

Fig. 5.16

| RET | : Return from the subroutine unconditionally. |
|---|---|
| **Operation** | : $PC_L \leftarrow (SP)$ |
| | $PC_H \leftarrow (SP + 1)$ |
| | $SP \leftarrow SP + 2$ |
| **Description** | : This instruction pops the return addr (address of the instruction next to CALL in the main program) from the stack and loads program counter with this return address. Thus transfers program control to the instruction next to CALL in the main program. |

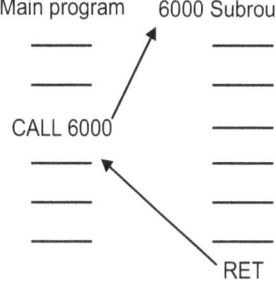

Fig. 5.17

**No. of Bytes** : 1 byte.
Opcode of RET.

**Addressing Mode** : Register indirect addressing.

**Flags** : Flag's are not affected.

**Example** : If SP = 27FDH and contents on the stack are as shown then

| SP → | 27FD | 00 |
|---|---|---|
| | 27 FE | 62 |
| | 27 FF | |

RET : This instruction will load PC with 6200H and it will transfer program control to the address 6200H. It will also increment the stack pointer by two.

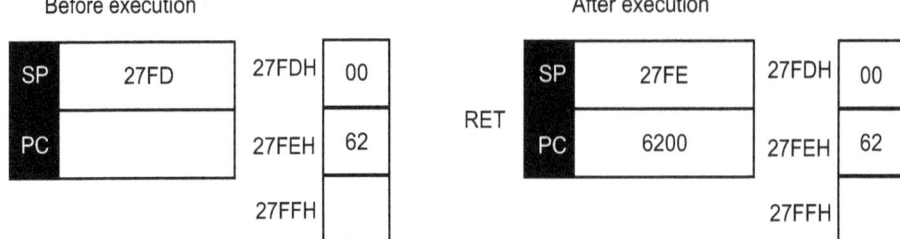

Fig. 5.18

## 5.4.3 Conditional Call and Return Instructions

In addition to the unconditional CALL and RET instructions, the 8085A instruction set includes eight conditional CALL instructions and eight conditional RET instructions. These conditions are checked by the reading the status of respective flags. If the condition associated with the conditional CALL is not' met, the instruction following the CALL is executed. If the condition ,is met, the program counter contents are saved on the stack, and the address contained in the CALL instruction is loaded into program counter. The number of machine cycles and T-states required by a conditional CALL depends on whether or not the condition is satisfied. When the condition is not. satisfied, two machine cycles with a total of nine T-state are required to fetch, decode -and execute the instruction. When the condition is satisfied, five machine T-states are required.

**C condition addr** : Call the subroutine conditionally at given addr.

**Operation** : If condition true $(SP - 1) \leftarrow PCH$
$(SP - 2) \leftarrow PC_L$
$SP \leftarrow SP - 2$
$PC \leftarrow addr$ else $PC \leftarrow PC + 3$

**Description** : This instruction calls the subroutine at the given address if a specified condition is satisfied. Before call it stores the address of instruction next to the call on the stack and decrements stack pointer by two. The table 5.1 shows the possible conditions for calls.

**Table 5.1 : Conditional calls**

| Instruction code | Description | Condition for CALL |
|---|---|---|
| CC | Call on carry | CY = 1 |
| CNC | Call on not carry | CY = 0 |
| CP | Call on positive | S = 0 |
| CM | Call on minus | S = 1 |
| CPE | Call on parity even | P = 1 |
| CPO | Call on parity odd | P = 0 |
| CZ | Call on zero | Z = 1 |
| CNZ | Call on not zero | Z = A |

**No. of Bytes** : 3 bytes.
First byte : Opcode of C condition.
Second byte : Low. order byte of the, address.
Third byte High order bytes of the address.

**Addressing Mode** : Immediate register indirect addressing.
**Flags** : Flags are not affected. Flags are checked.
**Example** : Carry flag = 1, stack pointer = 4000H.
**2000H CC 3000H** : This instruction will store the address of the next instruction
i.e. 2003H on the stack and load the program
; i.e. counter with 3000H.

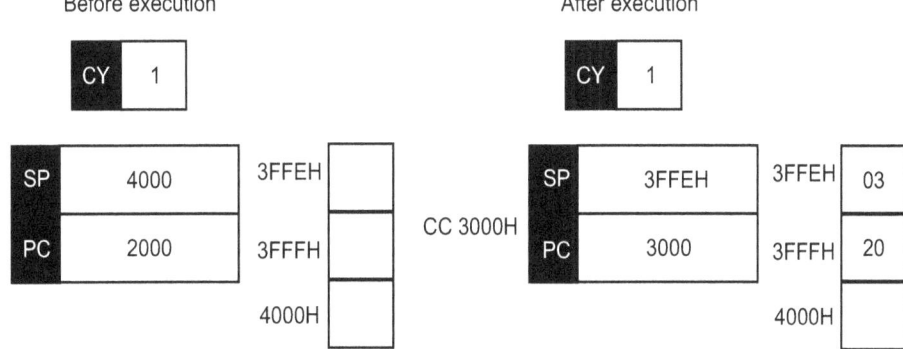

Fig. 5.19

**R condition** : Return from the subroutine conditionally.
**Operation** : If condition is true
$PC_L \leftarrow (SP)$
$PC_H \leftarrow (SP + 1)$
$SP \leftarrow SP + 2$
else
$PC \leftarrow PC + 1$

**Description** : This instruction returns the control to the main program if the specified condition is satisfied Table 5.2 shows the possible conditions for return.

Table 5.2 Conditions for return

| Instruction code | Description | Condition for REF |
|---|---|---|
| RC | Return on carry | CY = 1 |
| RNC | Return on not carry | CY = 0 |
| RP | Return on positive | S = 0 |

| RM | Return on minus | S = 1 |
|---|---|---|
| RPE | Return on parity even | P = 1 |
| RPO | Return on parity odd | P = 0 |
| RZ | Return on zero | Z = 1 |
| RNZ | Return on not zero | Z = 0 |

**No. of Bytes** : 1 byte.
Opcode of R condition

**Addressing Mode** : Register indirect addressing:

**Flags** : Flags are not affected.

## RESTART

This group consists of restart instructions.

1. **RSTT n** : Restart n (0 to 7)

    **Operation** : $(SP - 1) \leftarrow PC_H$
    $(SP - 2) \leftarrow PC_L$
    $SP \leftarrow SP - 2$, $PC \leftarrow (n \times 8)$ in hex

    **Description** : This instruction transfers the program control to the specific memory address as shown in Table 5.3. This instruction is like a fixed address CALL instruction. These fixed addresses are also referred to as vector addresses. The processor multiplies the RST number by 8 to calculate these vector addresses. Before transferring the program control to the instruction following the vector address RST instruction saves the current program counter contents on the stack like CALL instruction.

**Table 5.3 : Vector addresses for return instructions**

| Instruction Code | Vector Address |
|---|---|
| RST 0 | 0 × 8 = 0000H |
| RST 1 | 1 × 8 = 0008H |
| RST 2 | 2 × 8 = 0010ft |
| RST 3 | 3 × 8 = 0018H |
| RST 4 | 4 × 8 = 0020H |
| RST 5 | 5 × 8 = 0028H |
| RST 6 | 6 × 8 = 0030H |
| RST 7 | 7 × 8 = 0038H |

**No. of Bytes** : 1 byte.
Opcode of RST n.

**Addressing Mode** : Register indirect addressing.

**Flags** : Flags are not, affected.

**Example** :

**2000H RST 6** ; This instruction will save the current contents of the program
; counter (i.e. address of next instruction 2001H) on the stack and
; it will load the program counter with vector address
; (6 × 8 = 48₁₀ = 30H) 0030H.

Before execution          After execution

| SP | 3000 |
|----|------|
| PC | 2000 |

| 2FFEH | |
|-------|---|
| 2FFFH | |
| 3000H | |

RST 6

| SP | 2FFE |
|----|------|
| PC | 0030 |

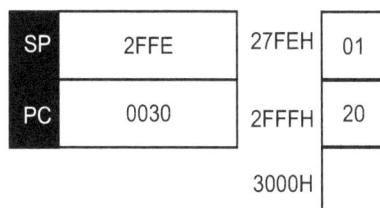

**Fig. 5.20**

**Input/Output** : This group consists of following set of instructions.
IN addr
OUT addr

1. **IN addr (8-bit)** : Copy data from input port into Accumulator.
   **Operation** : A ← (addr)
   **Description** : This instruction copies the data at the port whose address is specified in the instruction into the accumulator.
   **No. of Bytes.** : 2 bytes.
   First byte Opcode of IN.
   Second byte : 8-bit address.
   **Addressing Mode** : Direct addressing.
   **Flags** : Flags are not affected.
   **Example** : Port address = 80H data stored at port address 80H, (80H) 10H
   **IN 80H** ; This instruction will copy the data stored at address 80H, i.e. data 1011 in the accumulator.

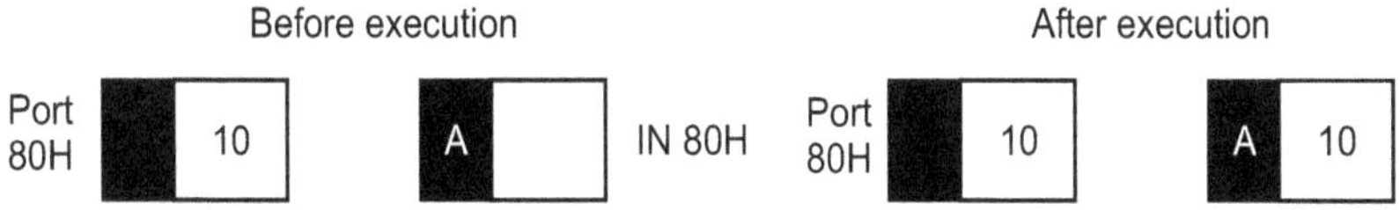

Before execution          After execution

| Port 80H | 10 |
|----------|----|

| A | |
|---|---|

IN 80H

| Port 80H | 10 |
|----------|----|

| A | 10 |
|---|----|

**Fig. 5.21**

2. **OUT addr (8-bit)** : Send data to the output port.
   **Operation** : (addr) ← A
   **Description** : This instruction sends the contents of accumulator to the output port whose address dress is specified within the instruction.

| | | |
|---|---|---|
| **No. of Bytes** | : | 2 bytes. |
| **First byte** | : | Opcode of OUT. |
| | | Second byte : 8-bit address. |
| **Addressing Mode** | : | Direct addressing. |
| **Flags** | : | Flags are not affected. |
| **Example** | : | A = 40H |
| **OUT 50H** | ; | This instruction will send the contents of accumulator (40H) to the output port whose address is 50H. |

Before execution          After execution

Port 50H [ ]    A | 40    OUT 50H    Port 50H | 40    A | 40

**Fig. 5.22**

3. **XTHL** : Exchange top of stack with H and L.
   **Operation** : L ↔ (SP)
                  H ↔ (SP + 1)
   **Description** : This instruction' exchanges the contents of memory location pointed by the stack pointer with the contents of L register and the contents of the next memory location with the contents of H register. This instruction does not modify stack pointer contents.
   **No. of Bytes** : 1 byte.
                    Opcode of XTHL.
   **Addressing Mode** : Register indirect addressing.
   **Flags** : Flags are not affected.
   **Example** : HL = 3040H and SP = 2700H, (2700H) 50H, (2701H) = 60H
   **XTHL** : This instruction will exchange the contents of L register (40H) with the contents of memory location 2700H (i.e. 50H) and the contents of H register (30H) with the contents of memory location 2701H (i.e. 60H).

4. **SPHL** : Move data from HL to stack pointer.
   **Operation** : SP ← HL
   **Description** : This instruction copies the contents of HL register pair into the stack pointer. The contents of H register are copied to higher order byte of stack pointer and contents of L register are copied to the lower byte of stack pointer.

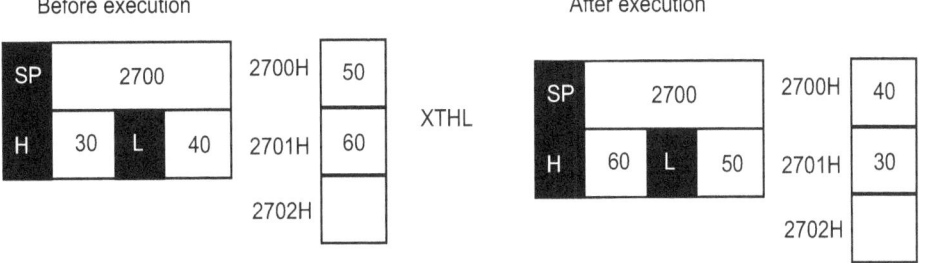

**Fig. 5.23**

**No. of Bytes** : 1 byte.,
Opcode of SPHL.
**Addressing Mode** : Register addressing.
**Flags** : Flags are not affected.
**Example** : HL = 2500H
**SPHL** : This instruction will copy 2500H into stack pointer. So after execution of instruction stack pointer contents will be 2500H.

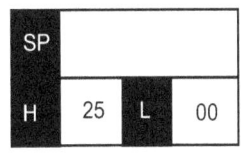 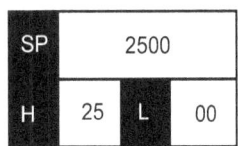

**Fig. 5.24**

## 5.4.4 Machine Control Instruction

This group consists of following set of instructions.
    (1) EI
    (2) DI
    (3) NOP
    (4) HLT
    (5) SIM
    (6) RIM

1. **EI**      : Enable Interrupt
   **Operation**      : IE (F/F) ← 1
   **Description**      : This instruction sets the interrupt enable flip flop to enable interrupts. When the microprocessor is reset or after interrupt acknowledge, the interrupt. enable flip-flop is reset. This instruction is used to reenable the interrupts.

**No. of Bytes** : 1 byte.
Opcode of EI.
**Addressing Mode** : None.
**Flags** : Flags are not affected.

Before execution          After execution

IE F/F               IE F/F

| | 0 | EI | A | 1 |

**Fig. 5.25**

2. **DI** : Disable Interrupts
   **Operation** : IE (F/F) ← 0
   **Description** : This instruction resets the interrupt enable flip flop to disable interrupts. This instruction disables all interrupts except TRAP since TRAP is non-maskable interrupt (cannot be disabled.. It is always enabled).
   **No. of Bytes** : 1 byte.
   Opcode of DI.
   **Addressing Mode** : None,
   **Flags** : Flags are . not affected.

3. **NOP** : No operation.
   **Description** : No operation is performed.
   **No. of Bytes** : 1 byte.
   Opcode of NOP.
   **Addressing Mode** : None.
   **Flags** : Flags are not affected.

4. **HLT** : Halts the processor.
   **Description** : This instruction halts the processor. It can be restarted by a valid interrupt or by applying a RESET signal.
   **No. of Bytes** : 1 byte.
   Opcode of HLT.
   **Addressing Mode** : None.
   **Flags** : Flags are not affected.

5. **SIM** : Set Interrupt Mask.
   **Description** : This instruction masks the interrupts ' as desired. It also sends out serial data through the SOD pin. For this instruction command byte must be loaded in the accumulator.

The pattern for command byte is

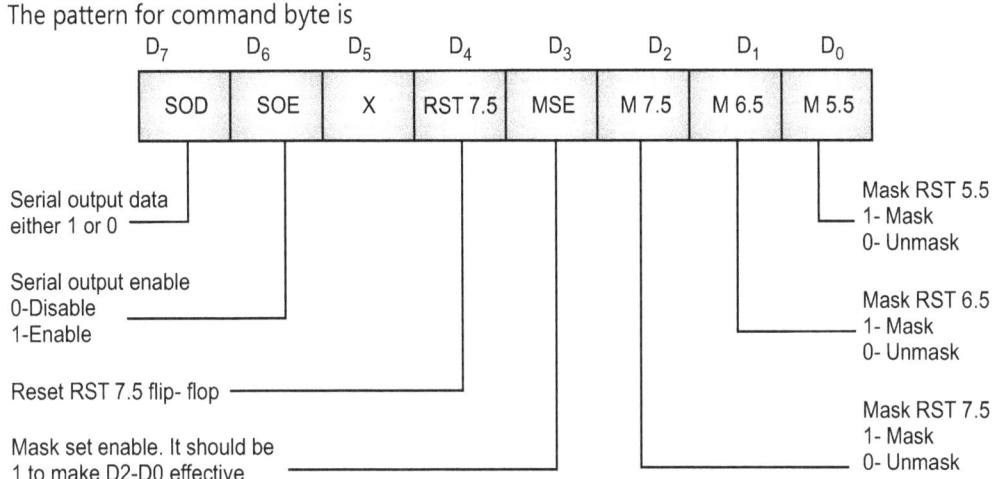

**Fig. 5.26**

**Example :**

; A = 0EH

| D7 | D6 | D5 | D4 | D3 | D2 | D1 | D0 |
|---|---|---|---|---|---|---|---|
| SOD | SOE | X | RST 7.5 | MSE | M 7.5 | M 6.5 | M 5.5 |
| 0 | 0 | 0 | 0 | 1 | 1 | 1 | 0 |

Register A = 0EH

SIM : This instruction will mask RST 7.5 and RST 6.5 interrupts where
; as RST,5.5 interrupt will be unmasked. It will also disable
; serial output.
; A = C0H

| D7 | D6 | D5 | D4 | D3 | D2 | D1 | D0 |
|---|---|---|---|---|---|---|---|
| SOD | SOE | X | RST 7.5 | MSE | M 7.5 | M 6.5 | M 5.5 |
| 1 | 1 | 0 | 0 | 0 | 0 | 0 | 0 |

Register A = C0H

SIM : This instruction will output one on the SOD pin of 8085.
; Masking will be ineffective because MSE bit is zero in the
; command byte.

6. **RIM** : Read Interrupt Mask.

   **Description** : This instruction copies the status of the interrupts into the accumulator. It also reads the serial data through the SID pin. The pattern of the status byte is

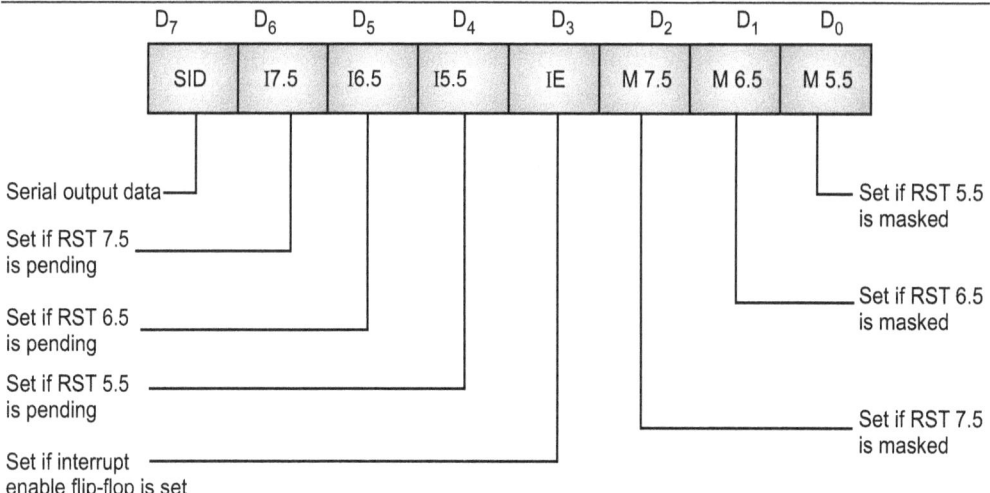

**Fig. 5.27**

### Example

**RIM** : After execution of RIM instruction if the contents of accumulator are 4BH then we get following information.

| D7 | D6 | D5 | D4 | D3 | D2 | D1 | D0 |
|---|---|---|---|---|---|---|---|
| SID | I7.5 | I6.5 | I5.5 | IE | M 7.5 | M 6.5 | M 5.5 |
| 0 | 1 | 0 | 0 | 1 | 0 | 1 | 1 |

Register
A = 4BH

i.e. (a) RST 7.5 is pending
    (b) RST 5.5 and RST 6.5 are masked
    (c) Interrupt Enable flip-flop is set
    (d) Serial i/p data is zero.

### Data Transfer Group Instructions

| Instruction | Description | Operation |
|---|---|---|
| MOV r1, r2 | (Move Data; Move the content of the one register to another) | [r1] <-- [r2] |
| MOV r, m | (Move the content of memory register). | r <-- [M] |
| MOV M, r | (Move the content of register to memory) | M <-- [r] |
| MVI r, data | (Move immediate data to register). | [r] <-- data |
| MVI M, data | (Move immediate data to memory) | M <-- data |

*(Contd.)*

| Instruction | Description | Operation |
|---|---|---|
| LXI rp, data 16 | (Load register pair immediate) | [rp] <-- data 16 bits, [rh] <-- 8 LSBs of data |
| LDA addr | (Load Accumulator direct) | [A] <-- [addr]. |
| STA addr. | (Store accumulator direct) | [addr] <-- [A] |
| LHLD addr. | (Load H-L pair direct) | [L] <-- [addr], [H] <-- [addr+1] |
| SHLD addr. | (Store H-L pair direct) | [addr] <-- [L], [addr+1] <-- [H] |
| LDAX rp. | (LOAD accumulator indirect) | [A] <-- [[rp]] |
| STAX rp. | (Store accumulator indirect) | [[rp]] <-- [A] |
| XCHG | (Exchange the contents of H-L with D-E pair) | [H-L] <--> [D-E] |

1. **MVI r, data (8)** : Move 8 bit immediate data to register r.

   **Operation** : r ← 8-bit data (byte)

   **Description** : This instruction directly loads a specified register with an 8-bit data given within the instruction. The register r is an 8-bit general purpose register such as A, B, C, D, E, H and L.

   **Number of Bytes** : 2 bytes.

   First byte : Opcode of MVI r.

   Second byte : 8-bit data.

   **Addressing Mode** : Immediate addressing.

   **Flags** : Flags are not affected.

   **Example** :

   MVI B, 60H : This instruction will load 60H directly into the B register.

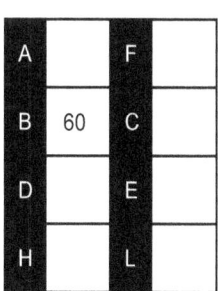

Fig. 5.28

2. **MVI M, data (8)** : Move 8 bit immediate data to memory whose address is in HL register pair.

   **Operation** : M ← byte or (HL) ← byte

   **Description** : This instruction directly loads an 8-bit data given within the instruction into a memory location. The memory location is specified by the contents of␣␣lit, register pair.

   **No. Bytes** : 2 bytes.

   First byte : Opcode of TVIVI M.

   Second byte : 8-bit data.

   **Addressing Mode** : Immediate and indirect addressing.

   **Flags** : Flags are not affected.

   **Example** : H = 20H and L = 50H

   MVI M. 40H ; This instruction will load 40H into
   ; memory whose address is 2050H.

   **Fig. 5.29**

3. **MOV rd, rs** : %love data from source register (rs) to destination register (rd).

   **Operation** : rd ← rs

   **Description** : This instruction copies data from the source register into destination register. The rs and rd are general purpose registers such as A, B, C, D, E, H and L. The contents of the source register remain unchanged after execution of the instruction.

   **No. of Bytes** : 1 byte.

   Op code of MOV rd, rs.

   **Addressing Mode** : Register addressing.

   **Flags** : Flags are not affected.

   **Example** : A = 20

   **MOV B, A** ; This instruction will copy the contents
   ; of register A (20H) into register B.

Fig. 5.30

4. **MOV M, rs** : Move data froth source register (rs) to memory whose address is in HL register pair.

   **Operation** : (HL) ← rs,

   **Description** : This instruction copies data form the source register into memory location pointed by the HL register pair. The rs is an 8-bit general purpose register such as A, B, C. D, E, H and L.

   **No. of Bytes** : 1 byte.

   Opcode of MOV M, rs.

   **Addressing Mode** : Indirect addressing.

   **Flags** : Flags are not affected.

   **Example** : If HL = 2050H, B = 30H.

   MOV M, B ; This instruction will, copy the contents
   ; of o B register (30H) into the memory location
   ; whose address is specified by HL (2050H)

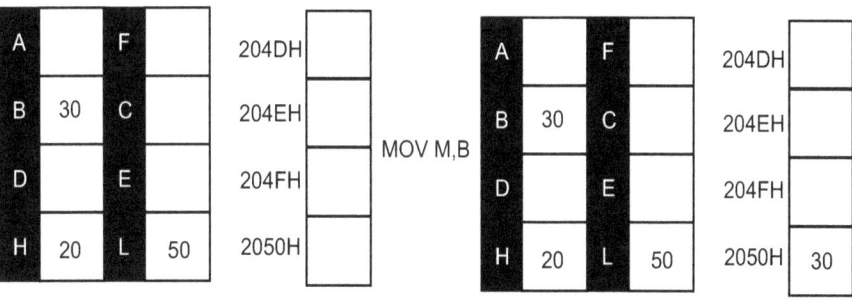

Fig. 5.31

5. **MOV rd, M** : Move data from memory location specified by HL register pair to the, destination register (rd).

   **Operation** : rd ← (HL)

   **Description** : This instruction copies data from memory location whose-address is specified by HL register into destination register. The contents of the "The rd is an 8-bit general he memory location remain unchanged The rd is an 8-bit general purpose register such as A, B, C, D, E, H and L.

   **No. of Bytes** : 1 byte.

   Opcode of MOV rd, M

**Addressing Mode** : Indirect addressing.

**Flags** : Flags are not affected.

**Example** : HL = 2050H, contents at 2050H memory location = 40H

MOV C, M ; This instruction will copy the contents
; of memory location pointed by HL
; register pair (40H) into the C register

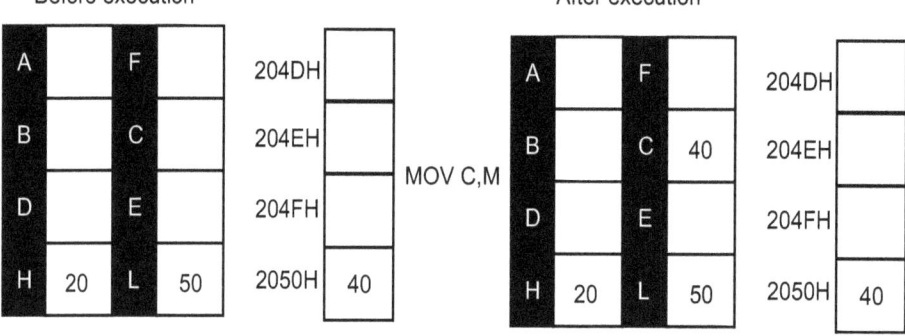

**Fig. 5.32 (a)**

6. **LXI rp, data (16)** : Load 16-bit immediate data to specified register pair.

   **Operation** : rp ← data (16)

   **Description** : This instruction loads immediate 16 bit data specified within the instruction i46 register pair or stack pointer. The rp is 16-bit register pair such- as BC, DE, HL or 16-bit stack pointer.

   **No. of Bytes** : 3 bytes.

   First byte : Opcode of LXI rp.

   Second byte : Low-order byte of 16-bit data.

   Third byte : High order byte of 16-bit data.

   **Addressing Mode** : Immediate addressing.

   **Flags** : Flags are not affected.

**Example** :

   i) **LXI B, 1020H** ; This instruction will load 10H into B
   ; register and 20H into C register.

   ii) **LXI SP, 27FFH** ; This instruction will load 27FFH into stack pointer.

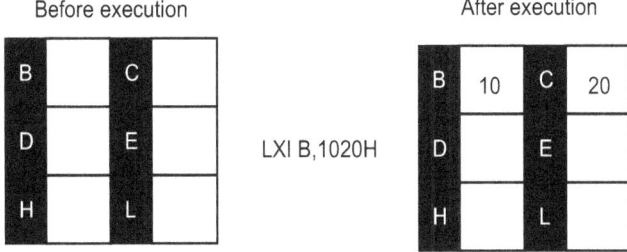

Fig. 5.32 (b)

7. **STA addr** : Store the contents of A register at address given within the instruction.

   **Operation** : (addr) ← A

   **Description** : This instruction stores the contents of- A, register into the memo location whose address is directly specified within the instruction, The contents of A register remain unchanged

   **No. of Bytes** : 3 bytes.
   First byte : Opcode of STA.
   Second byte: Low order byte of the address.
   Third byte : High order byte of the address.

   **Addressing Mode** : Direct addressing.

   **Flags** : Flags are not affected.

   **Example** : A 50H
   STA 2000H ; This instruction will store the
                  ; contents of A register (50H) to
                  ; memory location 2000H.

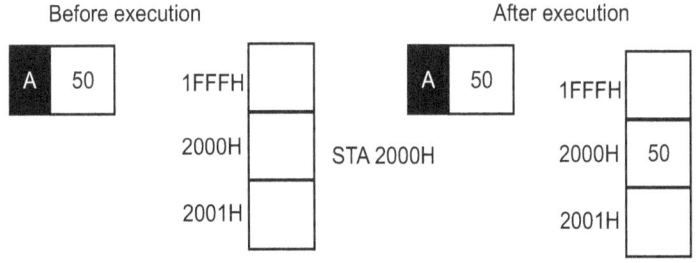

Fig. 5.33

8. **LDA addr** : Load data into A register directly from the address given within the instruction.

   **Operation** : A ← (addr)

   **Description** : This instruction copies the contents of the memory location address is given within the instruction into the accumulator. The contents of the memory location remain- unchanged

| | |
|---|---|
| **No. of Bytes** | : 3 bytes. |
| | First byte Opcode of LDA |
| | Second byte : Low order byte of the address. |
| | Third byte: High order byte of the address |
| **Addressing Mode** | : Direct addressing. |
| **Flags** | : Flags are not affected. |
| **Example** | : (2000H) = 30H |
| | LDA 2000H ; This instruction will copy the |
| | ; contents of memory location |
| | ; 2000H i.e. data 30H into the |
| | ; A register |

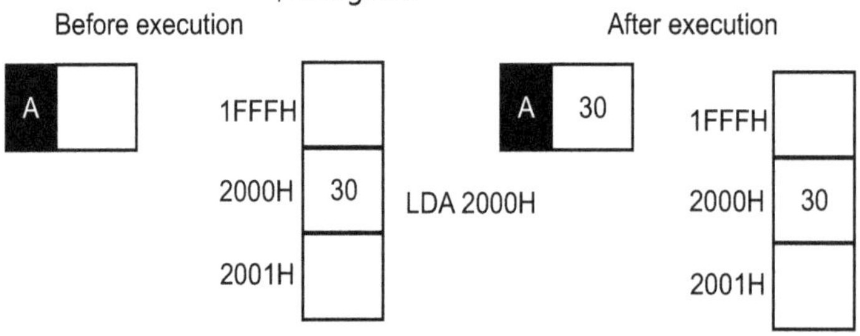

Before execution — After execution

A | 1FFFH     A  30 | 1FFFH
2000H 30  LDA 2000H  2000H 30
2001H                2001H

**Fig. 5.34**

9. **SKLD addr** : Store HL register pair in memory.
   **Operation** : (addr) ← L and (addr + 1) ← H
   **Description** : This instruction stores the contents of L register in the memory location given within the instruction and contents -of H register at address next to it. This instruction is used to store the contents of H and L registers directly into the memory. The contents of the H and L registers remain unchanged.
   **No. of Bytes** : 3 bytes.
   **First byte** : Opcode of SHLD
   Second byte : Low order byte of the address
   Third byte : High order byte of the address
   **Addressing Mode** : Direct addressing.
   **Flags** : Flags are not affected.
   **Example** : H = 30H, L = 60H
   SHLD 2500H ; This instruction will copy
   ; the contents of L register at
   ; address 2500H and the contents
   ; of H register at address 2501H.

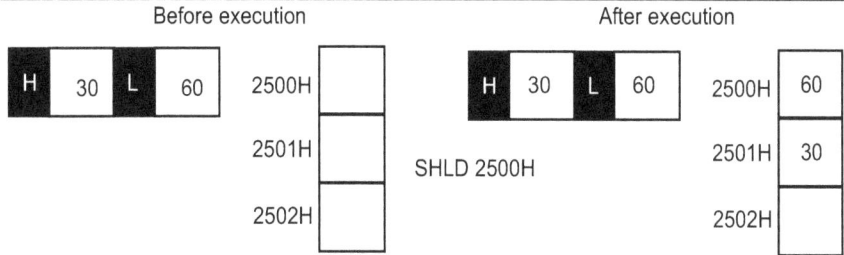

Fig. 5.35

**10. LRLD addr** : Load HL register pair from memory.
  **Operation** : L ← (addr), H ← (addr + 1)
  **Description** : This instruction copies the contents of the memory location given within the instruction into the L register and the contents of the next memory location into the H register.
  **No. of Bytes** : 3 bytes.
  First byte : Opcode of LHLD
  Second byte : Low order byte of the address
  Third byte : High-order byte of the address
  **Addressing Mode** : Direct addressing.
  **Flags** : Flags art not affected.
  **Example** :

  (2500H) = 30H, (2501H) = 60H
  LHLD 2500 H ; This instruction will copy the
  ; contents of memory location 2500H
  ; i.e. data 30H into the L register and
  ; the contents at memory location
  ; 2501H i.e. data 60H into the H register.

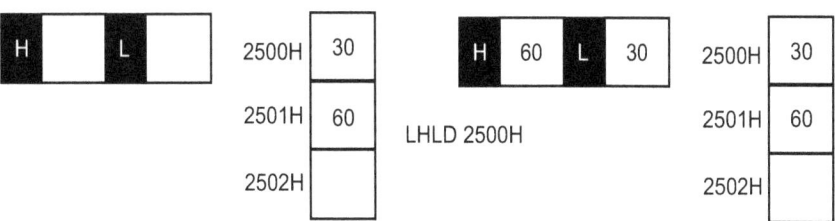

Fig. 5.36

**11. STAX rp** : Store the contents of A register in memory location whose address is specified by BC or DE register pair.

**Operation** : (rp) ← A

**Description** : This instruction copies the contents of accumulator into the memory location whose address is specified by the specified register pair. The rp is BC or DE register pair. This register pair is used as a memory pointer. The contents of the accumulator remain unchanged.

**No. of Bytes** : 1 byte.

Opcodc of STAR, rp

**Addressing Mode** : Register indirect addressing.

**Flags** : Flags are not affected.

**Example** : BC = 1020H, A = 50H

    **STAX B** ; This instruction will copy the
         ; contents of A register (50H) to the
         ; memory location specified
         ; by RC register pair (1020H).

Before execution
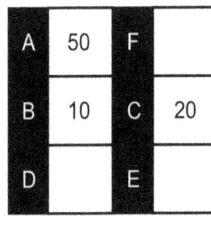 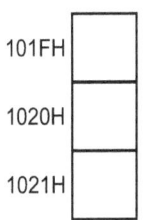

After execution
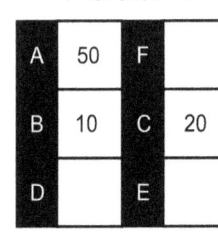 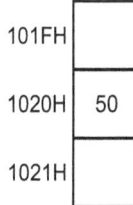

**Fig. 5.37**

**12. LDAX rp** : Load A register with the contents of memory location whose address is specified by AC or DE register pair.

**Operation** : A ← (rp)

**Description** : Ibis instruction copies the contents of memory location' whose address is specified by the register pair into the accumulator. The rp is BC or DE register pair. The register pair is used as a memory pointer.

**No. of Bytes** : 1 byte.

Opcode of LDAX rp

**Addressing Mode** : Register indirect addressing.

**Flags** : Flags are not affected.

**Example** : DE = 2030H, (2030H) = 80H

    LDAX D ; This instruction will copy the
         ; contents of memory location
         ; specified by DE register pair
         ; (2030H) into the accumulator.

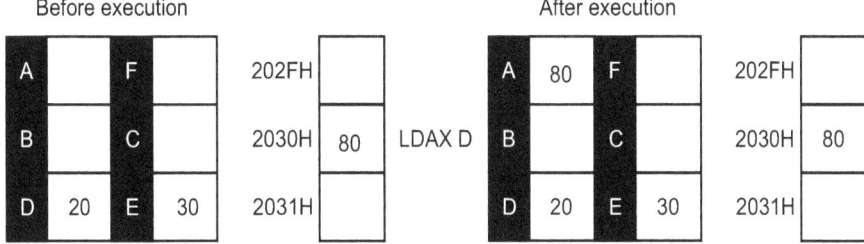

Fig. 5.38

**13. XCHG** : exchange the contents of H with D and L with E

**Operation** : H ↔ D and L ↔ E

**Description** : This instruction exchanges the contents of the -register H with that of D and of L with that of E.

**No. of Bytes** : 1 byte.

Opcode of XCHG

**Addressing Mode** : Register addressing.

**Flags** : Flags are not affected.

**Example** : DE = 2040H, HL = 7080H

**XCHG** : This instruction wilt load the data into registers as follows H = 20H, L = 40H, D = 70H and E = 80 H

**Note :**

- There is no single- instruction to transfer data from one memory location to another memory location in 8085.
- Data transfer instructions do not affect the flags.

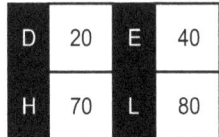

Fig. 5.39

## 5.5 ASSEMBLY LAGUAGE PROGRAMS

**Program 5.1:** Assembly Language program to Store the data byte 32H into memory location 4000H.

| MVI A, 32H | : Store 32H in the accumulator |
| STA 4000H | : Copy accumulator contents at address 4000H |
| HLT | : Terminate program execution |

**Program5.2: Assembly Language Program to add two 8-bit numbers.**

MVI A, 24H   // load Reg A=ACC with 24H
MVI B, 56H   // load Reg B with 56H
ADD B        // ACC= ACC+B
OUT 01H      // Display ACC contents on port 01H
HALT         // End the program
Result: 7A (All are in Hex)

**Program 5.3: Assembly Language Program to Multiply two 16-bit numbers**

LDA 2000   // Load multiplicant to accumulator
MOV B A,   // Move mul i li t p cant from A( ) acc to B register
LDA 2001   // Load multiplier to accumulator
MOV C A,   // Move multiplier multiplier from A to C
MVI A,00   // Load immediate value 00 to a
L: ADD B   // Add B( p) multiplier) with A
DCR C      // Decrement C, it act as a counter
JNZ L      // Jump to L if C reaches 0
STA 2010   // Store result in to memory
HLT        // End

**Program 5.4: Assembly Language program to Exchange the contents of memory locations 2000H and 4000H**

| | |
|---|---|
| LDA 2000H | : Get the contents of memory location 2000H into accumulator |
| MOV B, A | : Save the contents into B register |
| LDA 4000H | : Get the contents of memory location 4000H intoaccumulator |
| STA 2000H | : Store the contents of accumulator at address 2000H |
| MOV A, B | : Get the saved contents back into A register |
| STA 4000H | : Store the contents of accumulator at address 4000H |

**Program 5.5: Subtract the contents of memory location 4001H from the memory location 2000H and place the result in memory location 4002H.**

First number = (4000H) = 51H
Second number = (4001H) = 19H
Result = 51H - 19H = 38H

| | |
|---|---|
| LXI H, 4000H | : HL points 4000H |
| MOV A, M | : Get first operand |
| INX H | : HL points 4001H |

| | |
|---|---|
| SUB M | : Subtract second operand |
| INX H | : HL points 4002H |
| MOV M, A | : Store result at 4002H. |
| HLT | : Terminate program execution |

**Program 5.6: Add two 16-bit numbers**

(4000H) = 15H
(4001H) = 1CH
(4002H) = B7H
(4003H) = 5AH
Result = 1C15 + 5AB7H = 76CCH
(4004H) = CCH
(4005H) = 76H

| | |
|---|---|
| LHLD 4000H | : Get first 16-bit number in HL |
| XCHG | : Save first 16-bit number in DE |
| LHLD 4002H | : Get second 16-bit number in HL |
| MOV A, E | : Get lower byte of the first number |
| ADD L | : Add lower byte of the second number |
| MOV L, A | : Store result in L register |
| MOV A, D | : Get higher byte of the first number |
| ADC H | : Add higher byte of the second number with CARRY |
| MOV H, A | : Store result in H register |
| SHLD 4004H | : Store 16-bit result in memory locations 4004H and 4005H. |
| HLT | : Terminate program execution |

**Program 5.7: Add the contents of memory locations 40001H and 4001H and place the result in the memory locations 4002Hand 4003H.**

(4000H) = 7FH
(4001H) = 89H
Result = 7FH + 89H = 108H
(4002H) = 08H
(4003H) = 01H

| | |
|---|---|
| LXI H, 4000H | : HL Points 4000H |
| MOV A, M | : Get first operand |
| INX H | : HL Points 4001H |

| | |
|---|---|
| ADD M | : Add second operand |
| INX H | : HL Points 4002H |
| MOV M, A | : Store the lower byte of result at 4002H |
| MVIA, 00 byte result | : Initialize higher byte result with 00HADC A :Add carry in the high |
| INX H | : HL Points 4003H |
| MOV M, A | : Store the higher byte of result at 4003H |
| HLT | : Terminate program execution |

**Program 5.8:** Subtract the 16-bit number in memory locations 4002H and 4003H from the 16-bit number in memory locations 4000H and 4001H. The most significant eight bits of the two numbers are in memory locations 4001H and 4003H. Store the result in memory locations 4004H and 4005H with the most significant byte in memory location 4005H.

(4000H) = 19H  
(400IH) = 6AH  
(4004H) = I5H (4003H) = 5CH  
Result = 6A19H - 5C15H = OE04H, (4004H) = 04H, (4005H) = OEH

| | |
|---|---|
| LHLD 4000H | : Get first 16-bit number in HL |
| XCHG | : Save first 16-bit number in DE |
| LHLD 4002H | : Get second 16-bit number in HL |
| MOV A, E | : Get lower byte of the first number |
| SUB L | : Subtract lower byte of the second number |
| MOV L, A | : Store the result in L register |
| MOV A, D | : Get higher byte of the first number |
| SBB H | : Subtract higher byte of second number with borrow |
| MOV H, A | : Store l6-bit result in memory locations 4004H and 4005H. |
| SHLD 4004H | : Store l6-bit result in memory locations 4004H and 4005H. |
| HLT | : Terminate program execution |

**Program 5.9:** Find the l's complement of the number stored at memory location 4400H and store the complemented number at memory location 4300H.

(4400H) = 55H // Any number,   Result = (4300H) = AAH

| | |
|---|---|
| LDA 4400B | : Get the number |
| CMA | : Complement number |
| STA 4300H | : Store the result |
| HLT | : Terminate program execution |

**Program 5.10:** Find the 2's complement of the number stored at memory location 4200H and store the complemented number at memory location 4300H.

(4200H) = 55H, Result = (4300H) = AAH + 1 = ABH

| | |
|---|---|
| LDA 4200H | : Get the number |
| CMA | : Complement the number |
| ADI, 01 H | : Add one in the number |
| STA 4300H | : Store the result |
| HLT | : Terminate program execution |

**Program 5.11:** Calculate the sum of series of numbers. The length of the series is in memory location 4200H and the series begins from memory location 4201H. Consider the sum to be 8 bit number. So, ignore carries. Store the sum at memory location 4300H. and Consider the sum to be 16 bit number. Store the sum at memory locations 4300H and 4301H

4200H = 04H

4201H = 10H

4202H = 45H

4203H = 33H

4204H = 22H

Result = 10 + 41 + 30 + 12 = H, 4300H = H

Source program:

LDA 4200H

| | |
|---|---|
| MOV C, A | : Initialize counter |
| SUB A | : sum = 0 |
| LXI H, 420lH | : Initialize pointer |
| BACK | : ADD M : SUM = SUM + data |
| INX H | : increment pointer |
| DCR C | : Decrement counter |
| JNZ BACK | : if counter 0 repeat |
| STA 4300H | : Store sum |
| HLT | : Terminate program execution |

**Program 5.12:** Multiply two 8-bit numbers stored in memory locations 2200H and 2201H by repetitive addition and store the result in memory locations 2300H and 2301H.

(2200H) = 03H
(2201H) = B2H
Result = B2H + B2H + B2H = 216H, (2300H) = 16H, (2301H) = 02H

| | |
|---|---|
| LDA 2200H | |
| MOV E, A | |
| MVI D, 00 | : Get the first number in DE register pair |
| LDA 2201H | |
| MOV C, A | : Initialize counter |
| LXI H, 0000 H | : Result = 0 |
| BACK: DAD D | : Result = result + first number |
| DCR C | : Decrement count |
| JNZ BACK | : If count 0 repeat |
| SHLD 2300H | : Store result |
| HLT | : Terminate program execution |

**Program 5.13:** Divide 16 bit number stored in memory locations 2200H and 2201H by the 8 bit number stored at memory location 2202H. Store the quotient in memory locations 2300H and 2301H and remainder in memory locations 2302H and 2303H.

(2200H) = 60H
(2201H) = A0H
(2202H) = 12H
Result = A060H/12H = 8E8H Quotient and 10H remainder
(2300H) = E8H
(2301H) = 08H
(2302H = 10H
(2303H) 00H

Source program

| | |
|---|---|
| LHLD 2200H | : Get the dividend |
| LDA 2202H | : Get the divisor |
| MOV C, A | |
| LXI D, 0000H | : Quotient = 0 |
| BACK: MOV A, L | |

| SUB C | : Subtract divisor |
| MOV L, A | : Save partial result |
| JNC SKIP | : if CY 1 jump |
| DCR H | : Subtract borrow of previous subtraction |
| SKIP: INX D | : Increment quotient |
| MOV A, H | |
| CPI, 00 | : Check if dividend < divisor |
| JNZ BACK | : if no repeat |
| MOV A, L | |
| CMP C | |
| JNC BACK | |
| SHLD 2302H | : Store the remainder |
| XCHG | |
| SHLD 2300H | : Store the quotient |
| HLT | : Terminate program execution |

**Program 5.14:** Find the number of negative elements (most significant bit 1) in a block of data. The length of the block is in memory location 2200H and the block itself begins in memory location 2201H. Store the number of negative elements in memory location 2300H

(2200H) = 04H (2201H) = 56H
(2202H) = A9H
(2203H) = 73H
(2204H) = 82H

Result = 02 since 2202H and 2204H contain numbers with a MSB of 1.

Source program

| LDA 2200H | |
| MOV C, A | : Initialize count |
| MVI B, 00 | : Negative number = 0 |
| LXI H, 2201H | : Initialize pointer |
| BACK: MOV A, M | : Get the number |
| ANI 80H | : Check for MSB |
| JZ SKIP | : If MSB = 1 |
| INR B | : Increment negative number count |
| SKIP: INX H | : Increment pointer |

| | |
|---|---|
| DCR C | : Decrement count |
| JNZ BACK | : If count 0 repeat |
| MOV A, B | |
| STA 2300H | : Store the result |
| HLT | : Terminate program execution |

**Program 5.15 :** Find the largest number in a block of data. The length of the block is in memory location 2200H and the block itself starts from memory location 2201H. Store the maximum number in memory location 2300H. Assume that the numbers in the block are all 8 bit unsigned binary numbers.

(2200H) = 04
(2201H) = 34H
(2202H) = A9H
(2203H) = 78H
(2204H) = 56H
Result = (2202H) = A9H

Source program

| | |
|---|---|
| LDA 2200H | |
| MOV C, A | : Initialize counter |
| XRA A | : Maximum = Minimum possible value = 0 |
| LXI H, 2201H | : Initialize pointer |
| BACK: CMP M | : Is number> maximum |
| JNC SKIP | : Yes, replace maximum MOV A, M |
| SKIP: INX H | |
| DCR C | |
| JNZ BACK | |
| STA 2300H | : Store maximum number |
| HLT | : Terminate program execution |

**Program 5.16:** Write a program to count number of I's in the contents of D register and store the count in the B register.

Source program:
MVI B, 00H
MVI C, 08H
MOV A, D
BACK: RAR

JNC SKIP
INR B
SKIP: DCR C
JNZ BACK
HLT

**Program 5.17:** Write a program to sort given 10 numbers from memory location 2200H in the ascending order.

| | |
|---|---|
| MVI B, 09 | : Initialize counter |
| START | : LXI H, 2200H: Initialize memory pointer |
| MVI C, 09H | : Initialize counter 2 |
| BACK: MOV A, M | : Get the number |
| INX H | : Increment memory pointer |
| CMP M | : Compare number with next number |
| JC SKIP | : If less, don't interchange |
| JZ SKIP | : If equal, don't interchange |
| MOV D, M | |
| MOV M, A | |
| DCX H | |
| MOV M, D | |
| INX H | : Interchange two numbers |
| SKIP:DCR C | : Decrement counter 2 |
| JNZ BACK | : If not zero, repeat |
| DCR B | : Decrement counter 1 |
| JNZ START | |
| HLT | : Terminate program execution |

**Program 5.18:** Calculate the sum of series of even numbers from the list of numbers. The length of the list is in memory location 2200H and the series itself begins from memory location 2201H. Assume the sum to be 8 bit number so you can ignore carries and store the sum at memory location

Sample problem:
2200H= 4H
2201H= 20H
2202H= 15H
2203H= 13H
2204H= 22H

Result 2210H= 20 + 22 = 42H
= 42H

**Source program:**

| | |
|---|---|
| LDA 2200H | |
| MOV C, A | : Initialize counter |
| MVI B, 00H | : sum = 0 |
| LXI H, 2201H | : Initialize pointer |
| BACK: MOV A, M | : Get the number |
| ANI 01H | : Mask Bit 1 to Bit7 |
| JNZ SKIP | : Don't add if number is ODD |
| MOV A, B | : Get the sum |
| ADD M | : SUM = SUM + data |
| MOV B, A | : Store result in B register |
| SKIP: INX H | : increment pointer |
| DCR C | : Decrement counter |
| JNZ BACK | : if counter 0 repeat |
| STA 2210H | : store sum |
| HLT | : Terminate program execution |

**Program 5.19: Find the square of the given numbers from memory location 6100H and store the result from memory location 7000H**

| | |
|---|---|
| LXI H, 6200H | : Initialize lookup table pointer |
| LXI D, 6100H | : Initialize source memory pointer |
| LXI B, 7000H | : Initialize destination memory pointer |
| BACK: LDAX D | : Get the number |
| MOV L, A | : A point to the square |
| MOV A, M | : Get the square |
| STAX B | : Store the result at destination memory location |
| INX D | : Increment source memory pointer |
| INX B | : Increment destination memory pointer |
| MOV A, C | |
| CPI 05H | : Check for last number |
| JNZ BACK | : If not repeat |
| HLT | : Terminate program execution |

**Program 5.20:** Divide the 16-bit unsigned number in memory locations 2200H and 2201H (most significant bits in 2201H) by the B-bit unsigned number in memory location 2300H store the quotient in memory location 2400H and remainder in 2401H

Assumption: The most significant bits of both the divisor and dividend are zero.

| | |
|---|---|
| MVI E, 00 | : Quotient = 0 |
| LHLD 2200H | : Get dividend |
| LDA 2300 | : Get divisor |
| MOV B, A | : Store divisor |
| MVI C, 08 | : Count = 8 |
| NEXT: DAD H | : Dividend = Dividend x 2 |
| MOV A, E | |
| RLC | |
| MOV E, A | : Quotient = Quotient x 2MOV A, H |
| SUB B | : Is most significant byte of Dividend > divisor |
| JC SKIP | : No, go to Next step |
| MOV H, A | : Yes, subtract divisor |
| INR E | : and Quotient = Quotient + 1 |
| SKIP:DCR C | : Count = Count - 1 |
| JNZ NEXT | : Is count =0 repeat |
| MOV A, E | |
| STA 2401H | : Store Quotient |
| Mov A, H | |
| STA 2410H | : Store remainder |
| HLT | : End of program |

**Program 5.21:** Transfer ten bytes of data from one memory to another memory block. Source memory block starts from memory location 2200H where as destination memory block starts from memory location 2300H

| | |
|---|---|
| LXI H, 4150 | : Initialize memory pointer |
| MVI B, 08 | : count for 8-bit |
| MVI A, 54 | |
| LOOP | : RRC |
| JC LOOP1 | |
| MVI M, 00 | : store zero it no carry |
| JMP COMMON | |

LOOP2: MVI M, 01: store one if there is a carry
COMMON: INX H
DCR B        : check for carry
JNZ LOOP
HLT          : Terminate the program

## Questions

1. Draw and explain architecture of 8085 microprocessor.
2. What are the different types of registers used in 8085 microprocessor.
3. Explain different types of flags used in 8085 microprocessor.
4. What are the different types of instructions used in 8085 microprocessor.
5. Explain the function of following instructions
       STA addr    LDAX rp    SBB M    DAA    ANA M
       CMP r    RRC    JC    CALL    PUSH
6. Explain the addressing modes in 8085 microprocessor.
7. Write an assembly language program to add / substact / multiply / division / block transfer / finding largest number etc.
8. Explain the Data Addressing modes.
9. Explain the details MOV $r_1$ Data.
10. Explain PUSH | POP instruction and it's details.
11. What are stack memory Addressing modes ?
12. Explain the different Addressing modes.
13. Explain the stack operation. input / output and machine control group.
14. Explain in details following instructions
    (i) PUSH rp    (ii) POP rp    (iii) POP psw
15. What is CALL address and RET ?
    Explain the implements of substations
16. Explain in details STAX rp.

# Unit - VI

# INTERFACING I/O DEVICES

## 6.1 BASIC INTERFACING CONCEPTS

Microprocessor is the CPU of a computer. A microprocessor can perform some operation on a data and give the output. But to perform the operation we need an input to enter the data and an output to display the results of the operation. So we are using a keyboard and monitor as Input and output along with the processor. Microprocessors engineering involves a lot of other concepts and we also interface memory elements like ROM, EPROM to access the memory.

**Interfacing Types**

There are two types of interfacing in context of the 8085 processor.

- Memory Interfacing.
- I/O Interfacing.

**Memory Interfacing :**

There is a necessity for the microprocessor to access memory frequently for reading various instruction codes and data stored in the memory. The interfacing circuit aids in accessing the memory.

Memory requires some signals to read from and write to registers. Similarly the microprocessor transmits some signals for reading or writing a data.

The interfacing process involves matching the memory requirements with the microprocessor signals. The interfacing circuit therefore should be designed in such a way that it matches the memory signal requirements with the signals of the microprocessor. For example for carrying out a READ process, the microprocessor should initiate a read signal which the memory requires to read a data. In simple words, the primary function of a memory interfacing circuit is to aid the microprocessor in reading and writing a data to the given register of a memory chip.

**I/O Interfacing :**

We know that keyboard and Displays are used as communication channel with outside world. So it is necessary that we interface keyboard and displays with the microprocessor. This is called I/O interfacing. In this type of interfacing we use latches and buffers for interfacing the keyboards and displays with the microprocessor.

But the main disadvantage with this interfacing is that the microprocessor can perform only one function. It functions as an input device if it is connected to buffer and as an output device if it is connected to latch. Thus the capability is very limited in this type of interfacing.

## 6.2 PROGRAMMABLE PERIPHERAL DEVICES

Programmable peripheral devices were introduced by Intel to increase the overall performance of the system. These devices along with I/O functions, they perform various other functions such as time delays, counters and interrupt handling. These devices are nothing but a combination of many devices on a single chip. A programmable device can be set up to perform specific function by writing a code in the internal register. As this code controls the function of the device it's called control word and internal register in which it is stored is called Control Register.

INTEL developed some peripheral devices for processors like 8085/8086/8088. The peripheral devices includes

| IC No. | Application |
|---|---|
| 8255 | Parallel Communication Interface (PPI) |
| 8251 | Serial communication Interface (USART- Universal Synchronous / Asynchronous Receiver / Transmitter) |
| 8257 | DMA Controller |
| 8279 | Keyboard/Display Controller |
| 8259 | Programmable Interrupt controller |
| 8254 | Programmable Timer |

**Types of Communication Interface**

There are two ways in which a microprocessor can connect with outside world or other memory systems.
- Serial Communication Interface
- Parallel Communication interface

**Serial Communication Interface:**

In serial communication interface, the interface gets a single byte of data from the microprocessor and sends it bit by bit to other system serially (or) the interface receives data bit by bit serially from the external systems and converts the data into a single byte and transfers it to the microprocessor.

**Parallel Communication Interface:**

This interface gets a byte of data from microprocessor and sends it bit by bit to the other systems in simultaneous (or) parallel fashion. The interface also receives data bit by bit simultaneously from the external system and converts the data into a single byte and transfers it to microprocessor.

Consider that we have a microprocessor interfaced to both I/O device and also a memory chip. Now how to select between the two devices according to the requirement?

For this purpose an address decoding circuit is used. An address decoding circuit aids in selecting the required I/O device or a memory chip.

## Peripherals I/O Instructions

**Input/Output** : This group consists of following set of instructions.

IN addr
OUT addr

1. **IN addr (8-bit)** : Copy data from input port into Accumulator.
   **Operation** : A ← (addr)
   **Description** : This instruction copies the data at the port whose address is specified in the instruction into the accumulator.
   **No. of Bytes.** : 2 bytes.
   First byte Opcode of IN.
   Second byte : 8-bit address.
   **Addressing Mode** : Direct addressing.
   **Flags** : Flags are not affected.
   **Example** : Port address = 80H data stored at port address 80H, (80H) 10H
   **IN 80H** ; This instruction will copy the data stored at address 80H, i.e. data 1011 in the accumulator.

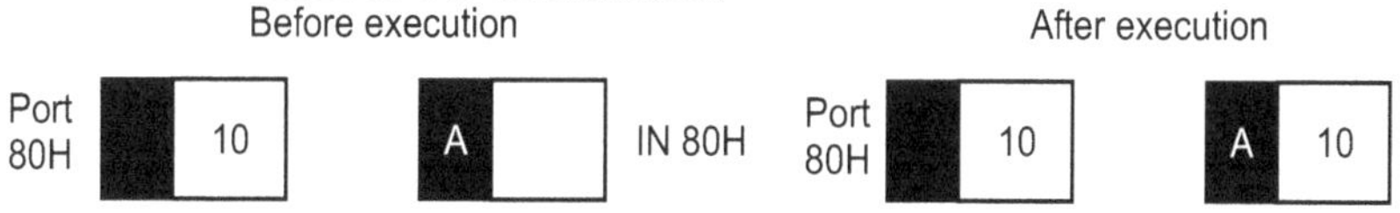

   Before execution | After execution

   Port 80H [10]   A [ ]   IN 80H   Port 80H [10]   A [10]

   **Fig. 6.1**

2. **OUT addr (8-bit)** : Send data to the output port.
   **Operation** : (addr) ← A
   **Description** : This instruction sends the contents of accumulator to the output port whose address dress is specified within the instruction.
   **No. of Bytes** : 2 bytes.
   **First byte** : Opcode of OUT.
   Second byte : 8-bit address.
   **Addressing Mode** : Direct addressing.
   **Flags** : Flags are not affected.
   **Example** : A = 40H
   **OUT 50H** ; This instruction will send the contents of accumulator (4011) to the output port whose address is 50H.

   Before execution | After execution

   Port 50H [ ]   A [40]   OUT 50H   Port 50H [40]   A [40]

   **Fig. 6.2**

## 6.3 INTERFACING MECHANISMS

### 6.3.1 Connecting a CPU to the Outside World

Most I/O devices interface to the CPU in a fashion quite similar to memory. Indeed, many devices appear to the CPU as though they were memory devices. To output data to the outside world the CPU simply stores data into a "memory" location and the data magically appears on some connectors external to the computer. Similarly, to input data from some external device, the CPU simply transfers data from a "memory" location into the CPU; this "memory" location holds the value found on the pins of some external connector.

An output port is a device that looks like a memory cell to the computer but contains connections to the outside world. An I/O port typically uses a latch rather than a flip-flop to implement the memory cell. When the CPU writes to the address associated with the latch, the latch device captures the data and makes it available on a set of wires external to the CPU and memory system Fig. 6.3. Note that output ports can be write-only, or read/write. The port in Fig. 6.3, for example, is a write-only port. Since the outputs on the latch do not loop back to the CPU's data bus, the CPU cannot read the data the latch contains. Both the address decode and write control lines must be active for the latch to operate; when reading from the latch's address the decode line is active, but the write control line is not.

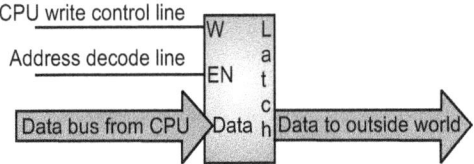

**Fig. 6.3 : A Typical Output Port**

Fig. 6.3 shows how to create a read/write input/output port. The data written to the output port loops back to a transparent latch. Whenever the CPU reads the decoded address the read and decode lines are active and this activates the lower latch. This places the data previously written to the output port on the CPU's data bus, allowing the CPU to read that data. A read-only (input) port is simply the lower half of Fig. 6.4; the system ignores any data written to an input port.

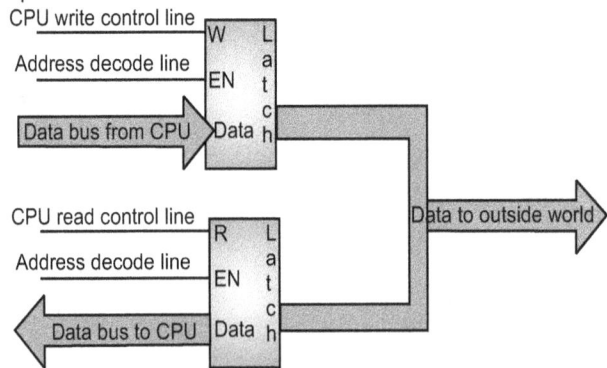

**Fig. 6.4 : An Output Port that Supports Read/Write Access**

Note that the port in Fig. 6.4 is not an input port. Although the CPU can read this data, this port organization simply lets the CPU read the data it previously wrote to the port. The data appearing on an external connector is an output port (only). One could create a (read-only) input port by using the lower half of the circuit in Fig. 6.4. The input to the latch would appear on the CPU's data bus whenever the CPU reads the latch data.

A perfect example of an output port is a parallel printer port. The CPU typically writes an ASCII character to a byte-wide output port that connects to the DB-25F connector on the back of the computer's case. A cable transmits this data to the printer where an input port (to the printer) receives the data. A processor inside the printer typically converts this ASCII character to a sequence of dots it prints on the paper.

Generally, a given peripheral device will use more than a single I/O port. A typical PC parallel printer interface, for example, uses three ports: a read/write port, an input port, and an output port. The read/write port is the data port. The input port returns control signals from the printer; these signals indicate whether the printer is ready to accept another character, is off-line, is out of paper, etc. The output port transmits control information to the printer such as whether data is available to print.

The first thing to learn about the input/output subsystem is that I/O in a typical computer system is radically different than I/O in a typical high level programming language. In a real computer system you will rarely find machine instructions that behave like writeln, cout, printf, or even the HLA stdin and stdout statements. In fact, most input / output instructions behave exactly like the 80x86's MOV instruction. To send data to an output device, the CPU simply moves that data to a special memory location. To read data from an input device, the CPU simply moves data from the address of that device into the CPU. Other than there are usually more wait states associated with a typical peripheral device than actual memory, the input or output operation looks very similar to a memory read or write operation.

## 6.3.2 Read-Only, Write-Only, Read/Write, and Dual I/O Ports

We can classify input/output ports into four categories based on the CPU's ability to read and write data at a given port address. These four categories are read-only ports, write-only ports, read/write ports, and dual I/O ports.

A read-only port is an input port. If the CPU can only read the data from the port, then that port is providing data appearing on lines external to the CPU. The system typically ignores any attempt to write data to a read only port1. A good example of a read only port is the status port on a PC's parallel printer interface. Reading data from this port lets you test the current condition of the printer. The system ignores any data written to this port.

A write only port is always an output port. Writing data to such a port presents the data for use by an external device. Attempting to read data from a write-only port generally returns garbage. You generally cannot depend on the meaning of any value read from a write-only port.

A read/write port is an output port as far as the outside world is concerned. However, the CPU can read as well as write data to such a port. Whenever the CPU reads data from a read/write port, it reads the data that was last written to the port. Reading the port does not affect the data the external peripheral device sees, reading the port is a simple convenience.

A dual I/O port is also a read/write port, but reading the port reads data from some external device while writing data to the port transmits data to a different external device. Fig. 6.5 shows how you could interface such a device to the system. Note that the input and output ports are actually a read-only and a write-only port that share the same address. Reading the address accesses one port while writing to the address accesses the other port. Essentially, this port arrangement uses the R/W control line(s) as an extra address bit when selecting these ports.

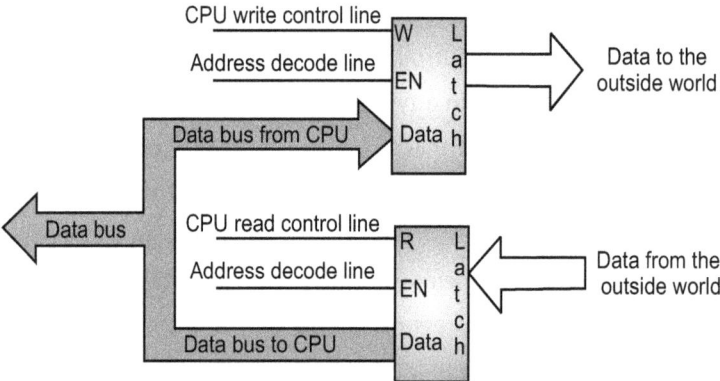

**Fig. 6.5 : An Input and an Output Device That Share the Same Address (a Dual I/O Port)**

The CPU always reads and writes data to peripheral devices using data on the data bus (that is, whatever data the CPU places on the data bus when it writes to an output port is the data actually written to that output port). While this is generally true for input ports, this isn't necessarily true for output ports. In fact, a very common output mechanism is simply accessing a port. Fig. 6.6 provides a very simple example. In this circuit, an address decoder decodes two separate addresses. Any access (read or write) to the first address sets the output line high; any read or write of the second address clears the output line. Note that this circuit ignores the data on the CPU's data lines. It is not important whether the CPU reads or writes data to these addresses, nor is the data written of any consequence. The only thing that matters is that the CPU access one of these two addresses.

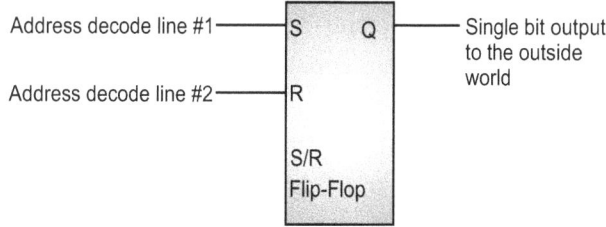

**Fig. 6.6 : Outputting Data to a Port by Simply Accessing That Port**

Another possible way to connect an output port to the CPU is to use a D flip-flop and connect the read/write status lines to the D input on the flip-flop. Fig. 6.7 shows how you could design such a device. In this diagram any read of the selected port sets the output bit to zero while a write to this output port sets the output bit to one.

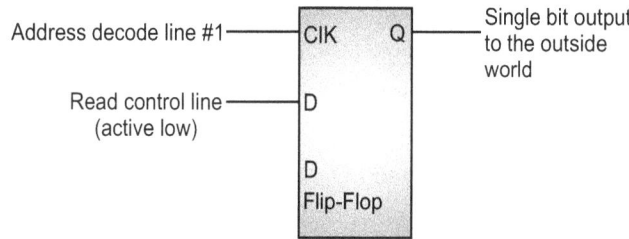

**Fig. 6.7 : Outputting Data Using the Read/Write Control as the Data to Output**

There are a wide variety of ways you can connect external devices to the CPU. This section only provides a few examples as a sampling of what is possible. In the real world, there are an amazing number of different ways that engineers connect external devices to the CPU. Unless otherwise noted, the rest of this chapter will assume that the CPU reads and writes data to an external device using the data bus.

## 6.3.3 I/O (Input/Output) Mechanisms

There are three basic forms of input and output that a typical computer system will use: I/O mapped I/O, memory-mapped I/O, and direct memory access (DMA). I/O-mapped input/output uses special instructions to transfer data between the computer system and the outside world; memory-mapped I/O uses special memory locations in the normal address space of the CPU to communicate with real world devices DMA is a special form of memory mapped I/O where the peripheral device reads and writes data in memory without going through the CPU.

## 6.4 MEMORY MAPPED INPUT/OUTPUT

A memory mapped peripheral device is connected to the CPU's address and data lines exactly like memory, so whenever the CPU reads or writes the address associated with the peripheral device, the CPU transfers data to or from the device. This mechanism has several benefits and only a few disadvantages.

The principle advantage of a memory-mapped I/O subsystem is that the CPU can use any instruction that accesses memory to transfer data between the CPU and a memory mapped I/O device. The MOV instruction is the one most commonly used to send and receive data from a memory mapped I/O device, but any instruction that reads or writes data in memory is also legal. For example, if you have an I/O port that is read/write, you can use the ADD instruction to read the port, add data to the value read, and then write data back to the port.

Of course, this feature is only usable if the port is a read/write port. If the port is read only or write only, an instruction that reads memory, modifies the value, and then writes the modified value back to memory will be of little use. You should use such read/modify/write instructions only with read/write ports.

Nevertheless, the fact that you can use any instruction that accesses memory to manipulate port data is often a big advantage since you can operate on the data with a single instruction rather than first moving the data into the CPU, manipulating the data, and then writing the data back to the I/O port.

The big disadvantage of memory mapped I/O devices is that they consume addresses in the memory map. Generally, the minimum amount of space you can allocate to a peripheral is a four kilobyte page. Therefore, a few independent peripherals can wind up consuming a fair amount of the physical address space. Fortunately, a typicalPC has only a couple dozen such devices, so this isn't much of a problem. However, some devices, like video cards, consume a large chunk of the address space.

## 6.5 I/O MAPPED INPUT/OUTPUT

I/O mapped input/output uses special instructions to access I/O ports. Many CPUs do not provide this type of I/O, though the 80x86 does. The Intel 80x86 family uses the IN and OUT instructions to provide I/O-mapped input/output capabilities. The 80x86 IN and OUT instructions behave somewhat like the MOV instruction except they transmit their data to and from a special I/O address space that is distinct from the memory address space. The IN and OUT instructions use the following syntax:

in( port, al ); // ... or AX or EAX, port is a constant in the range

out( al, port ); // 0..255.

in( dx, al ); // Or AX or EAX.

out( al, dx );

The 80x86 family uses a separate address bus for I/O transfers2. This bus is only 16-bits wide, so the 80x86 can access a maximum of 65,536 different bytes in the I/O space. The first two instructions encode the port address as an eight-bit constant, so they're actually limited to accessing only the first 256 I/O addresses in this address space. This makes the instruction shorter (two bytes instead of three). Unfortunately, most of the interesting peripheral devices are at addresses above 255, so the first pair of instructions above are only useful for accessing certain on-board peripherals in a PC system.

To access I/O ports at addresses beyond 255 you must use the latter two forms of the IN and OUT instructions above. These forms require that you load the 16-bit I/O address into the DX register and use DX as a pointer to the specified I/O address. For example, to write a byte to the I/O address $3783 you would use an instruction sequence like the following:

mov( $378, dx );

out( al, dx );

The advantage of an I/O address space is that peripheral devices mapped to this area do not consume space in the memory address space. This allows you to fully expand the memory address space with RAM or other memory. On the other hand, you cannot use arbitrary memory instructions to access peripherals in the I/O address space, you can only use the IN and OUT instructions.

Another disadvantage to the 80x86's I/O address space is that it is quite small. Although most peripheral devices only use a couple of I/O address, a few devices, like video display cards, can occupy millions of different I/O locations. As noted earlier, some video display cards have 32 megabytes of dual-ported RAM on board. Clearly we cannot easily map this many locations into the 64K I/O address space.

## 6.6 DIRECT MEMORY ACCESS

Memory mapped I/O subsystems and I/O-mapped subsystems both require the CPU to move data between the peripheral device and main memory. For this reason, we often call these two forms of input/output programmed I/O. For example, to input a sequence of ten bytes from an input port and store these bytes into memory the CPU must read each value and store it into memory. For very high-speed I/O devices the CPU may be too slow when processing this data a byte at a time. Such devices generally have an interface to the CPU's bus so they can directly read and write memory. This is known as direct memory access since the peripheral device accesses memory directly, without using the CPU as an intermediary. This often allows the I/O operation to proceed in parallel with other CPU operations, thereby increasing the overall speed of the system. Note, however, that the CPU and DMA device cannot both use the address and data busses at the same time. Therefore, concurrent processing only occurs if the CPU has a cache and is executing code and accessing data found in the cache. Nevertheless, even if the CPU must halt and wait for the DMA operation to complete, the I/O is still much faster since many of the bus operations during I/O or memory-mapped input/output consist of instruction fetches or I/O port accesses which are not present during DMA operations.

A typical DMA controller consists of a pair of counters and other circuitry that interfaces with memory and the peripheral device. One of the counters serves as an address register. This counter supplies an address on the address bus for each transfer. The second counter specifies the number of transfers to complete. Each time the peripheral device wants to transfer data to or from memory, it sends a signal to the DMA controller. The DMA controller places the value of the address counter on the address bus. At the same time, the peripheral device places data on the data bus or reads data from the data bus. After a successful data transfer, the DMA controller increments its address register and decrements the transfer counter. This process repeats until the transfer counter decrements to zero.

- Note, however, that some devices may fail if you attempt to write to their corresponding input ports, so it's never a good idea to write data to a read-only port.
- Physically, the I/O address bus is the same as the memory address bus, but additional control lines determine whether the address on the bus is accessing memory or and I/O device.
- This is typically the address of the data port on the parallel printer port.

Memory-mapped I/O (MMIO) and port-mapped I/O (PMIO) is also called isolated I/O are two complementary methods of performing input / output between the CPU and peripheral devices in a computer. An alternative approach is using dedicated I/O processors commonly known as channels on mainframe computers that execute their own instructions.

Memory-mapped I/O (not to be confused with memory-mapped file I/O) uses the same address bus to address both memory and I/O devices the memory and registers of the I/O devices are mapped to address values. So when an address is accessed by the CPU, it may refer to a portion of physical RAM, but it can also refer to memory of the I/O device. Thus, the CPU instructions used to access the memory can also be used for accessing devices. Each I/O device monitors the CPU's address bus and responds to any CPU access of an address assigned to that device, connecting the data bus to the desired device's hardware register. To accommodate the I/O devices, areas of the addresses used by the CPU must be reserved for I/O and must not be available for normal physical memory. The reservation might be temporary the Commodore 64 could bank switch between its I/O devices and regular memory or permanent.

Port-mapped I/O often uses a special class of CPU instructions designed specifically for performing I/O, such as the IN and OUT instructions found on microprocessors based on thex86 and x86-64 architectures. These two instructions can copy one, two or four bytes between the EAX register or one of that register's subdivisions on the CPU and a specified I/O port which is assigned to an I/O device. I/O devices have a separate address space from general memory, either accomplished by an extra "I/O" pin on the CPU's physical interface, or an entire bus dedicated to I/O. Because the address space for I/O is isolated from that for main memory, this is sometimes referred to as isolated I/O.

## 6.7 I/O MAPPED I/O

- In this technique, I/O device is treated as a I/Q device and memory as memory.
- Each I/Q device uses eight address lines.
- If eight address lines are used to interface to generate the address of the I/O port, then 256 input and 256 output devices can be interfaced with the microprocessor.
- The address bus of the 8085 microprocessor is 16 bit, so we can either use lower order address lines i.e. A0 to A7 or higher order address lines i.e. A8 to A15 to address I/O devices where the address available on A0 to A7 will be copied on the address lines A8 to A15.
- In I/O mapped I/O, the complete 64 Kbytes of memory can be interfaced as all address lines can be used to address memory locations as the address space is not shared among I/O devices and memory and 256 input and /or output devices.
- In this type, the data transfer is possible between accumulator A register and I/O devices only.
- Address decoding is simple, as less hardware is required.
- The separate control signals are used to access I/O devices and memory such as IOR, IOW for I/O port and MEMR,

MEMW for memory hence memory location are protected from the I/O access.
- But in this type, arithmetic and logical operation are not possible directly.
- Also we cannot use other register for data transfer between I/O device and microprocessor accepts A register.
- The Fig. 6.8 shows interfacing I/O devices in I/O mapped I/O.

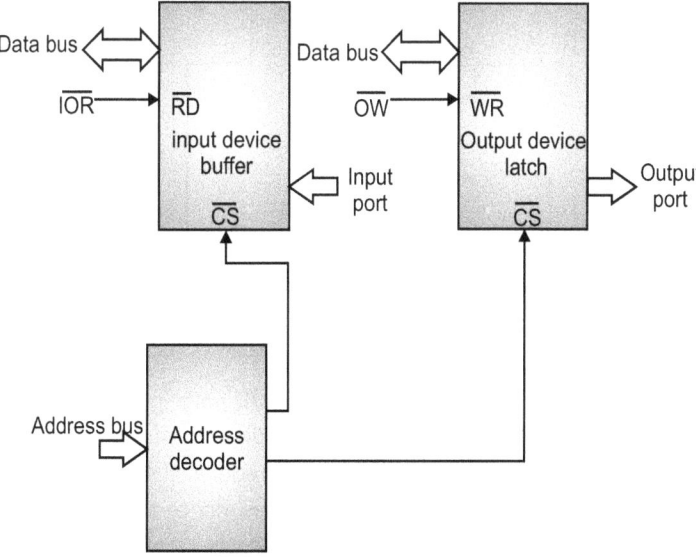

**Fig. 6.8 : I/O mapped I/O ports**

## 6.8 MEMORY MAPPED I/O

- In this technique, I/O devices are treated as memory and memory as memory, hence the address of the I/O devices are as same as that of memory i.e. 16 bit for 8085 microprocessor.
- So, the address space of the memory i.e. 64 Kbytes will be shared by the I/O devices as well as by memory.
- All 16 address lines i.e. A0 to A15 is used to address memory locations as well as I/O devices.
- The control signals MEMR and MEMW are used to access memory devices as well as I/O devices.
- The data transfer is possible between any register of the microprocessor and I/O device or memory device.
- Hence, all memory related instructions can be used to access devices as they are treated as memory devices.
- Address decoding of the I/O devices and memory devices are complicated and expensive as more hardware is required.
- The 8085 microprocessor can access either 64 K I/O ports or memory locations, hence the total numbers of the I/O ports and memory locations should not be greater than 64 K.
- I/O devices and memory locations are distinguished by the addresses only.

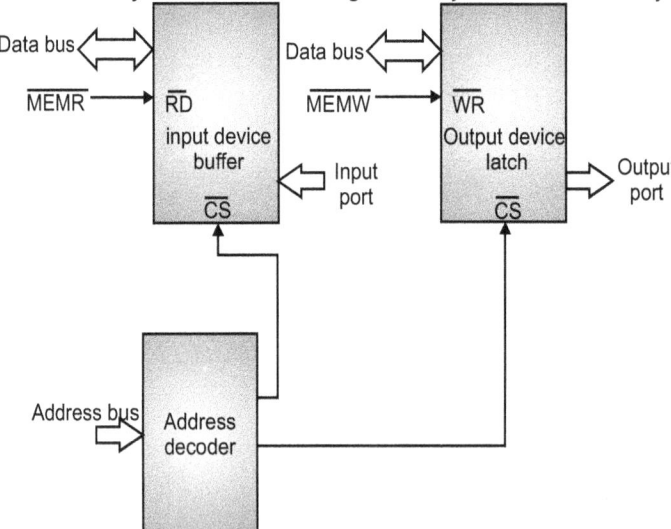

**Fig. 6.9 : Memory mapped I/O ports**

- Arithmetic and logical operation can be performed directly on the I/O devices.
- Most of the memory instructions are long; hence it reduces the speed of I/O.
- Normally, the speed of the I/O devices are very slow, hence the common interface used in memory mapped I/O will reduce the speed of memory access unnecessarily.
- The Fig. above shows interfacing of I/O devices in memory mapped I/O.

# 6.9 DIFFERENCE BETWEEN MEMORY MAPPED I/O AND I/O MAPPED I/O NO

| | I/O Mapped I/O | Memory Mapped I/O |
|---|---|---|
| 1 | I/O devices are treated as I/O devices and memory devices are treated as memory | I/O and memory devices are treated as memory devices. |
| 2 | Separate Control Signals for I/O devices are IOR, IOW and memory devices are MEMR, MEMW. | Control signals for memory as well as I/O devices are MEMR and MEMW. |
| 3 | IN and OUT instructions are required for I/O read and write operation. | All memory related instruction are used to Access I/O devices. |
| 4 | Data transfer is possible between I/O device and Accumulator only. | Data transfer is possible between any register and I/O devices. |
| 5 | Address decoding logic is simple. | Address decoding logic is complicated and expensive. |
| 6 | 8085 can access complete 64 Kbytes of Memory and 256 of Input and 256 output devices as address space is not shared. | 8085 can access 64 bytes maximum I/O devices or memory as address space is shared, so total numbers of I/O ports and memory locations should not more than 64K. |
| 7 | I/O Device address is 8 bit and memory address is 16 bit. | I/O device and memory address is 16 bit as I/O devices are treated as memory. |
| 8 | I/O devices and memory are distinguished by control signals and addresses. | I/O devices and memory are distinguished by only addresses. |
| 9 | Arithmetic and logical operations are not possible directly with I/O devices. | Arithmetic and logical operations are possible directly with I/O devices |

# 8.10 THE 8255 PROGRAMMABLE PERIPHERAL INTERFACE (PPI)

- Peripheral Interfacing is considered to be a main part of Microprocessor, as it is the only way to interact with the external world. The interfacing happens with the ports of the Microprocessor.

The main IC's which are to be interfaced with 8085 are:
- 8255 PPI
- 8259 PIC
- 8251 USART
- 8279 Key board display controller
- 8253 Timer/ Counter

- A/D and D/A converter interfacing.

Programmable Peripheral Interface Intel 8255

**Pins, Signals and internal block diagram of 8255:**

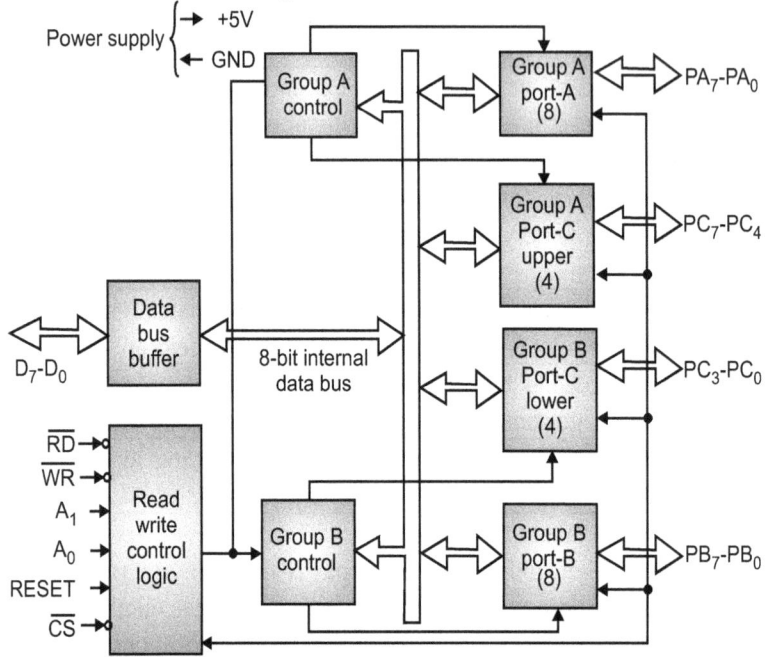

**Fig. 6.10 : Block diagram / Internal structure of 8255 PPI**

- It has 40 pins and requires a single +5V supply.

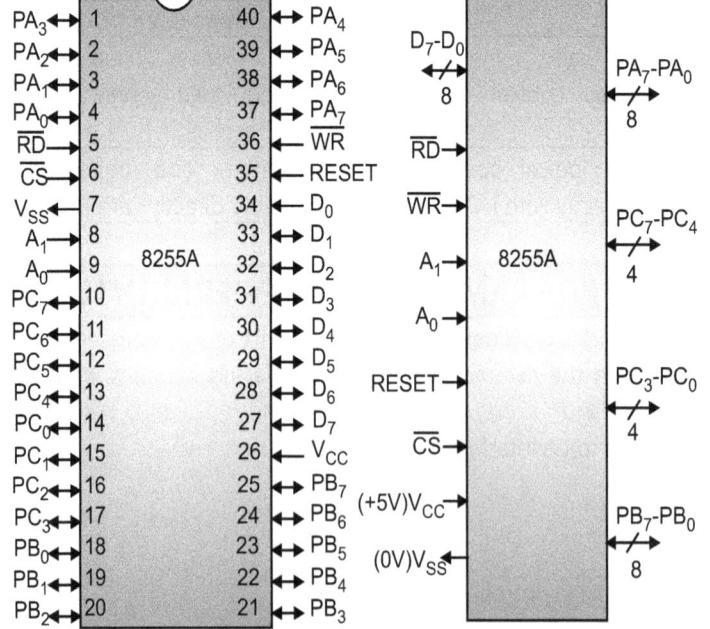

**Fig. 6.11**

- The INTEL 8255 is a device used to parallel data transfer between processor and slow peripheral devices like ADC, DAC, keyboard, 7-segment display, LCD, etc.
- The 8255 has three ports: Port-A, Port-B and Port-C.
- Port-A can be programmed to work in any one of the three operating modes mode-0, mode-1 and mode-2 as input or output port.
- Port-B can be programmed to work either in mode-0 or mode-1 as input or output port.
- Port-C (8-pins) has different assignments depending on the mode of port-A and port-B.
- If port-A and B are programmed in mode-0, then the port-C can perform any one of the following functions.
- As 8-bit parallel port in mode-0 for input or output.
- As two numbers of 4-bit parallel ports in mode-0 for input or output.
- The individual pins of port-C can be set or reset for various control applications.
- If port-A is programmed in mode- 1/mode-2 and port-B is programmed in mode-1 then some of the pins of port-C are used for handshake signals and the remaining pins can be used as input/ output lines or individually set/reset for control applications.
- The read/write control logic requires six control signals. These signals are given below.

1. **RD (Low)** : This control signal enables the read operation. When this signal is low, the microprocessor reads data from a selected I/O port of the 8255A.
2. **WR (Low)** : This control signal enables the write operation. When this signal goes low, the microprocessor writes into a selected I/O port or the control Register.
3. **RESET** : This is an active high signal. It clears the control register and set all ports in the input mode.
4. **CS (Low), A0 and A1:** These are device select signals.

## 6.11 INTERFACING OF 8255 WITH 8085 PROCESSOR:

A simple schematic for interfacing the 8255 with 8085 processor is shown in Fig.

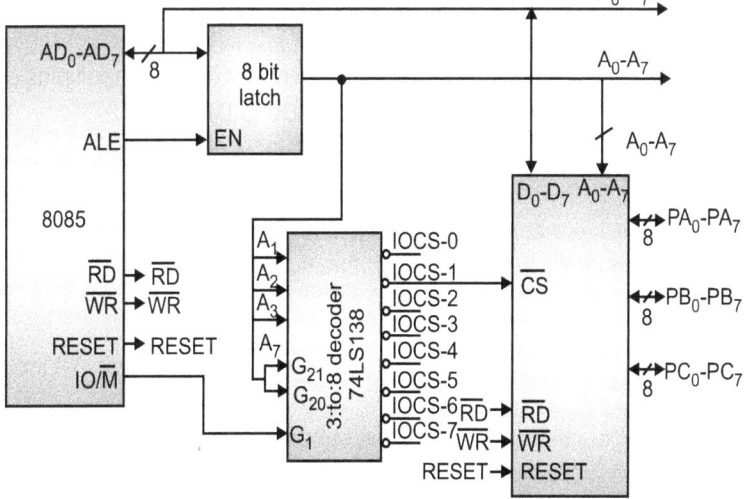

Fig. 6.12 : Enterfacing diagram of 8255 with 8085

- The 8255 can be either memory mapped or I/O mapped in the system. In the schematic shown in above is I/O mapped in the system.
- Using a 3-to-8 decoder generates the chip select signals for I/O mapped devices.
- The address lines A4, A5 and A6 are decoded to generate eight chip select signals and in this, the chip select IOCS- 1 is used to select 8255.
- The address line A7 and the control signal IO/M (low) are used as enable for the decoder.
- The address line A0 of 8085 is connected to A0 of 8255 and A1 of 8085 is connected to A1 of 8255 to provide the internal addresses.
- The data lines D0 to D7 are connected to D0 to D7 of the processor to achieve parallel data transfer.
- The I/O addresses allotted to the internal devices of 8255 are listed in table 6.1.

**Table 6.1**

| Internal Device | Binary address | | | | | | | | Hexa Address |
|---|---|---|---|---|---|---|---|---|---|
| | Decoder input and enable | | | | Input to address pins of 8255 | | | | |
| | $A_7$ | $A_6$ | $A_5$ | $A_4$ | $A_3$ | $A_2$ | $A_1$ | $A_0$ | |
| Port A | 0 | 0 | 0 | 1 | X | X | 0 | 0 | 10 |
| Port B | 0 | 0 | 0 | 1 | X | X | 0 | 1 | 11 |
| Port C | 0 | 0 | 0 | 1 | X | X | 1 | 0 | 12 |
| Control Register | 0 | 0 | 0 | 1 | X | X | 1 | 1 | 13 |

**Note :** Don't care "x" is considered as zero.

**Interfacing Steps**

**Step 1:**
- Lower order of 8-bit address A0 to A7 is separated from AD0 to AD7 using address latch/buffer Example IC 74373 and ALE signal.
- The separated address lines A0 to A7 are connected to A0 to A7 input pins of 8255 and the separated data bus D0 to D7 are connected to D0 to D7 pins of 8255.
- Reset out of 8085 is connected to reset pin of 8255.

**Step 2:**
- 8255 does not have internal control logic generator, hence the IO/M(bar), RD(bar) and WR(bar) control signals are not connected directly to 8255. These pins are 1st given to decoder and decoded using 3:8 decoder (IC 74IS138).
- The generated control signals $\overline{IOR}$ and $\overline{IOW}$ are connected to $\overline{RD}$ and $\overline{WR}$ input of 8155.

**Step 3:**
- An active low signal of chip select logic is obtained decoding remaining address lines of lower order addresses A2 to A7.
- Chip select logic and IO port address for this interfacing circuit are as:

**Table 6.2**

| Chip select address lines | Address lines to select port | | | | | | | Hex address | Selected I/O |
|---|---|---|---|---|---|---|---|---|---|
| $A_7$ | $A_6$ | $A_5$ | $A_4$ | $A_3$ | $A_2$ | $A_1$ | $A_0$ | | |
| 1 | 0 | 0 | 0 | 0 | 0 | 0 | 0 | 80H | Port A |
| 1 | 0 | 0 | 0 | 0 | 0 | 0 | 1 | 81H | Port B |
| 1 | 0 | 0 | 0 | 0 | 0 | 1 | 0 | 82H | Port C |
| 1 | 0 | 0 | 0 | 0 | 0 | 1 | 1 | 83H | Chip Select Register |

## 6.12 OPERATING MODES OF 8255 PPI

The 8255 has 24 input/output pins. These are divided into three 8-bit ports. Port A and port B can be used as 8-bit input/output ports. Port C can be used as an 8-bit input/output port or as two 4-bit input/output ports or to produce handshake signals for ports A and B.

The three ports are further grouped as follows:
- Group A consisting of port A and upper part of port C.
- Group B consisting of port B and lower part of port C.

Eight data lines (D0 to D7) are available to read/write data into the ports or control register under the status of the RD (pin 5) and WR (pin 36), which are active low signals for read and write operations respectively. The address lines A1 and A0 allow to successively access any one of the ports or the control register as listed following Table 6.3 :

**Table 6.3**

| $A_1$ | $A_0$ | Post Selected |
|---|---|---|
| 0 | 0 | Port A |
| 0 | 1 | Port B |
| 1 | 0 | Port C |
| 1 | 1 | Control register |

The control signal CS (pin 6) is used to enable the 8255 chip. It is an active low signal, i.e., when CS = '0', the 8255 is enabled. The RESET input (pin 35) is connected to the RESET line of system like 8085, 8086, etc., so that when the system is reset, all the ports are initialized as input lines. This is done to prevent 8255 and/or any peripheral connected to it, from being destroyed due to mismatch of ports. As an example, consider an input device connected to 8255 at port A. If from the previous operation, port A is initialized as an output port and if 8255 is not reset before using the current configuration, then there is a possibility of damage of either the input device connected or 8255 or both since both 8255 and the device connected will be sending out data.

The control register or the control logic or the command word register is an 8-bit register used to select the modes of operation and input/output designation of the ports.

## Control Word Register

Before going to discuss the detailed description about the usage of the 8255 in the MZ-700, you should see the bit definitions of the 8255 control word register port $E003 of the MZ-700. If bit 7 of the control word is a logical 1 then the 8255 will be configured. See the picture of the practicable configurations:

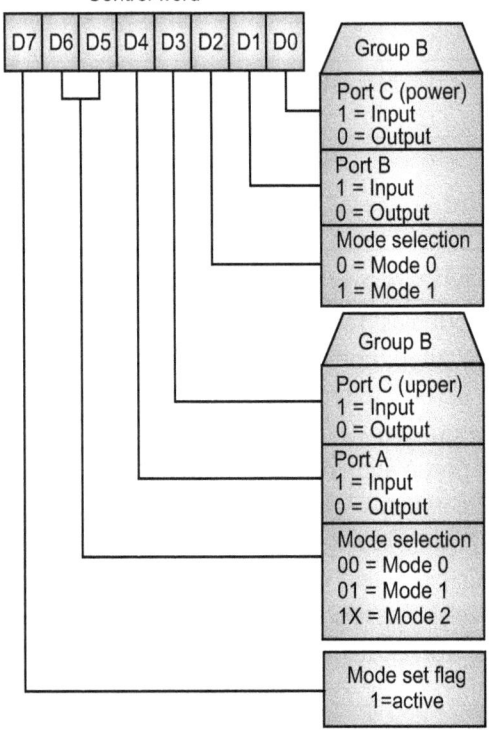

**Fig. 6.13 : Mode definition of the 8255 control REGISTER to configure the 8255.**

If bit 7 of the control word is a logical 0 then each bit of the port C can be set or reset. See the picture of the practicable possibilities:

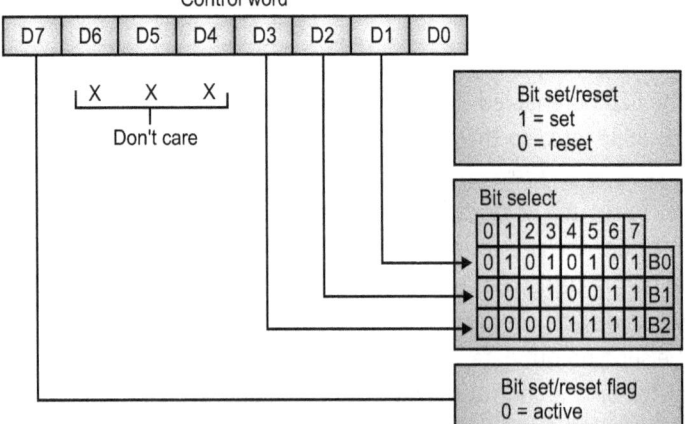

**Fig. 6.14 : Bit definitions of the 8255 control register to modify single bits of port C**

**Examples :**

If you want to set/reset bit 0 of port C then set D3 to D1 to 000.

Bit 1 of port C will be set/reset if you code 001 to D3 to D1.

Bit 6 of port C is set/reset if D3 to D1 is 110.

## 6.13 OPERATIONAL MODES OF 8255

There are two basic operational modes of 8255:

Bit set/reset Mode (BSR Mode).

Input/Output Mode (I/O Mode).

The two modes are selected on the basis of the value present at the D7 bit of the Control Word Register. When D7 = 1, 8255 operates in I/O mode and when D7 = 0, it operates in the BSR mode.

### 6.13.1 Bit set/reset (BSR) mode

The Bit Set/Reset (BSR) mode is applicable to port C only. Each line of port C (PC0 to PC7) can be set/reset by suitably loading the control word register. BSR mode and I/O mode are independent and selection of BSR mode does not affect the operation of other ports in I/O mode.

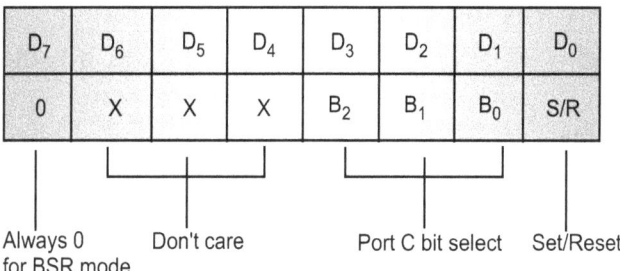

8255 control register format for BSR mode

**Fig. 6.15 : 8255 Control Register format for BSR mode**

8255 BSR mode

- D7 bit is always 0 for BSR mode.
- Bits D6, D5 and D4 are don't care bits.
- Bits D3, D2 and D1 are used to select the pin of Port C.
- Bit D0 is used to set/reset the selected pin of Port C.

Selection of port C pin is determined as following Table 6.4 :

**Table 6.4**

| B3 | B2 | B1 | Bit/pin of port C selected |
|---|---|---|---|
| 0 | 0 | 0 | PC0 |
| 0 | 0 | 1 | PC1 |

...Cont.

| | | | |
|---|---|---|---|
| 0 | 1 | 0 | PC2 |
| 0 | 1 | 1 | PC3 |
| 1 | 0 | 0 | PC4 |
| 1 | 0 | 1 | PC5 |
| 1 | 1 | 0 | PC6 |
| 1 | 1 | 1 | PC7 |

If it is needed that PC5 be set, then in the control word,
- Since it is BSR mode, D7 = '0'.
- Since D4, D5, D6 are not used, assume them to be '0'.
- PC5 has to be selected, hence, D3 = '1', D2 = '0', D1 = '1'.
- PC5 has to be set, hence, D0 = '1'.

Thus, as per the above values, 0B (Hex) will be loaded into the Control Word Register (CWR).

| D7 | D6 | D5 | D4 | D3 | D2 | D1 | D0 |
|---|---|---|---|---|---|---|---|
| 0 | 0 | 0 | 0 | 1 | 0 | 1 | 1 |

## 6.13.2 Input/Output mode

This mode is selected when D7 bit of the Control Word Register is 1. There are three I/O modes:
- Mode 0 : Simple I/O
- Mode 1 : Strobed I/O
- Mode 2 : Strobed Bi-directional I/O

**Control Word Format**

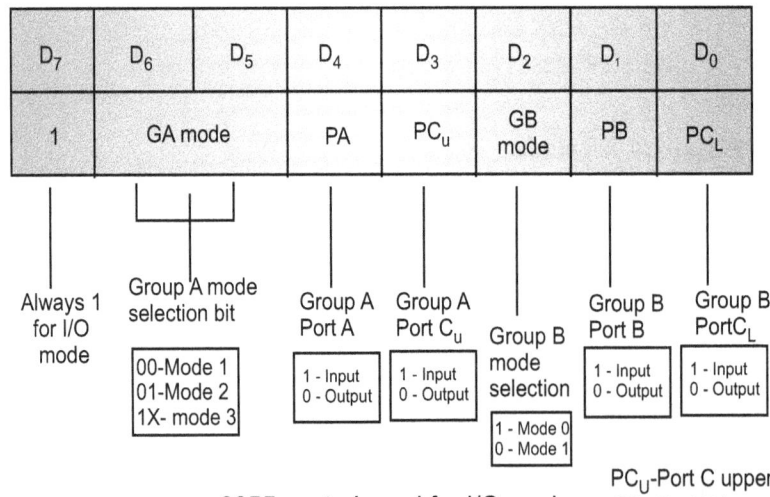

8255 control word for I/O mode

**Fig. 6.16 : 8255 control word for I/I mode**

## I/O Control Word Format

- $D_0$, $D_1$, $D_3$, $D_4$ are assigned for lower port C, port B, upper port C and port A respectively. When these bits are 1, the corresponding port acts as an input port. For e.g., if $D_0 = D_4 = 1$, then lower port C and port A act as input ports. If these bits are 0, then the corresponding port acts as an output port. For e.g., if $D_1 = D_3 = 0$, then port B and upper port C act as output ports.
- $D_2$ is used for mode selection of Group B (port B and lower port C). When $D_2 = 0$, mode 0 is selected and when $D_2 = 1$, mode 1 is selected.
- $D_5$ & $D_6$ are used for mode selection of Group A ( port A and upper port C). The selection is done as follows:

| $D_6$ | $D_5$ | Mode |
|---|---|---|
| 0 | 0 | 0 |
| 0 | 1 | 1 |
| 1 | X | 2 |

As it is I/O mode, $D7 = 1$.

For example, if port B and upper port C have to be initialized as input ports and lower port C and port A as output ports (all in mode 0):

1. Since it is an I/O mode, $D7 = 1$.
2. Mode selection bits, D2, D5, D6 are all 0 for mode 0 operation.
3. Port B and upper port C should operate as Input ports, hence, $D1 = D3 = 1$.
4. Port A and lower port C should operate as Output ports, hence, $D4 = D0 = 0$.

Hence, for the desired operation, the control word register will have to be loaded with 8A H.

### 6.13.2.1 Mode 0 : Simple I/O

In this mode, the ports can be used for simple I/O operations without handshaking signals. Port A, port B provide simple I/O operation. The two halves of port C can be either used together as an additional 8-bit port, or they can be used as individual 4-bit ports. Since the two halves of port C are independent, they may be used such that one-half is initialized as an input port while the other half is initialized as an output port.

The input/output features in mode 0 are as follows:

- Output ports are latched.
- Input ports are buffered, not latched.
- Ports do not have handshake or interrupt capability.
- With 4 ports, 16 different combinations of I/O are possible.

**Mode 0 : Input Mode**

- In the input mode, the 8255 gets data from the external peripheral ports and the CPU reads the received data via its data bus.

- The CPU first selects the 8255 chip by making CS low. Then it selects the desired port using A0 and A1 lines.
- The CPU then issues an RD signal to read the data from the external peripheral device via the system data bus.

**Mode 0 - Output Mode**

- In the output mode, the CPU sends data to 8255 via system data bus and then the external peripheral ports receive this data via 8255 port.
- CPU first selects the 8255 chip by making $\overline{CS}$ low. It then selects the desired port using A0 and A1 lines.
- CPU then issues a $\overline{WR}$ signal to write data to the selected port via the system data bus. This data is then received by the external peripheral device connected to the selected port.

### 6.13.2.2 Mode 1

- When we wish to use port A or port B for handshake input or output operation, we initialise that port in mode 1 port A and port B can be initialised to operate in different modes, i.e., for e.g., port A can operate in mode 0 and port B in mode 1. Some of the pins of port C function as handshake lines.
- For port B in this mode (irrespective of whether is acting as an input port or output port), PC0, PC1 and PC2 pins function as handshake lines.
- If port A is initialized as mode 1 input port, then, PC3, PC4 and PC5 function as handshake signals. Pins PC6 and PC7 are available for use as input/output lines.

The mode 1 which supports handshaking has following features:

- Two ports i.e. port A and B can be used as 8-bit i/o ports.
- Each port uses three lines of port c as handshake signal and remaining two signals can be used as i/o ports.
- Interrupt logic is supported.
- Input and Output data are latched.

**Input Handshaking Signals**

1. **IBF(Input Buffer Full)** : It is an output indicating that the input latch contains information.
2. **STB(Strobed Input)** : The strobe input loads data into the port latch, which holds the information until it is input to the microprocessor via the IN instruction.
3. **INTR(Interrupt Request)** : It is an output that requests an interrupt. The INTR pin becomes a logic 1 when the STB input returns to a logic 1, and is cleared when the data are input from the port by the microprocessor.
4. **INTE(Interrupt Enable)** : It is neither an input nor an output; it is an internal bit programmed via the port PC4(port A) or PC2(port B) bit position.

**Output Handshaking Signals**

1. **OBF(Output Buffer Full) :** It is an output that goes low whenever data are output(OUT) to the port A or port B latch. This signal is set to a logic 1 whenever the ACK pulse returns from the external device.

2. **ACK(Acknowledge) :** It causes the OBF pin to return to a logic 1 level. The ACK signal is a response from an external device, indicating that it has received the data from the 82C55 port.

3. **INTR(Interrupt Request) :** It is a signal that often interrupts the microprocessor when the external device receives the data via the signal. this pin is qualified by the internal INTE(interrupt enable) bit.

4. **INTE(Interrupt Enable) :** It is neither an input nor an output; it is an internal bit programmed to enable or disable the INTR pin. The INTE A bit is programmed using the PC6 bit and INTE B is programmed using the PC2 bit.

### 6.13.2.3 Mode 2

- Only group A can be initialised in this mode. Port A can be used for bidirectional handshake data transfer. This means that data can be input or output on the same eight lines (PA0 to PA7). Pins PC4 to PC7 are used as handshake lines for port A. The remaining pins of port C (PC0 to PC3) can be used as input/output lines if group B is initialised in mode 0 or as handshaking for port b if group B is initialised in mode 1. In this mode, the 8255 may be used to extend the system bus to a slave microprocessor or to transfer data bytes to and from a floppy disk controller.

## 6.14 APPLICATIONS OF MICROPROCESSOR

- Microprocessor are being used for numerous applications and the list of applications is becoming longer and longer. To give an idea of microprocessor applications few areas are given below.

1. Personal Computer
2. Numerical Control
3. Mobile Phones
4. Automobiles
5. Bending Machines
6. Medical Diagnostic Equipment
7. Automatic voice recognizing systems
8. Prosthetics
9. Traffic light Control

10. Entertainment Games
11. Digital Signal Processing
12. Communication terminals
13. Process Control
14. Calculators
15. Sophisticated Instruments
16. Telecommunication Switching Systems
17. Automatic Test Systems.

## QUESTIONS

1. What is interfacing? Why it is required.
2. What are the different Interfacing Chips / ICs are used for Interfacing.
3. Explain Memory mapped I/O.
4. Explain I/O mapped I/O.
5. Draw architecture of 8255 PPI. Explain.
6. What are the different modes of operations of 8255 PPI.

www.ingramcontent.com/pod-product-compliance
Lightning Source LLC
Chambersburg PA
CBHW081830170426
43191CB00047B/2219

ESSENTIAL VOCABULARY ORGANIZED BY TOPIC FOR IB DIPLOMA

French Ab Initio

DANIÈLE BOURDAIS

Published by Elemi International Schools Publisher Ltd

© Copyright 2021 Elemi International Schools Publisher Ltd

Author: Danièle Bourdais

> **Danièle Bourdais** is an award-winning author of French coursebooks and resources and an experienced tutor. She regularly tutors international students and writes resources to teach and support French Ab Initio and French B at Diploma level. She can be contacted at frenchmatters@outlook.com.

Series Editor: Mary James
Specialist Editor: Catherine Kaye

The author and publisher would like to acknowledge the very valuable input of Jenny Ollerenshaw, IB and language consultant. We would also like to thank Laura Kanyerezi who reviewed and commented on the manuscript. Laura is an experienced educator of the IB Diploma and currently teaches at North London Collegiate School Dubai.

First published 2021

All rights reserved. No part of this publication may be copied, reproduced, duplicated, stored in a retrieval system, or transmitted in any form or by any means, without the prior written permission of Elemi International Schools Publisher Ltd, or as permitted by law or by licence. Enquiries about permission for reproduction should be addressed to the publisher.

If you photocopy/scan this book, or if you are given a photocopied/scanned version of this book or any part of it, please be aware that you are denying the author and publisher the right to be appropriately paid for their work.

A catalogue record of this title is available from the British Library
British Library Cataloguing in Publication Data

ISBN 978-1-9164131-7-7

Page layout/design by EMC Design Ltd
Cover design by Jayne Martin-Kaye

We are an entirely independent publishing company. This resource has been developed independently from and is not endorsed by the International Baccalaureate Organization. International Baccalaureate, Baccalauréat International, Bachillerato Internacional and IB are registered trademarks owned by the International Baccalaureate Organization.